Mountain Elegance

presented by

The Junior League of Asheville, Inc.

A collection of favorite recipes
compiled and tested
by members and friends

D0048731

Bright Mountain Books, Inc.
Asheville, North Carolina

Dedication
In memory of the original cookbook chairman
Melanie Hudgins

Royalties from the sale of Mountain Elegance *will be returned to the community through projects of The Junior League of Asheville, Inc.*

Originally published by The Junior League of Asheville, Inc., 1982; reprinted with updated material by Bright Mountain Books, 1991; updated by Bright Mountain Books, Inc., 1997

Introduction

As a summer visitor, new resident, or old native, you may already know that the first white settlers ventured west of the Appalachian Mountains after the Revolutionary War when the new and impoverished American government offered its soldiers land grants in lieu of cash, and that in 1792 our county was named in honor of Colonel Edward Buncombe.

But you may not know that the colonel's name took on a different meaning out of the mouth of Representative Felix Walker, who persisted in making long-winded speeches. Weary of Mr. Walker's dull discourses, his colleagues began to say, "That's a lot of Buncombe." Thus was born the expression which in later usage became "bunkum" or "bunk," meaning nonsense.

Summer visitors may have heard about the region from other visitors, and they may leave here to spread the good word about area attractions—warm hospitality, wonderful climate, beautiful scenery. But they may not know that Asheville's first tourists arrived in 1827 over a muddy mountain track called the Buncombe Turnpike. Mostly they were wealthy folk from Georgia and South Carolina, fleeing the heat of the lowlands. In between, Asheville has entertained many notable guests, including Henry Ford, Thomas Edison, and assorted United States presidents.

A new resident may already have seen the Biltmore House and the Grove Park Inn. He may not know, however, that two buildings dating back to the 1840s still stand. The Smith-McDowell House and Ravenscroft School are thought to be the oldest buildings in Asheville, and they are definitely the oldest brick buildings in the county.

And an old native—if he is old enough—may have known Thomas Wolfe as a schoolmate. On the other hand, he may never have known that Asheville's Elizabeth Blackwell was the first woman in this country to earn a degree as a doctor of medicine.

Surely everyone knows that western North Carolina is an excellent place to live, work, play, learn, earn, and retire. It is also a marvelous place to eat. Whether you choose the dining room of a luxury hotel, a country inn or your own home, you can be sure the food will be good if an Asheville cook prepared it.

As my friend Margaret always says, it is a terrible thing to start a diet on an empty stomach. With this book in hand, the one may be necessary, but never the other.

Virginia C. Taylor
President, Junior League of Asheville
1957–1959

Cookbook Committee

Chairman	Melanie Hudgins
Co-chairman	Gail Rogers
Marketing Chairman	Barbara Nesbitt
Editorial Assistant	Sandi Holt
Recipe Chairman	Kathy Armstrong

Section Chairmen

Beverages	Gail Rogers
Hors d'oeuvres	Celine Lurey
Soups & Sauces	Diana Bilbrey
Bread	Molly Sandridge
	JoAnn Grimes
Fish & Seafood	Yvonne Day
Poultry & Game	Lelia Cort
Meat	Henny Steinfeld
Rice, Pasta, Eggs & Cheese	Joyce Cole
Vegetables	Dianna Goodman
Salads	Maureen Coleman
Desserts	Lynn Trotter
Chocolate	Jeanne Powell
Pickles & Jams	Joy Fitchett
Microwave	Alice Griffin

Restaurant Chairman	Martha Salisbury
Restaurant Artwork	Saralyn Spradling
Cover Design and Artwork	Wendy Simons-Mankey
Reprint Chairman	Fran Cogburn

Testers and Tasters

Jaime Armstrong	Emily Hollars	Laura Rogers
Linda Bell	Mary Claire Israel	Bea Russell
Betsy Biggers	Sara Lavelle	Jan Schulhof
Clara Bitter	Robyn Leslie	Sandy Sellers
Myra Bonner	Debbie Lyman	Mardi Shaw
Betsy Boys	Holly Mason	Carolyn Smith
Alice Britt	Carol Matthews	Linda Smith
Gay Coleman	Jean Moore	Yvonne Smith
Carol Costenbader	Lynn Moser	Barrie Sneed
Nancy Crosby	Sue McClinton	Carolyn Thompson
Susan Daniel	Jane McNeil	Betsy Thurlow
Sue Durham	Kathy Noyes	Helen Turner
Jean Frady	Ann Orr	Mary Ann Warlick
Elaine Gennett	Bitsy Powell	Ginny Webb
Gail Golding	Anne Rector	Becky York
Sherry Harbin	Betsy Rhodes	Kitty Young
Ann Heard	Debbie Robinson	

Table of Contents

Restaurants

The Market Place *Asheville*

TERRINE OF CRAB

Yield: 10 4-oz. servings
Baking Time: 45 minutes

2 # crabmeat
12 oz. heavy cream
4 eggs
2 teaspoons salt
1 teaspoon white pepper
2 teaspoons tarragon
1 Tablespoon parsley
Juice of 1 lemon

SAUCE: (if served cold)
5 Tablespoons sour cream
2 Tablespoons tomato ketchup
1 Tablespoon cognac
2 teaspoons lemon juice
3 drops Tabasco
Diced tomato

Puree crab through mouli legume. Blend cream into crab. Add eggs and seasonings. Add lemon juice. Mold in buttered 4-oz. molds.
Bake in a bain-marie (or place molds in larger pan of hot water) in 400° oven for 45 minutes until firm and brown on top.
Mix together all ingredients for sauce.
Note: Pink grapefruit juice may be substituted for lemon juice.

* * * * * * *

Fine Friends *Asheville*

APPLE ALMOND TORTE

CRUST:
4 oz. sugar
1/2 # sweet butter
1 # flour
2 eggs, well beaten

FILLING:
4 oz. almond paste
4 oz. flour
4 oz. sweet butter, softened
4 oz. sugar
2 eggs
2 apples

2 Tablespoons apple jelly
1 Tablespoon toasted almonds

Crust: Use a 1x9" torte pan with removable bottom and oil and flour it well. Cream the butter with the sugar; add the eggs. Slowly fold in the flour to create the dough. Knead the dough on a floured board until it is firm. Roll it out to fit the torte pan.
Filling: Mix the almond paste with the sugar adding 1 egg and beat well. Blend in the butter and the other egg and slowly mix in the flour. Pour filling into torte pan and smooth it down. Peel and slice the apples into 8 slices and press them into the filling.
Bake in a preheated 325° degree oven for 30 minutes or until the crust is browned. The filling will rise to almost cover the apples. Let the torte cool slightly before serving.
In a small saucepan, melt the apple jelly and spread over torte; top with toasted almonds.

High Hampton Inn *Cashiers*

SUNNY SILVER PIE

Must do ahead

1/3 cup cold water
Grated rind of 1 lemon
1/2 Tablespoon gelatin
1 cup sugar
4 eggs, separated
Few grains salt
3 Tablespoons lemon juice
1 cup whipping cream

Set gelatin to soak in 1/3 cup cold water. Place the 4 egg yolks, lemon juice, lemon rind and half cup of sugar in a rounded bottom enamel bowl. Set bowl in larger pan of boiling water. Keep boiling. Whip the egg mixture until it becomes quite firm and creamy. When it reaches this stage, turn the heat down and fold in the gelatin. Turn off stove. Beat the egg whites until very stiff and combine with remaining 1/2 cup of sugar. Then fold this into yolk mixture. Pour the filling into a baked pie shell and set in refrigerator for 2 hours. Whip cream until stiff and spread over top of pie just before serving.

Nu-Wray Inn *Burnsville*

CAROLINA RELISH

Makes about 5 quarts

2 large cabbages
6 onions
6 green peppers
6 apples
6 cucumbers
1 bunch celery
6 Tablespoons salt
6 cups vinegar
10 cups brown sugar
1 Tablespoon pickling spices
1 Tablespoon tumeric

Grind cabbage, onions, peppers, apples, and cucumbers coarsely in a food chopper, feeding vegetables into chopper alternately. Add salt, and put in a sack and let drip all night.
Chop celery and add next morning.
Mix vinegar, sugar, pickling spices and tumeric and add to drained vegetables.
Pack in sterile jars and seal. Keep in a cool place.

* * * * * * *

The Criterion Grill *Biltmore*

BLACKEYED PEA CAKES

2 15-oz. cans blackeyed peas, drained
Bread crumbs, to make firm
1/2 cup blue cornmeal
1/3 cup finely chopped red onions
1 teaspoon garlic
3 Tablespoons unsalted butter
2 Tablespoons minced pimentos
2 Tablespoons minced jalapenos
1 egg yolk
1-1/4 teaspoons Tabasco
2 Tablespoons cilantro
1/4 teaspoon cumin

Saute onions, garlic and pimentos in butter until soft. Add to peas. Mix in egg yolk and seasonings. Add bread crumbs until easy to work with.
Make 2-oz. patties, using biscuit cutter, if desired. Dredge in cornmeal. Melt butter in frying pan. Saute patties until brown on both sides.
Top with cooked black beans and tomato salsa. Drizzle top with a mixture of sour cream and buttermilk.

The Grove Park Inn   *Asheville*

ROAST RACK OF LAMB WITH HERBED DIJON CRUST AND LACED WITH NATURAL DRIPPINGS

Serves: 3

1 half side of domestic lamb rack
   (3-3 1/2 #)
1 teaspoon fresh minced garlic
1 teaspoon fresh chopped parsley
1/4 teaspoon fresh thyme
1/4 teaspoon fresh chopped rosemary
8 oz. white bread crumbs
2 oz. white wine
1 Tablespoon Dijon mustard
2 oz. melted butter

Remove deckel (fat covering) and chine bone completely. Scrape rib bones clean and cut rib bones one inch. Season with half of the garlic and salt and pepper to taste. Roast for about 5 minutes at 400° to seal meat.

Mix together bread crumbs, remaining garlic, white wine, Dijon mustard, melted butter and spices. Cover lamb loin completely with bread crumb mixture and roast for another 20 minutes.

NATURAL DRIPPINGS:
1 # lamb bones
Vegetable oil
1 medium carrot
1 small onion
1 stalk of celery
2 sprigs of rosemary
1 teaspoon tomato paste
1 cup red wine

Brown bones in vegetable oil along with vegetables which have been cut into 1/4-inch dice. Add tomato paste and saute. Add red wine and 3 cups water. Reduce liquid to 1/4 of original volume. Season with salt and pepper, then strain.

Magnolia's Raw Bar and Grille   Asheville

SEAFOOD "BOUILLABAISSE" OVER LINGUINI

Serves: 4

RED CLAM SAUCE:
4 cloves garlic, minced
2 shallots, minced
1 small white onion, peeled and slivered
2 cups plum tomatoes, peeled, seeded and chopped
2 cups chopped clams and juice
1 cup dry red wine
1 teaspoon Balsamic Vinegar
1 teaspoon dried oregano
1 teaspoon dried basil
1 teaspoon dried tarragon
Freshly grated Parmesan cheese
Salt and freshly ground pepper to taste
2-3 teaspoons quality olive oil

2 pounds linguini
1/2 lb. fresh shrimp (small, 40-50 count, peeled, deveined)
1/2 lb. fresh sea scallops
12-15 fresh mussels
8-10 fresh oysters

Drain clams and reserve clam juice. Saute garlic, shallots, onion, and clams in olive oil until onion is tender. Season with herbs. Add red wine, tomatoes, clam juice and vinegar. Simmer 20-30 minutes on low to combine everything evenly.

Cook linguini. Steam open mussels and oysters. In olive oil, saute shrimp and scallops, lightly, just until done. Combine with Red Clam Sauce.

Distribute linguini noodles evenly on plates. Arrange steamed seafood on borders, and top with a little sauce. Grate cheese over top and serve.

Note: Fresh herbs may be substituted and, of course, are more desirable.

*   *   *   *   *   *   *

The Jarrett House   Dillsboro

JARRETT HOUSE VINEGAR PIE

1 stick margarine, melted and cooled
1-1/2 cup sugar
1 Tablespoon flour
1 Tablespoon vanilla
2 Tablespoons apple cider vinegar
3 eggs
1 9" unbaked pie shell

Combine the first six ingredients. Pour into unbaked pie shell.
Bake at 300° for 45 minutes. Cool completely before slicing.

Great Smokies SunSpree Resort *Asheville*

SUNDAY BRUNCH DEEP DISH FRITTATA

Serves: 8-10

4 oz. lean bacon
4 oz. lean pork sausage with sage
1/2 # potatoes, peeled, cooked, cooled, and diced
10 eggs
1/4 teaspoon salt
1/8 teaspoon pepper
1 medium onion, diced
1 bell pepper, diced
minced garlic to taste
1/2 cup shredded Pepperjack cheese

Cook bacon and sausage completely in large skillet. Crumble bacon and sausage and add onions, peppers, and garlic. Saute one minute. Add potatoes and continue to saute until lightly browned.

While potatoes are sauteing, in a large mixing bowl beat eggs with salt and pepper.

Drain excess fat from saute mixture, pour egg mixture into skillet and stir. Reduce to low heat and cover. Cook until eggs are set, remove cover, top with cheese, and place under broiler until cheese is melted.

WARM PASTA SALAD

Serves 2 very well

1 cup fettucine, cooked according to package directions
2 Tablespoons unsalted butter, melted
1/2 teaspoon garlic, minced
1/2 cup domestic mushrooms, sliced
1 cup heavy whipping cream
1/2 cup chicken stock
1 boneless, skinless chicken breast, grilled and julienned
Salt and pepper to taste
1-1/2 cup fresh spinach, washed and stems removed
Parmesan cheese, freshly grated, to taste

Saute garlic and mushrooms in butter until soft. Add heavy cream and chicken stock and reduce to form a medium-thick consistency. Add salt and pepper to taste. Add fettucine. Heat throughout by swirling in pan. Add chicken. Continue to heat.

Just before serving, add fresh spinach and cook until just wilted. Top with freshly grated Parmesan.

✳ ✳ ✳ ✳ ✳ ✳ ✳

Pisgah Inn *Blue Ridge Parkway*

PARMESAN PEPPER SALAD DRESSING

Pisgah Inn's house dressing

1 cup mayonnaise
1/2 cup buttermilk
3/4 teaspoon onion powder
3/4 teaspoon garlic powder
2-1/4 teaspoons granulated sugar
1 teaspoon Heinz 57 sauce
1/2 cup grated Parmesan cheese
3/4 teaspoon cracked black pepper
Salt and white pepper to taste

Blend in mixer till blended. Let rest overnight in refrigerator.
Note: Use freshly grated Parmesan cheese; dry Parmesan will make the dressing gritty.

The Greenery Restaurant *Asheville*

MARYLAND CRABCAKES

Makes 10 crabcakes

1 # jumbo lump crabmeat,
  picked to remove all shells
2 whole eggs
1/4 cup chopped fresh parsley
1 Tablespoon freshly ground
  horseradish
1 Tablespoon Dijon-style mustard
1/4 to 1/2 cup mayonnaise
2-3 dashes Tabasco
1/2 teaspoon salt
1/4 teaspoon white pepper
Juice of 1 lemon
4-6 cups crushed saltine crackers
4-6 oz. clarified butter

Place eggs, parsley, horseradish, mustard, Tabasco, salt, white pepper, mayonnaise, and lemon juice in a mixing bowl; whip all together with wire whip; add picked crabmeat to mayonnaise mixture and mix.

Using a 2-oz. measure, scoop crab mixture and coat with crushed cracker crumbs. Form crabcakes into uniform cakes about 1/2 inch thick. Refrigerate until ready to cook.

Heat clarified butter in 10-inch saute pan. (Oil should be medium hot). Saute crabcakes until golden brown on each side. Remove and place in a preheated 350° oven for 10 minutes. Remove and serve immediately.

*   *   *   *   *   *   *

Céline and Company *Asheville*

CHICKEN, SPINACH, AND SUN-DRIED TOMATO CAKES

Serves 8

1 bunch scallions, thinly sliced
2 Tablespoons olive oil
1 cup sun-dried tomatoes
1-1/2 # skinless, boneless chicken
  breasts, cut into cubes
1 10 oz. package frozen spinach,
  thawed and squeezed dry
1/2 cup heavy cream
1/4 teaspoon cayenne, or more to
  taste
salt and pepper
1-1/2 cups fresh bread crumbs,
  divided
1 cup canola oil for sauteing

Saute scallions in olive oil; set aside. Soak sun-dried tomatoes in 2 cups boiling water; drain and chop.

In food processor, grind chicken. Combine ground chicken with 1/2 cup bread crumbs and all other ingredients except canola oil. Mix until thoroughly blended.

Form into 16 cakes, about 3 inches in diameter if serving as an entree; form into many smaller cakes if serving as an appetizer. Coat with remaining cup of bread crumbs. Fry in very hot canola oil in a nonstick skillet until well browned on each side.*

Serve with a mushroom sauce or any wine-based sauce.

*May be prepared in advance and refrigerated at this point. Bring back to room temperature and heat in a 400° oven for 10 minutes.

Deerpark Restaurant *Biltmore Estate, Asheville*

George Washington Vanderbilt was host for elaborate picnics at turn-of-the-century Biltmore Estate in Asheville, North Carolina, complete with silver tableware, china and plentiful food with fine wines. In addition to festive fare and libations, Vanderbilt and other Victorian-era picnickers would have enjoyed such gentile games as croquet and lawn bowling, or fishing and strolling near the picnic site.

Guests at Biltmore Estate enjoyed traveling by horse-drawn carriage to various scenic settings for outdoor dining. While picnics were less formal affairs than indoor dining, women might have changed clothes up to five times a day to suit the activities planned.

The delightful practice of simple-but-elegant picnics can be enjoyed today at a nearby park or lake, or even in your own backyard. Just as in Vanderbilt's day, what makes picnics special are the elements brought to them, including a variety of victuals and liquid refreshments, and, of course, the friends and family who make up the party.

To help you prepare for a festive but easy modern-day picnic, Biltmore estate Food and Beverage Manager Mike Harris selected the following recipes, created in the kitchens of the estate's Deerpark Restaurant. Winemaster Philippe Jourdain has paired each recipe with an appropriate wine for warm weather enjoyment. Add a crusty french bread to round out the outdoor feast.

CAESAR CHICKEN SALAD

Serve with Johannisburg Reisling

4 boneless chicken breasts
3 Tablespoons blackening spices
1 cup olive oil
1 head romaine lettuce
1 egg
2 garlic cloves, crushed
3 Tablespoons lemon juice
4 anchovy filets, drained and chopped
2 hard-boiled eggs, peeled and quartered
1/2 cup fresh grated Parmesan
3/4 cup garlic croutons

Mix 1/2 cup olive oil with blackening spices. Brush chicken generously with mixture and grill, taking care not to overcook. Rinse and dry lettuce, refrigerate. Whisk together the raw egg, garlic, lemon juice, and remaining 1/2 cup of olive oil. Then chill dressing in a jar until ready to serve. Once the dressing is placed in the salad bowl, add the lettuce, anchovies and hard-boiled eggs. Toss thoroughly, add Parmesan cheese and toss again. Slice chicken into strips and place on salad. Serve immediately.

Note: Blackening spices are available at gourmet food shops.

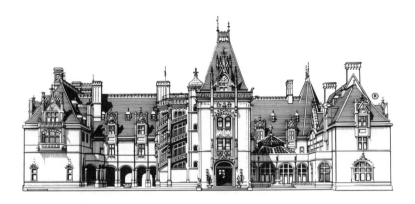

SUMMER LIME AND BLUEBERRY FRUIT TART

Serve with Sparkling Wine

LIME CURD:
Enough ripe limes (about 3) to yield 1 Tablespoon of grated zest and 1/2 cup of strained juice
1/2 cup (1 stick) plus 2 Tablespoons unsalted butter, cut up
Pinch of salt
4 egg yolks
1 whole egg
1-1/4 cups sugar

1 tart shell, fully baked and cooled
Fresh blueberries
Fine granulated sugar
Lightly whipped cream, unsweetened

Place two inches of water into the bottom of a double boiler and bring to a simmer over medium heat. Place 1 Tablespoon grated zest and 1/2 cup strained lime juice in the top pan of the double boiler. Add the butter and salt, then set aside.

Beat the egg yolks and whole egg together at high speed in a large bowl until foamy. Gradually add the sugar, continuing to mix for about 5 minutes until the substance is very thick.

Scrape the egg mixture into the double-boiler top (with the lime mixture) and place over simmering lower pan. Begin whisking immediately, stirring constantly for about 10 minutes, until the mixture is smooth, thick and steaming hot. Be cautious about overcooking the curd; it is done when it will coat a metal or wooden utensil heavily. Remove the upper pan from the hot water.

Pour the curd through a fine-meshed sieve over a bowl and press through with a rubber spatula, leaving the shreds of zest, which can be discarded. Scrape the curd into sterilized, dry jars and cap; then refrigerate.

To assemble fruit tart:
Spread half an inch of the lime curd in the tart shell. Top it with a layer of closely packed, fully ripe blueberries. Chill until serving time, preferably for no more than two to three hours. Just prior to serving, dust with fine granulated sugar. Garnish with unsweetened whipped cream.

Gabrielle's at Richmond Hill Inn *Asheville*

BRANDY MARINATED PORK TENDERLOIN WITH CHUTNEY

Serves: 6

3 pork tenderloins, trimmed and marinated overnight
1-1/2 cups bechamel sauce
4 oz. applejack brandy
1-1/2 cups prepared Apple-Raisin Chutney
12 sprigs fresh rosemary
6 fresh edible flowers

Preheat oven to 350°. Roast marinated pork tenderloins for 15-20 minutes depending on size. While tenderloins are roasting, prepare the bechamel sauce and add the brandy and simmer over low heat. To serve, ladle 2-3 oz. of brandy cream sauce onto plate, slice tenderloins and divide evenly and spoon apple chutney on an angle across pork. Garnish with fresh rosemary and a fresh edible flower.

MARINADE FOR PORK:
2 large sprigs of fresh rosemary, broken
2 shallots, chopped
6 Tablespoons jack brandy
1 cup soybean salad oil
1 Granny Smith apple, coarsely chopped
2 Tablespoons granulated sugar
6 cloves, crushed
Salt and cracked black pepper to taste

Combine all ingredients well and pour over trimmed pork tenderloins. Let marinate overnight.

APPLE-RAISIN CHUTNEY:
1 lb. Granny Smith apples, peeled, cored and diced into 1/2 in. cubes
1 small yellow onion, diced
3/4 cup apple cider vinegar
1/2 cup light brown sugar
1 Tablespoon ground ginger
2 teaspoons mustard seed
1/2 teaspoon Kosher salt
1 teaspoon cracked black pepper
1/4 teaspoon mace
1/4 teaspoon ground cloves
1 stick cinnamon

Combine all ingredients in a heavy saucepan and bring to a boil. Reduce heat and simmer until mixture is thickened. Cool and store in refrigerator until ready to use.

Pisgah View Ranch Candler

OATMEAL PIE

Baking time: 40 minutes

1 unbaked pie shell
1 stick butter, melted
2/3 cup sugar
2 eggs
2/3 cup dark Karo syrup
2/3 cup oatmeal
1 teaspoon vanilla

Blend ingredients. Pour into shell and bake in 325° oven for 40 minutes.

Charlotte Street Grill & Pub *Asheville*

GRILLED TUNA STEAK WITH VIDALIA ONION AND PINEAPPLE CHUTNEY

Serves 4-6

4-6 8-oz. tuna steaks
Salt
Pepper
1 Tablespoon vegetable oil
1/2 # Vidalia onions
1/4 # fresh pineapple
Finely chopped fresh parsley

Lightly salt and pepper tuna steaks. Grill 3 minutes per side for medium rare or 4 minutes per side for medium.

Chop onions and pineapple to medium fine dice. Saute onions in oil over medium heat until caramelized to a light brown. Add pineapple and continue to saute for 3 minutes longer. Add 2 pinches salt, 2 pinches pepper, and 4 pinches parsley. Mix well.

Top tuna steaks with chutney and serve with a wild rice pilaf.

Beverages

TIPS AND DECORATIONS

Use a fresh strawberry in each glass of wine or champagne.

For clear ice cubes, use boiled water.

Freeze a tiny violet in ice cubes.

At Christmas, tie tiny red and green velvet ribbons on the handles of punch cups.

Use a fresh wreath around a punch bowl.

Use a straw hat under a punch bowl.

For an ice mold, fill half of the mold with water; add fruit, flowers and freeze. Then add more water to fill so that items will not float to the top. Or if making several layers of items, add water one inch at a time. Freeze about 12 hours. To remove an ice mold, wet a turkish towel, wring it out and place in a microwave for 3 minutes to heat; remove with tongs and place on inverted ring. For clear ice rings, use distilled or very cold water.

WINE

Wine and food have a natural affinity, and food is nearly always enhanced by the addition of wine to the meal.

Wine can be divided into three types:

1. Sparkling wine
2. Fortified wine
3. Table wine

The first group, sparkling wine, of course includes Champagne which is the best. Real Champagne can only come from the region of Champagne in France. It is made in the special Champagne process and stands far ahead of other sparkling wines. A dry Champagne is a perfect aperitif. Semi-dry Champagne is fine with dessert. There are other very good sparkling wines which come from California, Germany, Spain, France and Italy, and are usually far less expensive than real Champagne.

The second group, fortified wines, include Sherry, Port and Madeira. Sherries can be very dry to very sweet. Dry Sherry is also considered a perfect aperitif. Port is excellent after dinner (with walnuts) as is a sweet Madeira. Never serve a fortified wine with a meal.

Table wines comprise the third and largest group of wines. *Table wine* simply means that it can be served with food, and is not a sparkling or fortified wine.

They can be sweet or dry; red, white or rosé; light or full-bodied; and contain from 7 to 15 percent alcohol. There is an endless variety of table wines from many countries, and a great deal of gastronomic pleasure can be derived from trying the many combinations of wine and food.

Although no one pretends to dictate which wines to drink with which foods, there are some time-honored combinations. It is also a good idea to note that some wines are best before or after others. Dry whites precede red; lighter reds precede full-bodied reds; lesser vintages precede better vintages; and sweet wines should come at the end of a meal.

A few of the best combinations are listed as follows:

Seafood—very dry whites, such as Chablis, Muscadel, Sancerre, white Bordeaux and Sauvignon Blanc (also called Fumé Blanc)

Chicken—depends on sauce or spiciness
mild white sauce—white Bordeaux, white Burgundy, Chardonnay, Riesling, Chenin Blanc
spicy—Gewurztraminer, white Cotes du Rhone
cooked in red wine—light Burgundy

Hamburger or stew—Beaujolais, Cotes du Rhone, or any dry red table wine

Steak or roast—full-bodied Burgundy or Bordeaux, Cabernet Sauvignon, Chateauneuf-du-Pape, Barolo

Veal—perfect with a light red Bordeaux, Cabernet Sauvignon, light red Burgundy, full-bodied white Burgundy or white Cotes du Rhone

Wild game—red Burgundy

Pork—dry Riesling, Gewurztraminer or any Alsatian wine

Ham—dry Riesling

Quiche—dry Riesling, Chenin Blanc

Soup—perfect with dry to medium dry Sherry

Pasta-with meat sauce—a good Italian red such as Chianti Classico, Valpolicella, Barbera

With white sauce or cheese—dry Italian white such as Frascati, Orvieto, Vernaccia di San Gimignano

Fruit—a good German Riesling, Vouvray, Chenin Blanc

Cheese—stronger cheeses such as ripe Brie, Roquefort, Fontina, Esrom, Tilsit and Cheddar go well with a dry red wine
Milder cheeses such as cream Havarti, Monterey Jack, Gouda, Muenster and Swiss go well with white wine

Dessert—Tokaji Aszu, Sauternes, German Auslese, Asti-Spumante
Note: Never serve wine with a chocolate dessert

Combinations to avoid:

Anchovies and any vinegar-based salad dressing are deadly to wine! Strong spices or heavy curry should be avoided with wine.

Just remember there are few foods that are not enhanced by serving wine with them. Try some different combinations and enjoy the experiences. Bon appetit!

Visit BON APPETIT and The Weinhaus at 86 Patton Avenue in Downtown Asheville!!

FRUIT PUNCH FOR CHILDREN
Children will lap it up!

Serves: 50

3 large cans frozen
    unsweetened orange juice
    (making 48 oz. each)
1 18-oz. can pineapple juice,
    unsweetened
1 46-oz. can apple juice,
    unsweetened

Mix orange juice according to directions on the package. Mix with other juices. Proportions may be altered according to taste. The pineapple juice and the orange juice combination is a happy one, however, and is sweet enough so that no sugar is needed. Pour into punch bowl filled with ice and an ice mold.

Ice mold: Fill ring mold with water and freeze. To decorate, freeze a layer of water, lay on sliced fruit or other decorations; add another layer of water; freeze.

Diana Roscoe Bilbrey (Mrs. George M., Jr.)

SMOOTHY
Children love this! Can be frozen as a popsicle for a treat.

Serves: 1 large glass
Preparation: Few minutes

1 carton Mandarin Orange
    yogurt
1 banana
1/4 cup orange juice
1/2 cup cracked ice

Combine ingredients in bowl of food processor or blender; process until smooth.

Lelia Kincaid Cort (Mrs. John)

INSTANT COCOA MIX
Makes lots!!

1 2-lb. box Nestle's Quik
1 8-quart box instant dry milk
6 oz. Cremora
1/2 cup powdered sugar

Mix and store in tightly covered jars.
Mix 1/4 cup of the mixture with hot water in a mug to serve.

Sara Oliver Bissette (Mrs. W. Louis)

24

SUNDAY PUNCH

Can do ahead
Serves: 40

1 46-oz. can pineapple juice
2 46-oz. cans apple juice
3 qts. ginger ale

Chill juices and ginger ale. Make ice ring of apple juice with cherries and orange slices. So easy and very good!!

Harriet Maybank Hutson (Mrs. Henry C.)

CAPPUCCINO COFFEE
Excellent gift

Can do ahead
Serves lots

1 cup instant coffee
2 cups (or more) nonfat
    dry milk
1-1/2 cup (or more) sugar
1-1/2 to 2 teaspoons ground
    orange peel
1/2 cup instant chocolate
    drink may be added for a
    different taste.

Mix together. To serve, use two teaspoons of the mixture with a cup of boiling water.

Lynn Holmes Trotter (Mrs. Benjamin)

COFFEE PUNCH

Do part ahead
Serves: 125
Preparation: 20 minutes

2 oz. instant coffee
4 cups boiling water
4 cups sugar
12 quarts milk
3 quarts vanilla ice cream,
    softened
3 quarts chocolate ice cream,
    softened
Optional: 3 pints
    Creme de Cacao

Mix the coffee, water and sugar; chill. Blend the milk, ice cream and, if you desire, the Creme de Cacao. Can be halved.

Nancy Sauer Crosby (Mrs. E. Brown)

SWEDISH BOILED EGG COFFEE

Serves: 6
Preparation: 10 minutes

6 cups cold water
6 slightly rounded tablespoons
    or regular grind coffee
About 1/4 beaten egg

Boil cold water and add coffee mixed with a little cold water and 1/4 beaten egg. Boil and stir with a fork about 3 minutes. Turn off heat and let it settle about 5 minutes. Serve. You may wish to use a strainer.

Mil Youngquist, Rockford, Illinois
by Sue Durham

RUSSIAN TEA

Yield: 1 gallon
Preparation: 15 minutes

2 lemon peels
3/4 cup honey
2 cups water
2 cinnamon sticks
1 Tablespoon whole cloves
2 lemons
2 oranges
12 oz. frozen orange juice
Tea

Boil together for 5 minutes the lemon peels, honey, water, cinnamon sticks and whole cloves. Let mixture cool with spices in it. Brew two quarts of very strong tea. Squeeze juice and insides out of two peeled lemons and add enough Real Lemon to make 3/4 cup. Squeeze juice and insides out of 2 sweet oranges and add to lemon juice. (You may wish to add less lemon/more orange depending on sweetness of oranges.) Thaw one 12 oz. container frozen orange juice. Combine strained spice mixture, tea, lemon-orange juice and thawed orange juice.
To serve: Heat and serve with fresh orange slice. Will keep 2 weeks refrigerated.

Emily Caddell Gordon (Mrs. Alan F.)

MORNING DRINK

Serves: 8
Preparation: Few minutes

1 can frozen orange juice
3 cans of Chablis wine

Mix together and serve over ice. I have also mixed the orange juice with 1 can of water and 2 cans of wine depending on how "spiked" you like your drink.

Yvonne Eriksson Day (Mrs. James K. M.)

STEVE'S BLOODY MARY
Glass size is important: use 14 ounce double old fashioned

TO MAKE ONE:

1-1/2 oz. vodka
3 shakes (generous)
Worcestershire sauce
1 drop Tabasco
Celery salt
Freshly ground pepper
1 lime wedge

Add ice to glass. Fill glass with V-8 (not tomato!!!) juice and stir to chill. Add a celery stick as garnish.

TO MAKE A BATCH:

Mix in a one-gallon jug:
2 cans (48 oz.) V-8 juice
1/4 cup Worcestershire sauce
3 to 4 drops Tabasco sauce
2 Tablespoons lime juice
26 oz. vodka

Mix well. Fill jug to top with more V-8 juice (about 12 ounces). Serve over ice in double old fashioned glass.

Clara Crumpler Bitter (Mrs. Stephen)

MUZZY'S FUZZ
Inspired by a stiff North Easter and fresh peaches on Carolina Shore

Easy
Can do ahead

1 quart Southern Comfort
1 quart fresh peaches, sliced
and juiced in blender
1/2 cup lemon juice
1/2 cup honey

Mix 1/3 of each ingredient together in blender. Combine all in a jug. Pour over many ice cubes. Enjoy!

Mrs. J. Robert McNeil

PINA COLADA

Serves: 2

2 oz. cream of coconut
3 oz. vodka
4 oz. pineapple juice

Mix the ingredients in a blender with a cup of ice and serve.

The Editors

ROCK STEADY

Serves: 3

1/2 oz. lemon juice,
   fresh
4 oz. pineapple juice
1 egg white
4 oz. rum
2 oz. Galliano
8 oz. orange juice

Put ingredients in a blender and mix. Put in tall glasses over ice cubes.

Gail Northen Rogers (Mrs. George H., Jr.)

FROZEN PEACH DAIQUIRI

Serves: 2
Preparation: 5 minutes

3/4 cup peaches
3 teaspoons frozen lemonade
3 teaspoons frozen limeade
4 to 5 oz. light rum

Slice peaches, toss with a little sugar. Put all of the ingredients in a blender, add ice to fill. Blend until it is smooth slush.

Marian MacEachran Boggs (Mrs. Walter J.)

JULGLOGG
Christmas Wine

Serves: 12
Preparation: 5 minutes

1/2 gallon burgundy
1-1/2 pints Swedish Aquavit
   or gin
3/4 cup raisins
1/2 cup sugar
1 Tablespoon cardamon seeds
1/2 teaspoon whole cloves
3-1/2 inch piece of cinnamon,
   broken

Pour 1/2 of the Aquavit or gin and all of the burgundy into a large saucepan. Add raisins, sugar and spices. Cover pan, bring very slowly to boiling point; let simmer about 30 minutes. Add remaining part of gin or aquavit, remove from heat and put a match to "gloggen" in saucepan. Using a long-handled ladle, spoon hot into punch glasses. Serve with raisins and almonds.

Yvonne Eriksson Day (Mrs. James K. M.)

PEACH FUZZIES
Delicious!

Serves: 4
Preparation: 10 minutes

2 large or 3 medium peaches
1 6-oz. can frozen pink
   lemonade
6 oz. vodka or white rum
Sugar to taste (about 1
   Tablespoon)

Wash and cut up peaches; do not peel. Put in blender with the rest of the ingredients. Finish filling blender with ice and blend until smooth.

Bettie Griffin Watts (Mrs. Nelson B.)

HOT MULLED CIDER

Can do ahead
Serves: 8
Preparation: 30 minutes

1/2 cup brown sugar
1 teaspoon whole allspice
1 teaspoon whole cloves
1/4 teaspoon salt
Dash ground nutmeg
3 inches stick cinnamon
2 quarts apple cider
Orange wedges

Combine sugar, allspice, cloves, salt, nutmeg, cinnamon, and cider in a large saucepan. Slowly bring to boiling; cover and simmer 20 minutes. Remove spices. Serve in warmed mugs with a clove-studded orange wedge in each.

Mary Jane Dillingham Westall
(Mrs. Jack W., Jr.)

HOLIDAY ODOR PUNCH
Not for Consumption!

1 quart pineapple juice
1 quart water
1 quart apple cider
4 pieces of ginger
3 3" sticks cinnamon
16 whole cloves
1 teaspoon allspice
1/2 teaspoon pickling spice

Combine all ingredients in a large cooking kettle and bring to boiling. Boil for several minutes. Reduce heat and simmer, allowing house to be filled with a wonderful Christmastime odor.

Helen King Turner (Mrs. Franklin H., Jr.)

EGG NOG

Can do 1 day ahead
Serves: About 24
Preparation: 30 minutes

1 dozen eggs, large
2 cups bourbon or more to taste
10 Tablespoons 4x sugar
1 pint whipping cream
1 pint milk

Separate eggs; whip egg whites. Beat egg yolks and very slowly dribble bourbon in; add sugar and beat. Whip the cream. Fold all ingredients together. If it is too thick, add a little more milk. Chill several hours and stir before serving. You can sprinkle a little nutmeg on top of each cup.

Kay Goode McGuire (Mrs. Walter R.)

CRANBERRY PERCOLATOR PUNCH
Delicious winter drink

Serves: 6

2 cups cranberry juice cocktail
2-1/2 cups unsweetened
*   pineapple juice*
1/2 cup water
1/3 cup brown sugar,
*   firmly packed*
1-1/2 teaspoon whole cloves
3 2" sticks of cinnamon,
*   broken*

Put cranberry juice cocktail, pineapple juice, water and brown sugar in a 6-8 cup percolator. Put whole cloves and cinnamon in basket of percolator and perk.

Nancy Mays Thrash (Mrs. Virgil)

ALL SAINTS RUM PUNCH

Serves: About 40 4-oz. drinks

1 quart dark rum
1 quart light rum
2 quarts apple juice
2 12-oz. cans frozen
*   limeade concentrate*

Refrigerate all ingredients several hours before serving. Make an ice mold, in which lemon and lime slices are arranged. Unmold ice ring into punch bowl and pour the chilled ingredients over it, adjusting to taste with fresh lemon juice. (See additional tips on ice molds in front of section.)

Jean Trainer Veach (Mrs. John B., Jr.)

SANGRIA

Must do part ahead
Serves: 25-30
Preparation: Few minutes

4 bottles Spanish red wine
    or light red wine
2 to 6 teaspoons sugar
    dissolved in a little water
1 Tablespoon lemon juice
6 Tablespoons brandy
4 peaches, sliced
1 orange, sliced
1 lemon, sliced
2 quarts club soda

Mix together and chill. At serving time add club soda and ice cubes.

Yvonne Eriksson Day (Mrs. James K. M.)

NEWFOUND SCHOOL PUNCH

This is the non-alcoholic, slightly tart, punch
we used at each of the schools' graduations.

Must do ahead
Serves: 20-30

1 quart cranberry juice
1 48-oz. can orange juice
1 48-oz. can pineapple juice
1 quart soda water
Lemon juice to taste

The day before serving, refrigerate all the ingredients. Arrange in a ring mold any combination of the following fruits: lemon slices, strawberries, chunks of pineapple, maraschino cherries. Add water and freeze. Just before serving, unmold the ice into a punch bowl and pour the chilled ingredients over it, adjusting the taste with lemon juice. Fresh mint leaves make a pretty garnish. (See additional tips on ice molds in front of section.)

Jean Trainer Veach (Mrs. John B., Jr.)

WHISKEY SOUR PUNCH

Can do ahead
Serves: About 25 4-oz. drinks

2-1/2 cups bourbon
2-1/4 quarts 7-Up
6 oz. lemon juice
6 oz. can frozen orange juice
6 oz. can frozen lemonade

Mix in a punch bowl and float a block of ice in it. (See additional tips on ice molds in front of section.)

Lynn Holmes Trotter (Mrs. Ben)

WHISKEY SOUR PUNCH

Must do ahead
Yield: 2 quarts
Preparation: 15 minutes

BASE:

1/3 cup citric acid
1 cup boiling water
2-1/2 cups pineapple juice
1 6-oz. can orange juice
  concentrate
1 6-oz. can lemonade
  concentrate
3 cups water
1 cup sugar

Dissolve citric acid in boiling water. Add juices, water and sugar and stir to blend. Refrigerate. To make punch use 1 quart of the base and the following:
5 28-oz bottles chilled ginger ale
Fifth of Canadian or bourbon

Nancy Kouns Worley (Mrs. Charles R.)

PINK SQUIRREL

FOR EACH DRINK:

2 oz. double cream
1 oz. grenadine
5/8 oz. white Creme de Cacao

Put ingredients in a blender and add some ice. Blend quickly and strain into a glass.

Gail Northen Rogers (Mrs. George H., Jr.)

JUSTINE SPECIAL
Wonderful in the summer

Serves: 8
Preparation: Few minutes

1/2 gallon vanilla ice cream,
  softened
1/2 fifth brandy

Mix half at a time in a blender and serve as a combination dessert and coffee.

Beverly Maury Bagley (Mrs. Carter S.)

EASY DESSERT BRANDY ALEXANDER

Serves: 4
Preparation: Few minutes

1-1/2 oz. Brandy
1-1/2 oz. Creme de Cacao
1 quart vanilla ice cream
  (or a little more)

Soften the ice cream. Mix in a blender the two liquors and add the ice cream. Mix well until smooth. Serve in champagne glasses.

Clara Crumpler Bitter (Mrs. Stephen)

LEMON LIQUEUR
Excellent gift

Must do ahead
Yield: About 2-1/2 cups

2 lemons
2 cups vodka
1 cup sugar

With a vegetable parer, peel lemons in continuous spirals. Place lemon peel and vodka in jar with a tight fitting lid. Let this stand one week. Shake occasionally. Remove lemon peel. Add sugar and shake until the sugar dissolves. Let stand 7 days before using. Serve straight or over crushed ice.

Lynn Holmes Trotter (Mrs. Benjamin)

NOTES

Hors d'oeuvres

APPETIZER PIE

Baking Time: 15 minutes

8 oz. cream cheese, softened
2 Tablespoons milk
1 pkg. dried beef shredded
2 Tablespoons instant
 minced onion
2 Tablespoons chopped green
 peppers
Dash pepper
1/2 cup sour cream
1/4 cup chopped walnuts

Blend cream cheese and milk. Stir in dried beef, onion, green pepper and pepper. Mix well. Stir in sour cream. Spoon into 8" pie plate or small, shallow baking dish. Sprinkle walnuts over top. Bake at 350° for 15 minutes. Serve hot with crackers.

Bea Smolka Russell (Mrs. Jeffrey)

APPETIZER QUICHE

Serves: 8 entrees, 24 appetizers or
50 to 60 cocktail bites
Baking Time: 30-40 minutes

Prepare piecrust to suit size
 of pan
1 lb. bacon, cooked and
 crumbled
2 onions, chopped and sauted
 in 2 Tablespoons bacon
 drippings
3 cups Swiss cheese, shredded
2 Tablespoons snipped parsley
6 eggs
1 quart half-and-half (or milk)
1-1/2 teaspoons salt
1/4 teaspoon nutmeg
1/4 teaspoon pepper
2 Tablespoons Dijon mustard

Bake pastry in oven at 425° for 6 minutes. Remove from oven and reduce heat to 375.° Sprinkle crust with: bacon, onions, cheese and parsley. Beat remaining ingredients together. Pour over filling. Bake in 375° oven for 30-40 minutes. Cool 10 minutes on rack before cutting.

Laura Littlejohn Rogers (Mrs. Bruce)

SHRIMP MOLD

Must do ahead

1 lb. peeled, coarsely chopped
shrimp (1 lb. can salmon
can be used instead)
1 can tomato soup
2 3-oz. pkg. cream cheese,
softened
3/4 cup finely chopped onions
3/4 cup finely chopped celery
2 cups mayonnaise
1-1/2 envelopes Knox
unflavored gelatin

Bring soup to boil—add cream cheese—stir and let cool. Mix remaining ingredients except gelatin. Add gelatin to 1/2 cup boiling water. Mix all together and place in greased mold. Chill several hours or overnight.

Jean Lipinsky Moore (Mrs. Michael)
Jean Moffat Frady (Mrs. A. Hampton, Jr.)

MARINATED SHRIMP

Must do ahead
Serves: 8-10

3 cups shrimp, cooked, shelled
and deveined
1/2 cup vinegar
1/4 cup salad oil
1 teaspoon salt
Few drops garlic juice
Dash of Tabasco
2 Tablespoons chopped olives
2 Tablespoons parsley
2 Tablespoons chopped
dill pickle

Put shrimp in a quart jar and add the remaining ingredients. Shake the jar well and store in refrigerator at least one day in advance of using. Shake the jar often. When ready to serve, the shrimp will have taken on a most delightful flavor. Serve with toothpicks. No sauce is needed.

Diana Roscoe Bilbrey (Mrs. George M., Jr.)

SHRIMP DIP

Can be frozen

2 lbs. cooked shrimp
2 (8 oz.) pkgs. cream cheese
2 Tablespoons lemon juice
1/3 cup catsup
1 teaspoon Worcestershire
sauce
Dash of Tabasco
1 Tablespoon grated onion
with juice
2 teaspoons horseradish

Mix all ingredients together except shrimp. Add the shrimp, after chipping in blender. To halve recipe, use 1/4 cup catsup and 1 full teaspoon horseradish. Serve with crackers.

Lynn Holmes Trotter (Mrs. Benjamin)

SEAFOOD CASSEROLE

Freezes well—thaws slowly
Yield: Approximately 6 quarts
Baking Time: At least 1 hour

1 lb. each: fillet of sole, sea
    scallops, shrimp, lobster
    tails or crab, swordfish
    or halibut
3/4 cup butter or margarine
1 lb. chopped onions
1/2 lb. diced fresh mushrooms
2 green peppers, chopped
1/2 lb. flour (8 oz.)
1/4 teaspoon nutmeg
2 Tablespoons dry mustard
3 Tablespoons Worcestershire
    sauce
3/4 oz. Tabasco
14 oz. light cream
1/2 teaspoon pepper
18 oz. fish stock (from boiled
    seafood)
2 Tablespoons salt
2 chopped pimentos
1/2 cup chopped parsley
1 lb. grated Cheddar
2 cups bread crumbs
Sprinkle of oregano
8 oz. sauterne wine

Combine and boil seafood. Drain, reserving stock. Cut seafood in bite-sized pieces. Melt butter in Dutch oven. Add dry ingredients and stir until slightly brown. Add all liquids gradually. Cook until smooth. Add cheese and blend. Combine seafood, sauce and remaining ingredients in Dutch oven. Cover with bread crumbs. Sprinkle with paprika and some melted butter. Bake at 325° to 350° until golden brown—at least one hour. May be used in the following ways:

1) As hot appetizer in chafing dish as a dip or filling for patty shells.
2) As a main dish over chow mein noodles.
3) As a filling for crêpes.

Linda Hinson Adams (Mrs. Alfred)

BARBEQUE SHRIMP APPETIZERS

Serves: 6-8 as main course or
16 as appetizer

3/4 cup chopped onion
1/2 cup salad oil
3/4 cup catsup
3/4 cup water
1/3 cup lemon juice
3 Tablespoons sugar
4 Tablespoons Worcestershire
3 Tablespoons mustard
2 teaspoons salt
1/2 teaspoon hot pepper sauce
1/4 teaspoon Tabasco
2 lbs. shrimp

Cook onion in oil until tender; add catsup, water, lemon juice, sugar, Worcestershire, mustard, salt, hot pepper sauce and Tabasco. Simmer 10-15 minutes. Peel and devein shrimp, leaving tail section on. Dip into sauce. Rotate over hot coals 5-8 minutes, brushing often with sauce. Serve with remaining sauce. Good with saffron rice, steamed fresh broccoli and spinach.

Sue Small Durham (Mrs. Cecil J., Jr.)

PICKLED SHRIMP

Must do ahead

3 lbs. fresh, cleaned, cooked
    shrimp
2 large onions, cut into rings
8 Tablespoons pickling spices
6 to 8 bay leaves
1 cup white vinegar
1-1/2 cups salad oil
2 teaspoons salt
2 teaspoons celery seed
4 Tablespoons capers,
    with juice
Several dashes Tabasco

Place shrimp, onions, bay leaves, pickling spices in large fruit jar alternately. Combine last six ingredients and pour into jar. Cover and shake. Store in refrigerator at least 24 hours (3-4 days is fine!) Shake occasionally.

Elizabeth B. Thurlow

SMOKEY SALMON SPREAD

Must do ahead
Yield: 2-1/2 cups

1 (7-3/4 oz.) can Sockeye
    Salmon
1 Tablespoon lemon juice
2 Tablespoons snipped parsley
2 teaspoons horseradish
1/4 teaspoon liquid smoke
Salt and pepper, to taste
1 (8 oz.) pkg. cream cheese
    with chives, softened
1/4 cup chopped pecans

Drain and flake salmon. Combine and blend well with the rest of the ingredients except the parsley and nuts. Shape into ball on waxed paper. Chill several hours. Combine nuts and parsley on wax paper and roll salmon ball in this. Chill. Garnish with additional parsley and serve with crisp crackers.

Elizabeth Shuford Nichols (Mrs. Herman G.)

SALMON MOUSSE

Must do ahead
Serves: 20 people
(Can be halved)

1 lb. smoked salmon
1/4 cup lemon juice
1/2 lb. butter
1 cup sour cream
Salt and pepper to taste
Lemon slices
Fresh dill
Capers

Purée salmon and lemon juice in food processor. Melt butter; add in steady stream while blending. Remove to a bowl; fold in remaining ingredients. Place in a mold or souffle dish and chill. Serve with toast points or melba toast.

Curry Wadopian (Mrs. Herbert)

SALMON SOUR CREAM MOLD

1 envelope unflavored gelatin
1/2 cup cold water
1 envelope sour cream
   sauce mix
1/2 cup mayonnaise
2 teaspoons lemon juice
1/2 teaspoon dill weed
1 16-oz. can salmon
1/2 cup finely chopped celery
Dash Tabasco

Soften gelatin in cold water; stir over boiling water until gelatin dissolves. Cool. Blend sour cream sauce mix, mayonnaise, lemon juice, and dill weed, gradually stir in gelatin. Drain salmon, discarding skin and large bones; flake. Fold salmon and celery into sour cream mixture. Turn into 3-cup mold. Chill 4 to 5 hours. Garnish with carrot curls, if desired. Serve with crackers.

Shirley Anne Freeman McCullough
(Mrs. Charles T.)

HOT CRAB BREAD

Partially do ahead
Yield: About 6 sandwiches
Baking Time: 25 minutes
Preparation: 30 minutes

1 7-1/2-oz. can crabmeat,
   drained and flaked
1/3 cup mayonnaise
1/3 cup commercial sour cream
2 Tablespoons chopped **fresh**
   parsley
2 teaspoons freshly squeezed
   lemon juice
Optional: 1/4 teaspoon
   garlic salt
1 loaf French/Italian bread
2 Tablespoons margarine
1/4 lb. sliced Swiss cheese

Combine crabmeat, mayonnaise, sour cream, parsley, lemon juice and garlic salt; chill. Slice bread in half lengthwise and place on baking sheet. Spread cut sides with margarine. Arrange cheese slices on bottom half of bread, and top with crab mixture. Cover with top half of bread. Bake in 350° oven about 25 minutes or until lightly browned. Cut crosswise into serving pieces.

Mary Jane Dillingham Westall (Mrs. Jack)

CRABMEAT DIP/SPREAD

Must do ahead

1 can crabmeat, drained
1 cup sour cream
Juice of 1 lemon
1 small onion, chopped
Dash Tabasco
1 Tablespoon Worcestershire
   sauce
Salt to taste

Squeeze juice of lemon over thoroughly drained crabmeat. Mix all ingredients together and refrigerate for several hours. Serve with your favorite crackers.

Louise Ready Hanks (Mrs. W. Neal)

CRAB ROUNDS

Yield: 32 appetizers
Baking Time: 10-12 minutes

1 can (7-1/2 oz.) crab, drained,
    boned and flaked
1 cup grated Swiss cheese
1/2 cup mayonnaise
1 Tablespoon dried green onion
    or 2 Tablespoons fresh,
    finely chopped onion
1 Tablespoon lemon juice
1/4 teaspoon curry powder
1/3 cup water chestnuts,
    thinly sliced
1/4 cup parsley
1 can Hungry Jack Buttermilk
    Biscuits

Mix crab, Swiss cheese, mayonnaise, onions, lemon juice and curry powder together. Separate layers of biscuits to get 32 rounds. Place on greased cookie sheet. Spread crab mixture on biscuits. Top with water chestnuts and sprinkle with parsley. Bake in 400° oven for 10 to 12 minutes.

Jeanne Forsyth Powell (Mrs. Benjamin)

CLAM-CRAB ROUNDS

Yield: 6-7 dozen rounds

6-7 dozen bread rounds
8 oz. softened cream cheese
1 7-1/2 oz. can raw minced
    clams, drained
3/4 cup fresh flaked crabmeat
2 teaspoons grated onion
2 Tablespoons minced chives
1 teaspoon Worcestershire
    sauce
1/2 teaspoon garlic powder
1/2 teaspoon pepper
1/2 teaspoon paprika

Toast rounds on one side and cool. Combine cream cheese, clams, crab, onions, chives, Worcestershire sauce and garlic powder. Spread mixture on untoasted side of bread. Sprinkle with paprika. Broil until bubbly.

Ellen Resnikoff Carr (Mrs. Robert J.)

GREEN GODDESS SPREAD

1 stick butter
1 8-oz. pkg. cream cheese
1/3 cup Green Goddess
    salad dressing
1 clove garlic, crushed

Mix well. Serve with Wheat Thins.

Mrs. Martin Hatcher

VEGETABLE DIP

Must do ahead
Preparation: 10 minutes

1/2 cup mayonnaise
1/2 cup sour cream
1/2 teaspoon marjoram
1/2 teaspoon dillweed
1/2 teaspoon summer savory
1/2 teaspoon minced garlic (or
    1/4 teaspoon garlic powder)
1/2 teaspoon sugar
1 teaspoon chives
1 teaspoon minced onions
1 teaspoon dried parsley
Juice of 1/2 lemon

Mix all ingredients together. Place in airtight container. Refrigerate. Serve with raw vegetables or crackers. Can thin with whipping cream and use as salad dressing.

Sue Small Durham (Mrs. Cecil J., Jr.)

SPINACH DIP

1 pkg. chopped spinach, cooked
    and drained
1 cup mayonnaise
1 cup sour cream
1/2 cup chopped green
    onions (or less)
2 Tablespoons lemon juice
1 Tablespoon oregano
1 Tablespoon McCormick
    Salad Supreme Seasoning
1/2 Tablespoon dillweed
1 pumpernickel round

Mix all ingredients together. Slice the top off the round of pumpernickel and hollow out. Pour the dip inside the bread and serve.

Elizabeth B. Thurlow
Beverly Maury Bagley (Mrs. Carter S.)

CRUNCHY DIP

Must do ahead

1 3-oz. pkg. cream cheese
1-1/2 cups sour cream
1/2 to 3/4 cup chopped water
    chestnuts
1/2 cup chopped stuffed olives
1 envelope Italian salad
    dressing mix

Blend cream cheese and sour cream. Add remaining ingredients. Chill. Serve with chips or crackers.

Candy Stell Shivers (Mrs. James A.)
from Mrs. Grey Shivers

HOT ARTICHOKE DIP

Can do ahead
Serves: 12
Preparation: 5 minutes
Baking Time: 20-25 minutes

1 14-oz. can artichokes,
  drained and chopped
1 clove garlic, mashed
1/2 to 3/4 cup mayonnaise
1/2 teaspoon Worcestershire
  sauce
1 cup grated Parmesan cheese
Freshly ground pepper, to taste

Combine all ingredients in small baking dish (greased). Bake in 350° oven for 20-25 minutes. If you wish you may sprinkle with paprika before baking. Serve hot with triscuits, taco flavored chips or your favorite crackers.

Sandra Bonjean Cagle (Mrs. W. B.)
Ruth Wellman Jameson (Mrs. J. L., Jr.)
Emmie Spencer Field (Mrs. Arthur)

ARTICHOKE SQUARES

Baking Time: 30 minutes
Yield: 30 squares

2 6-oz. jars of marinated
  artichokes
1 onion, chopped
1 clove garlic, minced
4 eggs
1/4 cup bread crumbs
Dash of Tabasco
1/2 teaspoon oregano
2 cups shredded Cheddar
  cheese
Salt and pepper

Drain juice from 1 jar of artichokes into skillet. Saute onion and garlic in juice. Drain away other jar of juice and chop all artichokes. In bowl, beat eggs and add remaining ingredients. Mix thoroughly. Bake in a 9x13" pan for 30 minutes in 325° oven. Cut into squares and serve hot.

Margaret Guy Dunn (Mrs. Francis H., Jr.)

HOUMMUS (CHICK PEA DIP)

Can do ahead
Serves: 6-8
Preparation: 5 minutes

1 can chick peas, drained
2 Tablespoons Tahini
1/3 cup oil
1/4 cup lemon juice
1 clove garlic, minced
1 or 2 teaspoons cumin, to taste
Salt
Pepper
Dash of cayenne

Mix all ingredients in food processor. Chill and serve with pita bread.

Celine Hanan Lurey (Mrs. Michael)

43

SPINACH BALLS

Can do ahead
Can freeze
Yield: 11 dozen
Preparation: 30 minutes
Baking Time: 15 to 20 minutes

2 (10-oz.) pkgs. frozen
  chopped spinach
3 cups herb-seasoned
  stuffing mix
1 large onion, finely chopped
6 eggs, well beaten
3/4 cup melted butter
1/2 cup grated Parmesan
  cheese
1 teaspoon pepper
1-1/2 teaspoon garlic salt
1/2 teaspoon thyme

Cook spinach; drain and squeeze. Combine all ingredients with spinach, mix well. Make 3/4" balls—bake at 325° on greased cookie sheet for 15-20 minutes.

Can be frozen before baking. Place on sheet, freeze until firm. Store in plastic bags. Thaw slightly. Bake for 20-25 minutes.

Melanie Huntsman Hudgins
(Mrs. Roderick M., Jr.)

TRIPLE CHEESE APPETIZER

Must do ahead
Can freeze
Yield: 3-1/4 cups (1 4-cup mold)

1 envelope unflavored gelatin
1/4 cup cold water
1/4 cup chopped pecans
3/4 cup mayonnaise
1/2 teaspoon salt
1-1/2 teaspoons prepared
  mustard
Dash hot sauce or cayenne
  (add enough to make spicy)
2 cups shredded cheese (8 oz.)
1/2 cup grated Parmesan
  (fresh)
1/4 cup crumbled blue cheese
1 cup whipping cream
Mayonnaise
Chopped parsley
Cherry tomatoes

Soften gelatin in water in small saucepan. Place over low heat, stirring until dissolved. combine next 9 ingredients in medium bowl, stirring; stir in gelatin mixture. Lightly coat 4 cup mold with mayonnaise; pour cheese mixture into mold. Chill overnight or until firm. Unmold on serving plate; garnish with chopped parsley and cherry tomatoes. Serve with crackers.

Renie Fridy
Sue Small Durham (Mrs. C. J., Jr.)

THE VINEYARD SPREAD

Must do ahead
Can freeze
Yield: 1 cheese ball
Preparation: 15 minutes

2 8-oz. pkgs. of cream cheese,
  softened
1-1/2 oz. crushed pineapple,
  drained well
1/4 cup green pepper, chopped
2 Tablespoons onion, chopped
1 Tablespoon seasoned salt
1 cup chopped pecans (save
  some to put on outside)

Mix ingredients as listed. Put in plastic bag. Chill and shape. This can be a cheese ball or served as a spread. Serve with your favorite crackers.

Lynn Holmes Trotter (Mrs. Benjamin)
Jane Brown McNeil (Mrs. M. Kerney)

STUFFED EDAM OR GOUDA CHEESE

Can do ahead

1 lb. Edam or Gouda cheese
  in red wax
1/2 cup beer
1 teaspoon Dijon mustard
1/8 teaspoon nutmeg
1/4 lb. soft butter, in chunks
1/2 teaspoon caraway seed

Cut a hole in the top of the cheese and scoop out insides, leaving the walls firm. Grate the cheese on a coarse grater. Place all ingredients, reserving 1/4 beer and caraway seeds, in the blender and mix. Place in bowl, add remaining beer and caraway seeds, mix well and set aside. Cut the open top of the cheese in points, pour in cheese mixture and refrigerate. Serve with crackers.

Diana Roscoe Bilbrey (Mrs. George)

SHERRY CHEESE PATÉ

2 3-oz. pkgs. cream cheese
4 oz. sharp Cheddar cheese,
  grated
1/2 teaspoon curry powder
1/2 teaspoon gelatin dissolved
  in 1/4 cup water
4 Tablespoons dry sherry
1 (8-oz.) jar chutney
2 green onions with tops
1/2 teaspoon salt

Mix cheese, wine, seasonings and gelatin thoroughly. Put on pie platter or mold into a flat ball. Chop up chutney and spread over cheese. Sprinkle with finely chopped green onions.

Jean Moffat Frady (Mrs. A. Hampton, Jr.)
Betty Lou McCarty Davis (Mrs. Philip C.)

NO BRAINER
Very good and easy!

Baking Time: 30 minutes

1 wheel Brie
1 box Pepperidge Farm puff
　pastry or patty shell,
　defrosted

Roll out pastry and put Brie in center; wrap. Use scraps to decorate the top with flowers, animals, etc. Bake approximately 30 minutes at 400° or until golden. Serve with pears poached in wine or plain fruit. Use a plate and fork to enjoy.

Carol Walton Costenbader (Mrs. William J. Jr.)

HOLIDAY CHEESE ROLL

Serves: 10

2 pkgs. (3 oz.) cream cheese
1/8 teaspoon Worcestershire
　sauce
1/8 teaspoon seasoned salt
1/8 teaspoon salt
4 drops hot pepper sauce
1 cup pecans
2 cloves garlic
1-1/2 teaspoons chili powder
1-1/2 teaspoons curry powder

Blend cream cheese, Worcestershire, seasoned salt, salt and hot pepper sauce. Put pecans and garlic in blender or food processor; chop fine. Blend into cheese mixture. Shape into roll. Mix chili and curry powders; sprinkle evenly over a piece of wax paper. Roll cheese roll in mixture, coating evenly. Wrap tightly in plastic wrap and chill about 4 hours or until roll is firm. Serve with crackers or apple slices dipped in lemon juice and water mixture.

Shirley Ann Freeman McCullough
(Mrs. Charles T.)

MOCK BOURSIN

Must do ahead

8 oz. whipped butter, softened
16 oz. cream cheese, softened
2 cloves garlic, pressed
1/2 teaspoon oregano
1/4 teaspoon basil
1/4 teaspoon dill weed
1/4 teaspoon marjoram
1/4 teaspoon black pepper
1/4 teaspoon thyme

Mix all ingredients thoroughly in food processor, but be careful not to over mix. Refrigerate overnight. Serve with assorted crackers.

Barrie Muilenburg Sneed (Mrs. Albert)

GOUGERE
Excellent for brunch as well

Can do ahead
Baking Time: 40 minutes

1/2 cup butter
1/2 teaspoon salt
Dash freshly ground pepper
1 cup sifted flour
4 eggs
3 oz. well-aged natural Swiss
  cheese, shredded
Dash of nutmeg

Combine 1 cup water and first three ingredients in saucepan; bring to boil. Add all flour. Heat over low heat until mixture leaves side of pan and does not separate (approximately 1 minute). Remove from heat; continue beating to cool mixture slightly (approximately 2 minutes). Add eggs one at a time, beating after each addition until mixture has satiny sheen. Stir in cheese. Spoon out in pieces the size of an egg and shape into high mounds on buttered baking sheet, forming a ring 8-9 inches in diameter or drop in teaspoon size for individual hot appetizers. Bake in moderate oven (375°) for 40 minutes or until puffy and golden brown. Serve while warm or make mixture one hour prior to baking and let sit at room temperature.

Magy Todd (Mrs. Christopher)

CHEESE POTPOURRI

Can do ahead
Can freeze
Yield: 5 cups

1-1/2 lbs. aged Cheddar cheese
1/4 lb. Roquefort, blue cheese
  or Gorgonzola, crumbled
1 teaspoon dry mustard
2 Tablespoons butter, softened
1 teaspoon Worcestershire
  sauce
1/8 teaspoon Tabasco
2 teaspoons onion, grated
1 12-oz. can of beer (flat)

Grate cheese. Place all ingredients, except beer, in bowl of electric mixer (or blender) and let stand at room temperature about 30 minutes to soften cheese. Mix slowly, gradually adding beer, until mixture is smooth and spreadable. Serve immediately, or store in a tightly-covered container in refrigerator or freezer.

Alice Bullard Britt (Mrs. Henry Joe, Jr.)
Barrie Muilenburg Sneed (Mrs. Albert Lee)

McNEIL LIVERWURST CONCOCTION

May do ahead
Can freeze

10 chicken livers
1 8-oz. pkg. liverwurst
2 Tablespoons chopped onion
1 Tablespoon mustard
Dash of Worcestershire
1/4 cup white wine or sherry
Salt and pepper, to taste
8 oz. softened cream cheese
Chopped parsley or chives,
    or both

Fry chicken livers in butter with onions. Add the mustard, Worcestershire, wine or sherry, salt and pepper and mix well. Put in refrigerator to cool and harden. Form liver mixture in a mound and cover with cream cheese which has been mixed with the parsley or chives. Serve with crackers or use as a sandwich spread.

Jane Brown McNeil (Mrs. M. Kerney)

PATÉ

Must do ahead

8 slices bacon
12 oz. liverwurst
2 Tablespoons butter, softened
3 Tablespoons sour cream
1 small onion, grated
1 clove garlic, pressed
2 Tablespoons chopped parsley
1-1/2 Tablespoons brandy
Salt to taste

Chop bacon and cook until crisp. Drain. Mash liverwurst with sour cream and butter. Add remaining ingredients and salt to taste. Press in crock. Cover and chill at least 2 hours.

Melanie Huntsman Hudgins
(Mrs. Roderick M., Jr.)

CAVIAR PIE

Must do ahead

6 eggs
Chopped white onion, to taste
1 cup sour cream
4 oz. jar or more of black caviar
Juice of half a lemon
2 Tablespoons minced parsley
Lemon wedges

Hard boil eggs and rice; mix with onions to taste. Butter a 9" pie plate and make a crust, using the eggs. Refrigerate for a day. Mix sour cream and more onions to taste. Place caviar in a bowl and season with lemon juice. Pour sour cream mixture into crust and top with caviar. Decorate the edges with minced parsley and arrange lemon wedges on top.

Yvonne Eriksson Day (Mrs. James K. M.)

GREEN CHILI AND CHEESE CANAPES

1 cup mayonnaise
1/2 lb. grated Monterey Jack
    cheese
1 4-oz. jar whole green or
    chopped chilies
1 cup butter, softened
1 clove garlic, minced
4" round loaf French bread,
    sliced thin

Combine mayonnaise and cheese. Set aside. Wash chilies, remove seeds and chop into small pieces. Add to butter and garlic. Spread on each bread slice. Top with a teaspoon of mayonnaise mixture. Place on cookie sheet. Broil 4 minutes —until bubbly and slightly brown.

Jeanne Forsyth Powell (Mrs. Benjamin)

HOT AND SPICY MEXICAN DIP

Can do ahead
Can freeze
Yield: 2 cups
Preparation: 5 minutes

1 pkg. (2 lbs.) Velveeta cheese
1 can (4 oz.) green chilies,
    drained
1 can (7-3/4 oz.) hot taco sauce
    OR
1 can Ro-Tel tomatoes

Slowly melt cheese in double boiler. Seed and chop green chilies. Stir chilies and sauce (or tomatoes) into cheese. Pour into chafing dish to keep warm. Serve with tostidos or large corn chips.

Jeanne Forsyth Powell (Mrs. Benjamin)

CHICKEN LIVER PATÉ

Yield: 3 cups
Preparation: 30 minutes

1/2 cup sweet butter
1-1/4 lb. chicken liver
2 teaspoons cognac
Chopped green onion
1 large sliced onion (1 cup)
1 hard-cooked egg
1/2 teaspoon salt
Dash pepper

In skillet saute sliced onion in 2 tablespoons butter until tender (10 minutes)—remove cooked onion. Heat remaining butter in same skillet. Add livers and saute 3 to 5 minutes—liver should be pink inside. Put 1/2 onion, livers, egg and cognac in blender. Blend at low speed until smooth. Turn into bowl. Repeat with other half of everything. Add salt and pepper. Put into crock and refrigerate overnight. Garnish with green onion.

Jean Moffat Frady (Mrs. A. Hampton)

CHEESE AND OLIVE EMPANADITAS (or TARTS)
These are worth the trouble!

Can be made ahead
Can freeze
Yield: About 4 dozen
Baking Time: 20-25 minutes

CREAM CHEESE PASTRY:

1 cup butter
8 oz. cream cheese
2 cups flour
1 egg yolk, mixed with 2
  teaspoons milk

FILLING:

6 oz. grated Cheddar cheese
1/4 cup soft butter
1/4 cup sour cream
1 4-1/2 oz. can chopped
  ripe olives
2 to 4 Tablespoons hot
  taco sauce
OR
2 to 4 Tablespoons roasted
  green chilies

For Pastry: Soften butter and cream cheese and mix well. Stir in flour and mix well. Wrap in wax paper and chill 1/2 hour or longer.
For Filling: Grate cheese into bowl and let stand to soften. Drain ripe olives. If using peeled chilies, drain, seed and chop finely. Mix all filling ingredients well.
Take half of chilled pastry and roll out to 1/8" thickness on a well-floured surface. Cut into rounds with biscuit cutter. Moisten edges of rounds with water. Place a scant teaspoon of filling in each. Fold over into half-moon shapes and press edges well to seal, using a fork if desired. Transfer to buttered baking sheets. Repeat with remaining dough and re-roll scraps. Chill until ready to bake, up to a day if desired. Preheat oven to 350° Brush tops of pastries with egg-milk mixture and bake 20-25 minutes. Pastries should turn golden, but not brown.
Can be made ahead and frozen unbaked...bake *without* thawing.

Celine Hanan Lurey (Mrs. Michael)

AUNT JUDY'S CHILI CON CASA
Have plenty of cold drinks on hand!

Can do ahead
Appetizer
Preparation: 20 minutes

2 lbs. American cheese (Kraft)
1 tomato, peeled, seeded,
  chopped
1/4 lb. bacon, fried
  and crumbled
1 4-oz. can green chilies
  (seeded if you do not want
  it too hot)

Cook ingredients together. Place in chafing dish. Serve with doritos or fry tortillas (cut in wedges) until crisp. Salt.

Lynell Bell (Mrs. C. Robert, Jr.)

ARTICHOKE AND CLAM PUFFS

Can do ahead

2 pkgs. frozen artichoke
   hearts
1 can (8 oz.) minced clams
1 8-oz. pkg. cream cheese
1/2 cup mayonnaise
1 teaspoon grated onion
2 dashes Tabasco

One to three hours before serving—cook artichoke hearts as directed, slightly undercooking. Drain clams and mix with remaining ingredients. Spread mixture on cut sides of artichokes. At this point you may cover and leave at room temperature for an hour or refrigerate for several hours.

If refrigerated, bring to room temperature; broil under medium heat until puffy and brown.

Note: If you have a heat-proof serving tray, use it. They are quite difficult to transfer from a cookie sheet.

Celine Hanan Lurey (Mrs. Michael)

WHEAT THINS

Can do ahead
Yield: 3 dozen
Preparation: 20 minutes
Baking Time: 10 minutes

2 cups whole wheat flour
2 Tablespoons wheat germ
1 teaspoon salt
1 teaspoon baking powder
2 Tablespoons brown sugar
2 Tablespoons dry milk powder
6 Tablespoons margarine
1/2 cup water
1 Tablespoon molasses
Cornmeal

In a mixing bowl combine the flour, wheat germ, salt, baking powder, brown sugar and dry milk. Cut in the margarine with a pastry blender. Combine separately and stir in the water and molasses. Turn out on a board and knead until smooth. Grease 2 cookie sheets (10x15″) and sprinkle each with cornmeal. Divide the dough in half. Roll out half the dough directly onto the cookie sheet with a floured pin, rolling dime thin. Sprinkle lightly with paprika, garlic, onion, or seasoned salt. Run rolling pin over once more. Prick with a fork. Cut into squares or triangles. Bake 10 minutes or until lightly browned. Makes 2/3 lb.

Mary Berg

PARMESAN COCKTAIL BISCUITS

Must do ahead
Yield: 48 (4 dozen)
Baking Time: 12-15 minutes

1-1/4 cup Parmesan cheese
1 cup flour
1 stick butter, softened
1/2 teaspoon marjoram
1/2 teaspoon basil
1/2 teasoon oregano
1/2 teaspoon Worcestershire
    sauce
2 to 3 Tablespoons dry
    white wine

In a bowl, combine cheese, flour, herbs and butter. Blend to resemble coarse meal. Add Worcestershire sauce and enough wine to just form a ball. Roll dough into 1-1/2 inch log. Wrap in plastic wrap and chill one hour or until firm. Slice dough into 1/4" slices and place on lightly greased baking sheet. Bake in 350° oven for 12-15 minutes. Cool on wire rack and store in airtight tins.

Jo Ann McGowan Grimes (Mrs. Charles)

SESAME CHEESESTICKS

Must do ahead
Baking Time: 45-60 minutes

6 slices firm bread
1/4 stick butter
3 Tablespoons Parmesan
    cheese
2 teaspoons oregano
1/4 teaspoon garlic salt
3 Tablespoons sesame seeds

Freeze bread. Cut crust from frozen bread. Spread with mixture of butter, Parmesan cheese, oregano, garlic salt and sesame seeds blended into a paste. Cut bread into halves—then half again. Place on cookie sheet and bake in 275° oven for 45-60 minutes. Check in 30 minutes. Move around if browning too fast. Cool and store in glass jars. Keep indefinitely. May be reheated to crisp but never seem to last long enough.

Jean Croxton Moran (Mrs. Raymond F.)

CHEESE BENNIES

Can freeze
Bake: 350°
Preparation: 30 minutes

1 lb. grated sharp cheese
1/2 lb. butter or margarine
2-1/2 cups sifted flour
Pinch of red pepper
1 tsp. salt
1/2 cup or more toasted
    sesame seeds

Cream together cheese, butter, pepper and salt. Add flour and sesame seeds. Make into a roll and wrap in waxed paper, refrigerate. Slice and bake in moderate oven.

Harriet Maybank Hutson (Mrs. Henry C.)

HOT CHEESE PUFFS

Can do ahead
Yield: 32
Preparation: 30 minutes

3/4 lb. sharp natural Cheddar
    cheese, grated
4-1/2 Tablespoons unsifted
    all-purpose flour
1/2 teaspoon salt
1/4 teaspoon pepper
5 egg whites
1/2 cup pkg. dry bread crumbs
Salad oil or shortening for
    deep frying

Combine cheese, flour, salt and pepper. Mix thoroughly. In large bowl beat egg whites until stiff peaks form. Shape into balls using level teaspoon for each. Roll in bread crumbs. Meanwhile slowly heat oil or shortening 1-1/2" to 2" deep in electric skillet or heavy deep sauce pan to 375° on deep fry thermometer. Deep fry balls until golden, about one-half minute. Lift out with slotted spoon. Drain on paper towels. Can be refrigerated uncooked overnight. Fry just before serving.

Jean Moffat Frady (Mrs. A. Hampton, Jr.)

4 IN 1 COCKTAIL STICKS

Yield: 32 sticks
Baking Time: 8-10 minutes

2 pkgs. frozen patty shells
1 slightly beaten egg yolk
2 Tablespoons shelled
    sunflower seeds
1 Tablespoon sesame seeds,
    toasted
2 teaspoons poppy seeds
1 Tablespoon grated Parmesan
    cheese
1 Tablespoon milk
1/4 teaspoon onion powder

Thaw patty shells in refrigerator; place one on top of the other and press together. Roll to 8x6" rectangle. Combine egg yolk, milk and onion powder; brush over pastry. Cut dough into four equal portions. Sprinkle each portion with a different seed and the cheese. Cut into 3x1-1/2" strips. Place on baking sheet. Bake in 400° oven for 8 to 10 minutes or until lightly browned. Cool on rack.

Jean Moffat Frady (Mrs. A. Hampton, Jr.)

MUSHROOM TURNOVERS

May be made ahead
Can be frozen
Baking Time: 15 minutes
Yield: 3 dozen

3 (3 oz.) pkgs. cream cheese,
   softened
1/2 cup margarine or butter,
   softened
1-1/2 cups flour

MUSHROOM FILLING:

3 Tablespoons butter or
   margarine
1 large onion, finely chopped
1 lb. mushrooms, chopped
1/4 teaspoon thyme
1/2 teaspoon salt
Pepper to taste
2 Tablespoons flour
1/4 cup sweet or sour cream

Mix cheese and margarine or butter thoroughly; add flour and stir until smooth. Chill at least 30 minutes. In a skillet heat butter; add onions and cook until lightly brown. Add mushrooms and cook, stirring often, about 3 minutes. Add thyme, salt, pepper and cream. Sprinkle with flour and cook until thick. Roll dough on floured board to 1/8" thickness. Cut with a small round glass (about 2"). Place one-half to one teaspoon mushroom mixture on round. Fold dough over the filling. Press edges together with a fork. Prick top of dough with fork. Bake on ungreased cookie sheet for 15 minutes in 350° oven. For a nice variation—you may shape the dough in 1" balls. Use fingers to press against sides and bottoms of ungreased small muffin tins—may be made ahead and frozen unbaked—thaw before cooking.

Martha Blackshear Salisbury (Mrs. Kent)
Ann Williams Martin (Mrs. Hayes)
Mary Bruce Rhodes Woody (Mrs. Stephen W.)

CHEESE CRISPIES

Can do ahead
Can freeze
Yields: 90

1 stick butter (not oleo)
1 cup flour
1/2 teaspoon red pepper
1/2 lb. grated extra sharp
   Cheddar cheese
1 cup very crisp
   Rice Crispies

Melt butter, add flour with one-half heaping teaspoon red pepper. Add grated cheese and Rice Crispies. Pinch a ball of mixture the size of a nickel and roll in palm of your hand. Place on a cookie sheet and press with thumb. Bake in 350° oven for 20 minutes or until light brown. Store in tightly covered tins.

Elsie Allport Bennett (Mrs. Harold K.)

SWEET-SOUR MEATBALLS

Can be frozen
Yield: 50-60 meatballs

2 lbs. ground meat
1 large grated onion
1 slightly beaten egg
Salt to taste

Mix together ground meat, onion, egg and salt. Shape into 50 to 60 balls; place in sauce. Simmer until brown.

SAUCE:

1 bottle chili sauce
Juice of 1 lemon
1/2 large (16 oz.) jar grape jelly

Brenda Seagrove McGuire (Mrs. Leslie)

HAM MOUSSE
Mrs. Richard M. Nixon's recipe

1/2 cup cooked ham, finely
*   ground*
1 cup tomato juice
1 cup beef consomme
1/2 teaspoon paprika
4 Tablespoons cold water
1 envelope gelatin
2 cups whipping cream
*   (whipped until it stands)*
Salt to taste

Mix together and bring to a boil 4 tablespoons cold water and envelope of gelatin; add to ham mixture (first 4 ingredients). Put into refrigerator to cool, stirring occasionally. When it begins to slightly congeal, fold in 2 cups whipping cream. Add salt to taste. Pour into 1 large mold or individual molds. Let set in refrigerator until firm. Unmold and garnish with watercress. Serve with mayonnaise thinned with a few drops of lemon juice and a little heavy cream, adding finely chopped chives.

Helen King Turner (Mrs. Franklin H., Jr.)

COCKTAIL SAUSAGE BALLS
A hot hors d'oeuvres—to go with anything

Can do ahead
Can freeze
Yield: 100 round balls
Preparation: 1 hour
Baking Time: 20 minutes

cups Bisquick
lb. medium or regular
*   sausage*
/4 lb. sharp Cheddar cheese,
*   shredded*

Mix (pastry blender helps) and roll (size 1/2 of a ping pong ball) in the palm of your hand. Place on ungreased cookie sheet. Bake in 350° oven for 10 minutes. Freeze for future use. Bake 20 minutes longer for serving hot.

Jean Fitzhenry Coughlin (Mrs. J. Desmond)

COCKTAIL MEATBALLS WITH CURRY SAUCE
Men love this!

MEATBALLS:

1 lb ground beef
1/2 cup grated soft
    bread crumbs
1/4 cup milk
1/4 cup sherry
1 egg, beaten
2 Tablespoons grated onion
1 teaspoon salt
1/4 teaspoon pepper

Mix meatball ingredients well and shape into small balls, using 1 level teaspoon. Melt 4 tablespoons bacon drippings in large, heavy skillet and add a single layer of meatballs. Cook slowly for about 10 minutes or until done. These can be frozen. Combine sauce and heat until piping hot. Pour over meatballs in chafing dish.

SAUCE:

1/4 cup sherry
1 can mushroom soup
1/2 teaspoon curry powder

Gail Southwood Golding (Mrs. James N.)

CHICKEN CURRY MOUSSE

Can do ahead
Serves: 6 for lunch
Preparation: 30 minutes

1 envelope plain gelatin
1/4 cup white wine
1 can vichyssoise
1 Tablespoon freeze dried
    chives
1/2 Tablespoon curry powder
2 cups cooked chicken (about
    1 fryer) chopped fine
1 cup heavy cream, whipped
1/2 teaspoon seasoned salt
1/2 teaspoon seasoned pepper
1/2 cup chutney (may add
    more chutney)
Optional: 1 stalk chopped
    celery

Mix ingredients and pour into 1-1/2 quart ring mold, oiled.
Refrigerate.
Serve with cold rice salad inside ring—sliced tomatoes; hot spinach turnovers.

Renie Fridy
Sue Small Durham (Mrs. C. J., Jr.)

TUNA TEASERS

Can be made ahead and frozen
Yield: 3 dozen
Preparation: 20 minutes
Baking Time: 10-15 minutes

1 cup all-purpose flour
1-1/2 teaspoons baking powder
1 teaspoon onion salt
1/2 teaspoon curry powder
Dash cayenne pepper
1/2 cup butter, or margarine
1/2 cup milk
1 6-1/2 oz. can tuna
1 cup shredded Cheddar cheese
1 teaspoon minced green
    pepper

Mix first five ingredients. Cut in the 1/2 cup of butter. Stir in the rest of the ingredients. Drop by the teaspoonful on a greased baking sheet. Bake in 450° oven for 10-15 minutes.

Martha Osborne Enloe (Mrs. Harold)

MONT BLANC CHICKEN SPREAD

Make a day or two ahead— flavor
improves as ingredients mellow
Freezes well

2 (4-3/4 oz.) cans Underwood
    Chicken Spread
1 cup toasted walnuts,
    chopped fine
1/4 cup chopped green onion,
    or chives
1-1/2 Tablespoons soy sauce
1 Tablespoon garlic flavored
    vinegar or wine vinegar
    with dash of garlic
1/3 cup mayonnaise
1/2 to 1 cup sour cream

Mix, cover and refrigerate. Turn onto plate and shape into a mold. Cover completely with sour cream. Serve with crackers or as a sandwich spread.

Betty Bryan Coleman (Mrs. Richard L.)

TAPENADE WITH FRESH VEGETABLES

1 (7-oz.) can tuna
8 canned anchovy fillets,
    drained and chopped
2 Tablespoons lemon juice
1 Tablespoon capers and
    some juice
1/2 cup olive oil

MAYONNAISE:

2 egg yolks
2 Tablespoons lemon juice
1/4 teaspoon white pepper
1/2 teaspoon dry mustard
1 teaspoon salt
1-3/4 cup salad oil

Combine tuna, anchovies, lemon juice and capers in blender. Combine well. Gradually blend in olive oil until sauce is smooth and creamy. Chill. To make mayonnaise: Combine all ingredients except oil in mixer bowl. Gradually stir in oil, drop by drop at first and in a stream at the end to form a thick paste. Beat in a tablespoon or two of boiling water to thin and improve keeping ability. Combine 1 cup of the mayonnaise with the tuna mixture and use as a dip for fresh vegetables.
Note: The tuna mixture without mayonnaise may be used as a tonnato sauce for hard-cooked eggs, tomatoes, veal or chicken cubes. Garnish with black olives.

Celine Hanan Lurey (Mrs. Michael)

TUNA PATÉ

Must do ahead
Yield: 4 cups

8 oz. pkg. cream cheese,
    softened
2 Tablespoons chili sauce
2 Tablespoons parsley
1 teaspoon minced onion
1/2 teaspoon hot sauce
2 (7 oz.) cans white tuna,
    drained and flaked

Blend cream cheese, chili sauce, parsley, onion and hot sauce. Add tuna and mix well. Pack firmly in a 4-cup serving bowl or mold. Chill 4 hours. Unmold and serve with crackers.
Variation: Fold chopped nuts into paté.

Libba Shuford
Bettie Griffin Watts (Mrs. Nelson B.)

PARMESAN MUSHROOMS
Good as meat accompaniment or hors d'oeuvres

Can do ahead
Serves: 4-6
Preparation: 10 minutes
Baking Time: 15-20 minutes

12 medium mushrooms
2 Tablespoons olive oil
1/4 cup chopped onions
2 cloves garlic, chopped
1/3 cup seasoned bread crumbs
3 Tablespoons Parmesan
   cheese
1/8 teaspoon oregano
1/2 teaspoon salt
1 Tablespoon parsley, chopped
2 Tablespoons olive oil

Wash mushrooms; break off stems and remove a little meat to make a deeper cavity for the stuffing. Chop stems and scraped meat. Saute onions, garlic and chopped mushrooms in olive oil. Combine remaining ingredients except additional oil with the sauteed mixture. Pile into mushroom caps. Place mushrooms in a casserole greased with additional oil. Bake in 400° oven for 15-20 minutes.

Celine Hanan Lurey (Mrs. Michael)

STUFFED MUSHROOMS

Baking Time: 15-20 minutes

12 large, fresh whole
   mushrooms
3 Tablespoons melted butter
Salt and pepper
1/4 cup minced onion
3 Tablespoons bread crumbs
1/4 cup grated Swiss cheese
Minced parsley
1/4 teaspoon tarragon
2 or 3 Tablespoons heavy cream
3 Tablespoons Parmesan
   cheese for topping
2 Tablespoons melted butter

Remove stems from mushrooms; chop stems. Brush caps with melted butter; salt and pepper. Dry chopped stems and saute with the onions in the butter. Do not brown. Mix bread crumbs, cheese, parsley, tarragon, salt, pepper, onion and mushrooms. Blend in the heavy cream, just to moisten. Fill mushroom caps with the stuffing; top with Parmesan and melted butter. Bake in 375° oven until lightly brown on top about 15-20 minutes.

Ann Williams Martin (Mrs. Hayes)

MARINATED VEGETABLES
Great for buffets as a salad!

Must do ahead
Serves: 8-10

1 8-oz. can button mushrooms,
  drained
1 green pepper, cut into
  1/2" strips
3 carrots, cut lengthwise
  into eighths
2 cups cauliflower florets, raw
6 green onions (top with a small
  part of green left on)
1 cup broccoli florets, raw
1-1/2 cups wine vinegar
1 teaspoon sugar
1-1/2 teaspoon salt
1/2 teaspoon black pepper
2 teaspoons oregano, crushed
  in palm of hand
1 teaspoon basil
1/2 cup salad oil
1/2 cup olive oil

Combine all vegetables in large bowl. Heat vinegar; stir in seasonings. Cool slightly; combine with oils. Pour over vegetables and mix well. Cover and refrigerate at least 24 hours before serving. To serve, drain vegetables. Other vegetables may be added, if desired, such as artichoke hearts, cherry tomatoes, squash, zucchini, etc. Double amount of marinade, as needed.

Celine Hanan Lurey (Mrs. Michael)

MUSHROOM ROLL-UPS

Can freeze
Baking Time: 20 minutes

1 lb. fresh mushrooms, finely
  chopped
1/2 cup butter
6 Tablespoons flour
1-1/2 teaspoon salt
1/2 teaspoon Accent
2 cups half and half
1-1/4 Tablespoons chopped
  chives
2 loaves white bread,
  crust trimmed off, rolled
  thin with rolling pin

Saute mushrooms for 5 minutes in butter. Blend in flour, salt and Accent. Stir in half and half and simmer until thick. Add chives and lemon juice. Spread on bread and roll like a jelly roll. Cut in two pieces. Freeze if desired. Defrost and toast in 400° oven for about 20 minutes.

Bettie Griffin Watts (Mrs. Nelson B)

FUNGUSALLAS
Hors d'oeuvres

Must do ahead
Yield: 24 hors d'oeuvres
Preparation: 20 minutes

24 approximately 2"
mushrooms
1 4-oz. pkg. cream cheese
1-1/4 lb. block blue cheese
or Roquefort cheese
4 Tablespoons sour cream
4 whole truffles, thinly sliced
OR
Black olives, pitted if truffles
not available

Remove stems from mushrooms and save. Wash mushrooms, dry thoroughly and refrigerate, covered.
Combine washed and dried 8 mushroom stems, softened cream cheese, softened blue cheese, and sour cream in a blender or food processor. Using an iced teaspoon, press ingredients and heap mixture into mushroom caps. Top with a thin slice of truffle (or substitute). Chill for at least 12 hours in refrigerator. Serve cold on platter decorated with sliced large mushrooms and parsley.
Note: Do not add salt or pepper.

Carl Biggers

SPICED NUTS

Can do ahead
Yield: 4 cups
Preparation: 10 minutes
Baking Time: 20-25 minutes

1 egg white, beaten
1 teaspoon water
4 cups mixed nuts
1 cup sugar
1 Tablespoon pumpkin pie
spice

Combine egg white and water; add nuts to coat. Combine sugar and spice; toss nuts in mixture. Place in single layer on lightly greased baking sheet. Bake in 300° oven for 20-25 minutes. Remove and place on waxed paper and break up large clusters. Store in airtight container.

Bonnie Tyler Brannon (Mrs. Russell)

CAVIAR RING

Must do ahead
Serves: 4-6
Preparation: 30 minutes

1 teaspoon unflavored gelatin
2 Tablespoons dry sherry
2 Tablespoons fresh lemon juice
6 hard-cooked eggs
1 cup mayonnaise
1 teaspoon anchovy paste
1 teaspoon Worcestershire
    sauce
1 2-1/2-oz. jar lumpfish caviar
Parsley sprigs (garnish)
Sesame rice crackers or black
    bread

Generously grease two-cup mold. Soften gelatin in sherry and lemon juice in small, heat-proof container about 5 minutes; then place over very low heat until dissolved, stirring several times. Chop eggs in food processor or blender. Transfer to mixing bowl. Stir in gelatin, mayonnaise, anchovy paste and Worcestershire sauce and mix thoroughly.

Gently fold in caviar until well blended. Turn into mold, cover and refrigerate until firm. Unmold and garnish with parsley sprigs. Surround with crackers or thin slices of black bread.

Ellen Resnikoff Carr (Mrs. Robert J.)

MARINATED BROCCOLI

Do ahead
Refrigerate
Serves: 6-8 as salad or vegetable
Makes more for hors d'oeuvres

3 bunches fresh broccoli
1 cup cider vinegar
1 Tablespoon dill weed
1 Tablespoon sugar
1 teaspoon salt
1 teaspoon coarsely ground
    pepper
1 teaspoon garlic salt
1-1/2 cups vegetable oil

Cut broccoli into small flowerettes. (Leave stems slightly longer if using for pick up hors d'oeuvres). Mix remaining ingredients and shake well. Pour over broccoli and refrigerate for 24 hours. Stir occasionally. Drain and serve. Keeps for a week in the refrigerator.

Sandra Tucker Holt (Mrs. Stanley E.)

Soups & Sauces

SOUPS AND SAUCES

Although soups and sauces are part of the foundations of our cooking traditions, they are not always treated in today's kitchen with the respect they deserve. Many cooks, seduced by the plethora of canned, packaged and dehydrated products that pass under the guise of soup and sauce, have forgotten how delicious the real thing is. But anyone who can cut up a vegetable or wield a spoon can make a soup or sauce in only a little more time than it takes to open a can and heat the contents.

This chapter starts with the premise that soups are the most versatile and variable item on the menu. Served hot, they will banish the cold on a winter evening; served chilled, they refresh the palate on a summer afternoon. They can be made with every category of food— meats, poultry, fish, fruits and vegetables, and they encourage the cook to experiment with the entire range of herbs, spices and seasonings.

Though soup may be the kindest course, sauces are the basis of most cuisines. The sauce recipes included in this chapter are the basic ones that should be a part of any good cook's kitchen. The blender can produce superior sauces and soups with less effort than the long, hand-blended, or sieved methods. But we have included both the standard and the modern techniques so that you may choose for yourself. We have also included some special sauces, mayonnaises and butters.

The following pages will teach you how to explore new culinary possibilities and will enable you to execute all of the recipes that make up this chapter of *Mountain Elegance*. The recipes presented here include the best soups and sauces from our "mountain" cuisines; they provide both an introduction and a guide to an elemental aspect of cookery.

EVERYDAY HINTS FOR SOUPS AND SAUCES

Sauces are the basis of most cuisines, and stocks are the foundation of many of the most important sauces as well as of soups and stews. The richer the stock, the better the flavor of the dish to which it is added; and long, slow cooking is the secret of extracting the flavor from the bones and vegetables used to make the stock. You may find that you prefer to use our recipe to make your own homemade stocks rather than buying the canned kind. If so, we suggest that you try to put aside a day every six weeks or so to spend making basic stocks and sauces. You can freeze the stock in one- or two-cup containers with wide mouths, so that the frozen liquid may be easily removed by rotating the container under hot water for a few minutes.

The basic stocks and sauces can be frozen in ice cube trays and packed into moisture-vaporproof bags. These are a great convenience when a recipe calls for a few tablespoons of a basic ingredient. Each ice cube equals two or three tablespoons of stock or sauce.

You can keep a constant supply of bechamel, chicken veloute, brown, tomato and hollandaise sauces in the freezer. The recipes for these are found in this chapter. In addition to these essential sauces, pots of roux and clarified butter will keep well in the freezer.

There are some simple kitchen tools that help create a better texture, flavor and color of sauces. A whisk will make lumps vanish. Kitchen shears with a self-releasing hinge are easy to keep clean and unrusted. Use them to snip herbs quickly, right into the sauce. A garlic press will squeeze enough juice to give an ineffable flavor to your sauces, and the hand grater is good for a shaving of lemon rind or nutmeg. By all means, have some very hard wooden spoons for delicate sauces which may be broken down by the more vigorous metal tools. A sauce spoon with one pointed end will scrape the pan edges clean easily and help avoid lumping. If you should use a metal spoon, make sure it is stainless steel, so as not to discolor a delicate sauce.

There are two basic kinds of soup, clear and cream.

Clear soups are usually a meal in themselves, chock full of meats and vegetables. If you're short on time, and caught without your own homemade version, make the stock from commercial bouillon or consomme. (And if you think your homemade stock is a little short on flavor, add a bouillon cube for more body.)

Cream soups, the easiest and quickest to make, are excellent main dishes or appetizers. To make sure they're really creamy, stir the flour into the melted butter before adding liquids, or shake the flour in a jar with some of the liquid before mixing with the soup. A blender adds protection against lumpy cream soup.

How do you freeze soup? Divide it into the portions you'll be using later and freeze in plastic containers or small jars. One hint for clear soups: If you're planning on serving part and freezing the rest, put only half the amount of potatoes in and include them in the first serving. Later, when you're preparing the frozen portion, add diced raw potatoes and simmer for 20 minutes until potatoes are cooked. Your other hearty vegetables, such as peas, corn, beans and carrots, can be frozen without losing their texture.

Cream soups may look curdled while thawing, but will become smooth when reheated. If you feel more liquid is needed, stir it in.

Fast cooling and freezing help preserve the flavor and retard bacterial growth. Frozen soups will keep well up to six months, but rarely longer. Therefore, label and mark your containers of soup clearly before you start putting them in the freezer.

Generally, allow 1-1/2 cups of soup per person when it's to be the main course, and half a cup per person for a light soup served as an appetizer.

BASIC SOUP STOCKS

The object of making a stock is to produce a liquid brimming with flavor and nutrition. From this basic broth, diverse soups and sauces can be created. Flavor is imparted automatically through the simmering process, but to extract the maximum nutrition there are a few rules that must be carefully followed.

1. Save bits of raw vegetables, tops of scallions and celery, tender leaves of beets, tough spinach, stems of watercress and dill, limp outer leaves of lettuce and cabbage—in other words, all of the otherwise good foodstuffs you normally throw away because they are not aesthetically pleasing or simply because you are accustomed to treating them as scraps. These should be well washed and refrigerated in a large jar with a lid. They can be kept up to a week and a half.

2. Freeze scraps of leftover meat in plastic containers. Meat bones and the carcasses of game birds, chickens, turkeys or ducks may also be frozen for use in soup stocks. If poultry has been stuffed, carefully remove any remaining bits from the carcass before freezing.

3. Bones contain no vitamins, but are high in minerals which may be extracted from the connective tissue by simmering at about 200° F. for at least one hour.

4. After you have simmered your soup stock, don't feel guilty about straining out and discarding the bones and vegetables used to flavor it. The nutrition has passed from these ingredients into the soup liquid where they await your pleasure.

5. Simmering means cooking without letting the liquid boil. Turn your burner as low as possible and only partially cover the soup kettle to keep the soup from boiling.

6. If stocks are simmered with a tight-fitting lid, they may cloud. To overcome this and still retain the nutritional value, cover with a loose-fitting lid or leave the lid slightly ajar. (The lid is important, however, to keep the vitamins from being lost.)

7. Simmer the broth gently without disturbing it; stirring would release protein and mineral particles that could cloud the broth. Just push any floating pieces down below the surface of the liquid.

8. The herbs you use to enhance the flavor of the stock need to be "tied down" so they will not float to the surface. Smaller herbs can be bound inside an informal tube made from the overlapping celery stalks and tightly tied with white string. Herbs can also be tied between a leek that has been sliced lengthwise. A bay leaf can be fastened to an onion with a clove. Herbs can be placed in a 4-inch square of cheesecloth tied into a bag. The herbs are much easier to remove when made into a bouquet garni.

9. Some of the herbs and flavors good for stock are bay leaf, peppercorns, thyme, parsley stems, celery tops, turnips, onion, leeks (white portion only), parsnips, clove, carrots, mushrooms, and garlic.

10. If you plan to freeze your stock, do not add extra cloves to the pot. Freezing will enhance the flavor of cloves. Also, carrots tend to color and sweeten a white stock.

11. As the stock heats, quite a heavy scum rises to the surface. If a clear soup is wanted, it is imperative to skim this foamy albuminous material before the first half-hour of cooking. After the last skimming, wipe the edge of the stock pot at the level of the soup. Some nutritionists advise against skimming stocks to be used for brown sauces.

12. Another way to help keep your stock clear is to empty the pot by ladling instead of pouring. Or use a stock pot with a spigot.

13. Never salt heavily at the beginning of stock-making. The great reduction both in original cooking and in subsequent cooking—if the stock is used as an ingredient—makes it almost impossible to judge the amount you will need. And a little extra salt can so easily ruin your results. If stocks are stored, the salt and seasonings are apt to intensify; and if any wine is used in dishes made from stock, the salt flavor will be increased.

The following ingredients may be substituted as indicated:

1. One soup stock may be substituted for another in many cases. Use your own judgment and imagination.

2. Frozen vegetables may be substituted for fresh, but never use soggy, devitalized, canned vegetables unless you are snow-bound in an Arctic log cabin.

3. Canned consomme, chicken broth, beef broth, and clam broth may be used in place of basic stocks or consommes.

But of all these elements, the hand is the most important. You add the onion, the turnip, the parsnip, and what you add is your choice. Follow the recipe if you wish; it becomes your recipe. Or omit whatever you choose; that also becomes your recipe. Your broth simmering on your stove, producing pools of flavor, strained and clear, is the backbone of nutritious soups and sauces.

BROWN STOCK (Fonds Brun)

Must do ahead
Can freeze
Yield: 3 quarts
Preparation: 4-1/2 hours (includes cooking time)

Please read about
Basic Soup Stocks
2 lbs. beef shin, cubed
3 lbs. veal knuckle, cubed
1/2 lb. lean raw ham, diced
2 Tablespoons cooking oil
3 carrots, sliced
2 onions, sliced
2 stalks celery, sliced
3 cloves garlic
Water
Bouquet garni of parsley,
* 1/2 teaspoon thyme, 2 bay*
* leaves and 1 teaspoon*
* crushed peppercorns*
2 teaspoons salt (add last and
* adjust to taste)*

Preheat oven to very hot 475°. Spread in flat baking pan beef shin, veal knuckle and ham. Sprinkle with cooking oil and bake in the very hot oven for 45 minutes, stirring occasionally. Add carrots, onions, celery, and garlic and bake 15 minutes more. Transfer meat and vegetables to a large soup kettle. Rinse baking pan with 2 cups water and add to kettle. Add 4-1/2 quarts water and the Bouquet garni. Bring water to a boil slowly, skimming the scum from the surface when necessary. Reduce heat and simmer for 3 hours. Double a large piece of muslin or cheesecloth and dampen it so that it will hold back fat. Line a colander or strainer with the fabric then strain the broth into a bowl. Discard the solids. Let the broth cool to room temperature. If you want to use the broth immediately, blot up the remaining liquid fat from the surface by touching the globules lightly with a folded paper towel. If you do not intend to use the broth the same day, refrigerate it and spoon off the fat when it solidifies on the surface. Store the broth, tightly covered, in the refrigerator or pour into containers and freeze. Refrigerated stock will keep for 5 days; frozen stock for 12 weeks.

BEEF CONSOMME

Can do ahead
Can freeze
Serves: 8
Preparation: 25 minutes

8 cups beef bouillon (see index)
3 egg whites and shells

Place the beef bouillon in a saucepan and bring to a boil. Beat the egg whites until they are frothy and add, together with the crushed egg shells, to the boiling soup, stirring constantly. Lower the heat slightly and continue to stir while the soup boils for 10 minutes. Remove from heat and allow to stand for 10 minutes while the particles settle to the bottom of the pan. Strain the consomme into another pan through a linen dish towel. Reheat before serving.

CHICKEN STOCK (White Stock or Fonds Blanc)

Must do ahead
Can freeze
Yield: 3 quarts
Preparation: 4 hours (including cooking time)

Please read about
Basic Soup Stocks
5 lb. roasting or stewing
chicken, ready to cook
1 lb. veal knuckle bones,
cracked
1 medium carrot, coarsely cut
1 onion, stuck with 3
whole cloves
6 peppercorns
1 stalk celery with leaves,
coarsely cut
4 sprigs parsley
1 bay leaf
1/4 teaspoon thyme
5 quarts cold water
2 teaspoons salt (Add last
and adjust to taste)

Into large kettle, put chicken, veal knuckle bones, carrot, onion stuck with cloves, peppercorns, celery, parsley, bay leaf (may attach bay leaf to onion with cloves), thyme and water. Bring water slowly to a boil, reduce heat, and simmer for 3 hours, skimming the scum from the surface when necessary. Remove the chicken and use for chicken salad or some other purpose. Strain the stock through a colander or strainer lined with a doubled piece of muslin or cheesecloth. (Dampen the material used so that it will hold back the fat.) Discard the solids. Let the broth cool to room temperature. If you want to use the broth immediately, blot up the remaining liquid fat from the surface by touching the globules lightly with a folded paper towel. If you do not intend to use the broth the same day, refrigerate it and spoon off the fat when it solidifies on the surface. Store the broth tightly covered in the refrigerator or pour into containers and freeze. Refrigerated stock will keep for 5 days; frozen stock for 12 weeks.

CHICKEN CONSOMME

Serves: 8

3 quarts chicken stock
(see index)
2 egg whites and shells

Bring the chicken stock to a boil in a large kettle. Continue to boil over medium heat for one hour, or until the stock is reduced by one-third and the flavor becomes more concentrated. To clarify the stock, stir in the egg whites and egg shell. Cook for 11 minutes, remove from heat, and allow the consomme to stand for an additional 10 minutes while the egg particles sink to the bottom of the kettle. Strain the consomme through several layers of cheesecloth. Heat briefly before serving.

FISH STOCK (Fonds de Poisson Blanc)

Must do ahead
Can freeze
Yield: About 2 quarts
Preparation: 1 hour (includes cooking time)

Please read about
Basic Soup Stocks
2-1/2 quarts water
2 lbs. bones and trimmings of
*   white-fleshed fish*
2 onions, sliced
5 sprigs parsley
1/4 teaspoon peppercorns
Juice of 1/2 lemon
1 teaspoon salt (Add last and
*   adjust to taste)*

Into large kettle put water, fish, onion, parsley, peppercorns, and lemon. Bring water slowly to a boil, reduce heat and simmer for 30 minutes, skimming the scum from the surface when necessary. Double a large piece of muslin or cheesecloth and dampen it so that it will hold back fat. Line a colander or strainer with the fabric, then strain the broth into a bowl. Discard the solids. Let the broth cool to room temperature. If you want to use the broth immediately, blot up the remaining liquid fat from the surface by touching the globules lightly with a folded paper towel. If you do not intend to use the broth the same day, refrigerate it and spoon off the fat when it solidifies on the surface. Store the broth, tightly covered, in the refrigerator or pour into containers and freeze. Refrigerated stock will keep for 5 days; frozen stock for 12 weeks.

MUSHROOM CONSOMME

Serves: 10

1-1/2 lbs. young fresh
*   mushrooms*
2 leeks
2 stalks celery with leaves
2 medium sized carrots
4 cups water
2 quarts beef consomme
Salt and pepper, to taste
1/2 cup dry sherry

Rinse mushrooms and dry thoroughly. (Young fresh mushrooms do not have to be peeled.) Slice each leek down the center without cutting through, and wash thoroughly. Rinse celery stalks and peel carrots. Chop all vegetables coarsely. Place in a saucepan and cover with the water. Cover and simmer slowly for 40 minutes, or until the vegetables are cooked through. Strain the broth and discard the vegetables. Stir broth into the hot beef consomme, and season with salt and pepper to taste. Lace consomme with sherry before serving.

Hint:
To remove excess fat from soup, place a lettuce leaf in hot soup and remove when it has absorbed the grease.

CONSOMME CHIFFONADE

Serves: 8

1 cup lettuce leaves (or sorrel)
  finely shredded
2-1/2 quarts beef consomme

Place the finely shredded lettuce leaves in a small saucepan. Add salted water to cover and boil for 1 minute. Drain lettuce and divide the shredded strips among 8 soup plates. Pour hot beef consomme over and serve immediately.

Diana Roscoe Bilbrey (Mrs. George M., Jr.)

CONSOMME ARGENTEUIL

Serves: 8

8 cups beef consomme
1 cup fresh cooked asparagus
  tips

Heat the beef consomme just to the boiling point. Add the cooked asparagus tips. Serve immediately.

Diana Roscoe Bilbrey (Mrs. George M., Jr.)

NAVY BEAN SOUP
Recipe takes time, but it is easy to prepare

Must do ahead
Yield: Approximately 3-1/2 quarts
Serves: 8-10
Preparation: 1 hour
Cooking Time: 2-3 hours

1 lb. dry navy beans
2 quarts water
2 teaspoons salt
1 grated carrot
1 onion, cut up
1 teaspoon butter
Ham bone or ham pieces
1 cup diced potatoes
Pepper

Rinse and sort beans. Cover with water and soak overnight; drain. (Or simmer 2 minutes and soak covered 1 hour; drain.) Put beans in soup pot, add water and salt. Heat to boiling. Saute onion and carrot in butter; add to beans. Add pepper and ham bone or pieces. Cover and cook slowly 2 to 3 hours, adding potatoes last hour. Remove meat if ham hock is used. Remove about 1 cup of the beans and mash or process in blender. Return to pot. Cut meat into pieces and return to pot. Serve hot.

Jeannie Renick Davis (Mrs. John N., Jr.)

Hint:
Citrus peel can be saved and frozen...it's wonderful added to soup.

CREAM SOUPS

Can do ahead
Can freeze
Preparation and cooking time: 15 minutes

BASIC CREAM SAUCE: *Yield: 3 cups*

6 Tablespoons butter
1 medium onion, sliced
3 Tablespoons flour
1 teaspoon salt
Pinch of white pepper
3 cups milk

Melt butter and saute onions until soft (about 5 minutes). Discard onion. Stir in flour, salt and pepper. Add milk slowly, stirring constantly over low heat. Bring to a boil, but do not boil. The cream sauce thickens slightly as it cools. All cream soups may be thinned by adding milk or water as they are heated.

CREAM OF ASPARAGUS SOUP *Yield: 12 1/2-cup servings*

2 cups asparagus
1 cup water
3 cups basic cream sauce
1/4 teaspoon nutmeg

Cut asparagus in small pieces. Cook in water until soft; save tips for garnish. Press asparagus and liquid through a sieve or whirl in blender. Combine with cream sauce and nutmeg; heat. Sprinkle with a few tips over each serving.

CREAM OF BROCCOLI SOUP *Yield: 12 1/2-cup servings*

2 cups broccoli, chopped
1 cup milk
3 cups basic cream sauce

Cook broccoli in milk in double boiler for about 20 minutes, until tender. Puree in blender or press through sieve. Add cream sauce and heat slowly. Garnish with almond slivers.

CORN CHOWDER *Yield: 5 1-1/2-cup servings*

Several cubes of salt pork
1 medium onion, diced
2 cups water
1 cup potatoes, diced
2 cups corn
3 cups basic cream sauce

Fry salt pork in large saucepan until crisp. Add onion and saute 3 minutes. Stir in water, potatoes and corn, and simmer covered for 20 minutes, or until potatoes are soft. Add cream sauce and continue heating. A diced tomato can be added with the other vegetables.

PARSNIP AND POTATO CHOWDER *Yield: 7 1-1/2-cup servings*

3 cups potatoes, diced
Small cube salt pork
3 cups sliced parsnips
2 cups water
3 cups basic cream sauce

Fry salt pork until crisp, add potatoes, parsnips and water. Cook until vegetables are tender. Stir in cream sauce and continue heating.

BORSCH

Must be made ahead
Yield: 3-1/2 quarts
Preparation: 30 minutes
Cooking Time: 3-1/2 hours (on 2 separate days)

4 lb. shin of beef
1 large marrowbone
Salt
1 can (1 lb.) tomatoes,
    undrained
1 medium onion, peeled,
    quartered
1 stalk celery, cut up
3 parsley sprigs
10 whole black peppers
2 bay leaves
3 cups coarsely shredded
    cabbage (1 lb.)
1-1/2 cups thickly sliced,
    pared carrot (4 medium)
1 cup chopped onion
2 teaspoons snipped fresh dill
    or three teaspoons dried
    dill weed
1/3 cup cider vinegar
2 teaspoons sugar
1 can (1 lb.) julienne beets,
    undrained
Dairy sour cream

Day before: in eight-quart kettle, place beef, marrowbone, 1 teaspoon salt and 2 quarts of water. Bring to boiling; reduce heat, simmer, covered, 1 hour. Add tomatoes, quartered onion, celery, parsley, black peppercorns and bay leaves simmer, covered, 2 hours.

Remove from heat. Lift out beef. Discard marrowbone. Strain soup. Place beef and soup back in kettle. Add cabbage, carrot, onion, dill, the vinegar, sugar, and salt, bring to boiling. Reduce heat; simmer, covered, 30 minutes or until beef and vegetables are tender. Refrigerate overnight. Next day, skim off fat. Remove beef; cut into 1" cubes; return to soup, along with beets. (If making piroshki, reserve 1-1/2 cups of beef.)

This is a favorite with men. Serve with piroshi (see index) or black bread. Sour cream and additional dill make a good garnish.

Mary Claire Krause Israel (Mrs. Thomas M., II)

CARROT SOUP

A good first course in the winter time.

Can do ahead
Can freeze
Serves: 4-8
Yield: 2-1/2 quarts
Preparation: 30 minutes
Cooking Time: 80 minutes

4 Tablespoons butter
6 carrots, sliced
1 onion, chopped
2 quarts chicken stock
3 Tablespoons Farina (rice or
    mashed potatoes)
1/2 teaspoon pepper
Dash nutmeg
2 Tablespoons chopped parsley

Melt butter; add carrots and onion. Saute for 15 minutes. Add stock; cover and simmer for 45 minutes. Put in blender to puree. Return to stove; add Farina and spices. Cook over low heat for 20 minutes.

Mrs. Charles Utesch

CHEESE SOUP
Great while watching football!

Can do ahead, but do not boil
Serves: 6
Preparation: 40 minutes

3/4 cup finely chopped carrot
2/3 cup finely chopped celery
1/3 cup finely chopped
    green onion
1/4 cup melted butter
1/3 cup all-purpose flour
2 cups chicken broth
2 cups half and half
1/4 teaspoon salt
1-1/2 cups shredded sharp
    Cheddar cheese
1 teaspoon brandy
Chopped fresh parsley, green
    onions, crumbled bacon,
    for garnish

Saute vegetables in butter until soft but not brown; blend in flour. Gradually stir in broth, then half and half; cook, stirring constantly, until mixture thickens and boils. Stir in salt, cheese and brandy; heat just until cheese melts. Sprinkle with parsley.
Serve with roast beef sandwiches and raw vegetables.

Mary Claire Krause Israel (Mrs. Thomas M., II)

JANE'S GARDEN FRESH GAZPACHO

Use processor
Best to do ahead
Yield: Approximately 1-1/2 quarts
Preparation: 20 minutes

1/2 medium onion
1/4 cup salad stuffed olives
1 small cucumber
2 banana peppers
6 medium tomatoes, skinned
2 cloves garlic, minced
1/4 cup dry red wine
Pinch tarragon, basil and cumin
1 Tablespoon fresh parsley
2 teaspoons paprika
1/2 teaspoon salt
Coarse black pepper
Juice of 1 lemon
2 Tablespoons wine vinegar
2 Tablespoons olive oil
2 teaspoons granulated chicken
    bouillon, crushed

Process onion, olives, cucumber and pepper together. Add tomatoes and process. Add rest of ingredients. Chill well before serving. Sprinkle croutons on top of individual servings.

Lelia Kincaid Cort (Mrs. John)

CHICKEN-CAVIAR SOUP

Must do ahead—jell chicken broth
for 4 hours before serving
Serves: 8
Preparation: 15 minutes

4 12-1/2-oz. cans chicken broth
1 4-oz. jar black caviar
1/2 cup sour cream
2 Tablespoons finely cut chives

Jell chicken broth in cans*. Put two tablespoons black caviar and 1 tablespoon sour cream in bottom of each of 8 soup cups. Divide jellied stock into cups. Stir well, sprinkle with chopped chives and serve. It is not necessary to use the expensive caviar.

*If canned broth or consomme is from a new pack it has enough gelatin in it to respond favorably to mere chilling. If the pack is as old as two years, it must be treated as though it had no gelatin. Do not freeze it, but try it out by refrigerating for at least 4 hours, to see how much additional thickening it will need. Keep in mind that, if too stiff, soup jellies are not very attractive. Allow, if necessary, 1/2 teaspoon gelatin to each 2 cups consomme or broth.

Menu suggestion: Chicken-caviar soup, cold poached salmon (caught by your husband) surrounded by cucumbers and dilled mayonnaise, asparagus vinaigrette, couer a la creme with strawberries and raspberries.

Jean Moffat Frady (Mrs. A Hampton, Jr.)

ROMAINE LETTUCE SOUP

This is also good cold. Serve as a first course. Good with something spicy.

Can be made ahead partially
Can be frozen, partially
Serves: 8
Preparation: 20 minutes

2 Tablespoons butter
1 small onion, minced
1 quart chicken broth
2 quarts chopped romaine
2 teaspoons salt
Dash pepper
4 egg yolks
1 cup heavy cream

Saute onion and romaine in butter until tender. Add chicken broth. Cool soup and puree in food processor. The soup may be made ahead and frozen at this point. Return to saucepan over medium-low heat. Slowly add beaten egg yolks and cream. Do not let the mixture boil or it will curdle. Should this happen, add 1 tablespoon of boiling water.

Betsy Lynn Ivey (Mrs. George E.)
Mary Claire Krause Israel (Mrs. Thomas M., II)

75

EGG DROP SOUP

From Chinese cooking class taken in Okinawa, Ryukyu Islands

Can partially do ahead
Servings: 8 side servings or 4 main servings

STOCK MIXTURE:

2 quarts chicken stock
 (see index)
3 slices ginger
1 Tablespoon wine
2 Tablespoons soy sauce
1/2 teaspoon Accent
Salt to taste

MEAT MIXTURE:

1/2 cup chicken shredded (or
 any kind of meat)
1 teaspoon cornstarch
1-1/2 teaspoon wine

VEGETABLES:

2 cups any **one** of these: chinese
 cabbage shredded, lettuce
 shredded, fresh spinach; or
 1/2 cup sliced dried
 mushrooms

EGG MIXTURE:

2 eggs beaten with a fork
1/2 cup green onion, chopped
Salt and pepper, to taste

Bring to boil blended stock mixture and cook 5 minutes on high heat. Mix ingredients for meat mixture well. Add meat and vegetable mixtures to boiled stock and cook 5 minutes. (Can do this much ahead.)

Add to soup chopped onion, salt and pepper to taste. Stir and then turn off heat. Immediately drizzle beaten eggs into soup. Stir slightly and very gently. Serve hot.

Menu suggestion: I serve this with beef and green peppers (or variation), rice, fried cabbage, almond cookies, chilled mandarin oranges, hot tea.

Diana Roscoe Bilbrey (Mrs. George M., Jr.)

SHERRIED LOBSTER SOUP

Fix lobster tails ahead
Serves: 8
Preparation: 20 minutes (includes cooking time)

2 cans mushroom soup
2 cans asparagus soup
3 cans milk
2 lobster tails, cooked and cut
 to bite size
1 box of mushrooms (sliced,
 but add to soup uncooked)
1/2 cup sherry

Combine mushroom and asparagus soup in top of double boiler. Mix well. Stir in sherry, milk and mushrooms. Add lobster to soup. Bring just to boiling over medum heat, stirring occasionally. To serve, pour soup into a warm tureen or soup cups. Garnish with sliced, green onion.

Nancy Sauer Crosby (Mrs. E. Brown)

ONION SOUP WITH RED WINE

Can do ahead
Serves: 6
Preparation: 30 minutes
Cooking time: 30 minutes

3 Tablespoons butter
1 Tablespoon salad oil
5 to 6 cups large yellow
  onions, sliced
1/2 teaspoon salt
1/2 teaspoon sugar
1 heaping Tablespoon flour
2 10-3/4-oz. cans beef broth
2 soup cans water (water can be
  decreased to 1-1/2 cans for
  richer soup)
1 soup can dry red wine
1 bay leaf
1/2 teaspoon sage
Salt and pepper, to taste
1/4 teaspoon Kitchen Bouquet
French bread slices
Swiss or mozzarella cheese

Melt butter and oil in casserole or pan. Add onions, cook over medium heat until tender. Add sugar and salt and raise heat to medium high. Cook until onions are golden. Lower heat to medium. Stir in flour. Add broth and water a little at a time, whisking as you add. Add wine, bay leaf and sage and simmer 3 to 4 minutes. Add Kitchen Bouquet for richer, brown color. Cut and toast slices of French bread to fit individual soup crocks. Pour soup into crocks, add a slice of bread to each. Cover with cheese. Bake in 350° oven for 30 minutes until cheese is melted. Menu suggestion: Can use as main course or appetizer.

Beth Walker Hill (Mrs. Haywood N.)

POTAGE CRESSONAIRE

Can do ahead
Can freeze
Yield: 8 cups
Preparation: 30 minutes
Cooking Time: 25 minutes

2 Tablespoons butter
2 leeks, cleaned and chopped
3 medium potatoes, peeled
  and sliced
2 cans Campbells chicken broth
  plus 2 cans water
  OR
5 cups homemade chicken
  broth (index)
1 bunch watercress
Salt and pepper, to taste
1 cup heavy cream
Watercress leaves

Heat the butter in a saucepan without letting it brown. Then add the leeks and saute them for a few minutes without browning them. Add the potatoes, chicken broth and water (or homemade broth), bring to a boil and simmer for 20 minutes. Add the watercress and salt and pepper, to taste. Simmer for another 2 minutes. Cool the soup and put through a blender. Add the cream and reheat gently before serving, or refrigerate and serve cold. Garnish with watercress leaves.

Joyce Lichtenfels Cole

OYSTER SOUP ST. CROIX
(or clam, shrimp or mushroom)

Can be done ahead
Serves: 6
Preparation: 30 minutes

4 Tablespoons butter, melted
4 Tablepoons onion, chopped
2 stalks celery, chopped
    very fine
1 28-oz. can tomatoes
4 teaspoons flour
1 can chicken broth
1 Tablespoon soy sauce
1/2 teaspoon sugar
3 Tablespoons tomato paste
2 8-oz. cans oysters cut into
    little pieces (clams, shrimp
    or mushrooms may be
    substituted for oysters)
2 Tablespoons chopped parsley
Salt to taste
Lemon pepper to taste
4 oz. butter or sour cream
    for garnish

Saute onions and celery in butter in large saucepan. Blend tomatoes in blender or processor; slowly add to vegetables. Shake flour and 1/2 cup of chicken broth in jar until blended. Then add flour and broth mixture, remaining broth, soy sauce, sugar, tomato paste, oysters and parsley to vegetable mixture. Bring to boil over medium heat, stirring frequently. Add salt and lemon pepper to taste. To serve, pour soup into warm tureen or soup cups. Garnish with pat of butter or dollop of sour cream.
Menu suggestion: Try this with spinach salad and good bread.

Mary Claire Krause Israel (Mrs. Thomas M., II)

COLD MINTED PEA SOUP
Can also be served hot

Can do ahead
Serves: 6
Preparation: 45 minutes plus chilling time

1 teaspoon butter
1/4 cup chopped onion
1-1/2 cups chicken broth
2 cups frozen peas, cooked
2 outside lettuce leaves
1/4 cup chopped parsley
2 sprigs fresh mint
    (or more to taste)
    dried can be bought at
    health food stores
1 cup milk

Melt butter in saucepan, add onions and 1/2 cup chicken broth. Cook until onions are soft. Add peas, lettuce, parsley and mint. Cover and cook 2 minutes. Add remaining broth and bring to boil. Remove from heat and cool. Put soup in blender or processor and blend until smooth. Add milk and stir. Chill well in refrigerator. Garnish with chopped mint, chives or grated orange zest.

Lindsay Huffman Healy (Mrs. Raymond R.)

CREAM OF SPINACH SOUP

Can do ahead
Can freeze
Serves: 8
Preparation: 30 minutes

3/4 lb. young spinach
1/4 cup butter
4 scallions, thinly sliced
1 quart chicken broth
  (see index)
3 Tablespoons flour
Salt to taste
1/4 teaspoon pepper
Pinch of nutmeg and basil
1 cup light cream

Wash spinach and pull off tough stems. Melt 1 tablespoon of the butter in a large saucepan. Add scallions and cook, stirring, about 1 minute. Add spinach with just the water that clings to the leaves; cover and cook about 2 minutes or until spinach is barely wilted and is still a bright green. Turn the contents of the saucepan into a blender, add 1 cup of the broth and whirl until smooth. Add the remaining 3 tablespoons butter to the saucepan and melt over medium heat. Add flour and cook, stirring, 1 to 2 minutes; do not brown. Gradually stir in remaining broth and bring to a boil. Simmer 5 minutes. Add the pureed spinach and the seasonings. Return to a boil. Stir in cream and heat, *but do not boil.*

Menu suggestion: Cream of spinach soup; roast beef or rack of lamb; risi bisi (see index); baked tomatoes; butter rolls; dry red wine; light dessert—such as sherbet.

Patricia Anders Coggins (Mrs. Gregory)

WILD RICE SOUP

Can do ahead
Can partially do ahead
Can freeze
Serves: 8 generous servings
Yield: 3 quarts
Preparation: 40 minutes
Cooking Time: 50 minutes

1/2 cup celery, chopped
1/2 cup onion, chopped
1/2 cup carrot, chopped
1/4 cup green pepper, chopped
1/4 cup pimento, chopped
2 quarts chicken broth
  (see index)
3 cups cooked chicken,
  cut into pieces
1 box wild rice
1/2 lb. fresh mushrooms,
  sauteed in butter
1/2 cup flour
1/2 cup butter
1 quart milk

Saute chopped vegetables. Add to pan (Dutch oven) with 2 quarts of chicken broth and contents of wild rice box. Simmer 30 to 40 minutes. While rice cooks, make white sauce. Melt butter in pan. Whisk in flour. Slowly add milk. Stir until thick. (Takes approximately 8 to 10 minutes.) Add white sauce, cooked chicken, sauteed mushrooms to Dutch oven containing rice. This makes 3 quarts—freezes—and is a meal in itself.

Menu suggestion: Wild rice soup, French bread, spinach salad, a Chablis or Pinot Chardonnay.

Candy Stell Shivers (Mrs. James A.)

79

SAUSAGE AND LENTIL SOUP
A lot of work, but well worth the effort

Must be made ahead
Can be frozen
Serves: 6-8
Preparation: 1 hour
Cooking Time: 1 hour, 50 minutes

2 cups lentils, rinsed and
   picked over
7 cups water
1-1/2 teaspoons minced fresh
   thyme or 1/2 teaspoon dried
1/2 teaspoon salt
1/2 teaspoon pepper
1 bay leaf
2 pinches Herbs de Provence or
   any mixture you like
1 lb. sausage meat
1 lb. hot Italian sausages
1 28-oz. can plum tomatoes,
   drained and chopped
1 cup sliced carrot
1 cup sliced celery
1 cup sliced onion
1/2 cup dried pasta,
   cut into bits
1 pkg. Knorr Oxtail Soup Mix
   (2-5/8 oz.)

In a kettle cover lentils with water and add seasonings. Bring the water to a boil over medium heat, skimming the froth as it rises, and simmer the mixture, covered, for about 40 minutes. (While lentils are simmering, prepare sausage, tomatoes, pasta and vegetables). In a large skillet, brown sausage meat, crumbled, over moderately high heat. Transfer it with a slotted spoon to the kettle and pour off the fat in the skillet. In the same skillet, brown the Italian sausages, pricked lightly, over moderately high heat. Transfer them with the slotted spoon to a cutting board and cut them into 1/4 inch sections. Add sausage to the kettle with tomatoes and the other vegetables and dried pasta. Add soup mixture to thicken base and enhance flavor. Bring liquid to a boil over medium heat and simmer the soup for one hour. Stir frequently.

Lane Weaver Byrd (Mrs. R.W.H.)

BLENDER BEARNAISE
Quick and easy

Can do ahead
Yield: 3/4 cup
Preparation: 30 minutes

1/2 cup white wine
1 Tablespoon tarragon vinegar
Pinch of dried tarragon
Ground pepper, to taste
3 egg yolks
1/4 lb. butter (1 stick)

In blender place 3 egg yolks and beat well. Slowly add one stick of melted butter and continue beating. Add wine and vinegar mixture and dried tarragon. Cook in double boiler until reduced to one-half the original volume.
Can be stored in refrigerator and reheated.

Beverly Maury Bagley (Mrs. Carter S.)

BECHAMEL SAUCE
Basic thick white sauce

Can do ahead
Can freeze
Yield: 1 pint
Preparation: 20 to 25 minutes

1/4 cup softened butter
1 teaspoon salt
6 Tablespoons flour
1/4 teaspoon white pepper
2 cups hot milk

Into container of an electric blender put butter, salt, flour, white pepper and hot milk. Cover container and turn motor on low speed. When blades have reached full momentum, switch motor to high and blend for 30 seconds. Pour sauce into double boiler and cook over simmering water for 15 minutes, stirring occasionally.

Medium white sauce: Make as above, using only 4 tablespoons flour.

Thin sauce: Make as above, using only 2 tablespoons butter and 2 tablespoons flour.

Cream sauce: Makes 3 cups. Make thick white sauce. When cooked, stir in 1 cup cream and heat through.

Mornay sauce: Makes 2-1/2 cups. Make medium white sauce, adding to container, along with the hot milk, 4 tablespoons diced Gruyere cheese and 4 tablespoons grated Parmesan cheese. Cook over simmering water for 15 minutes, stirring occasionally. Stir in gradually 2 tablespoons butter.

BEARNAISE SAUCE

Can do ahead
Can freeze
Preparation: 20 to 25 minutes

Blender Hollandaise
   (see index)
1/4 cup white wine
2 Tablespoons tarragon vinegar
2 teaspoons chopped fresh
   tarragon (or 1 teaspoon
   dried tarragon)
1 Tablespoon chopped shallots
1/4 teaspoon freshly ground
   pepper

Make Blender Hollandaise and leave it in the container. In small saucepan, combine wine, tarragon vinegar, fresh (or dried) tarragon, chopped shallots and pepper. Bring liquid to a boil and cook rapidly until liquid is reduced to about 2 tablespoons or less. Pour remaining liquid and seasonings into container, stir to blend, cover and blend on high speed for 8 seconds.

BROWN SAUCE

Can do ahead
Can freeze
Yield: 1 quart
Preparation: 45 minutes

1/2 cup butter
8 Tablespoons flour
4 cups brown stock (see index)
1 cup dry white wine
1 carrot, sliced
1 medium onion, coarsely cut
1 leek, the white part,
   quartered
1 clove garlic
2 Tablespoons tomato puree
1/2 teaspoon thyme
1 large bay leaf
Salt and pepper
1/2 cup sherry or Madeira

In heavy skillet melt one-half cup of butter. Add 8 tablespoons flour and cook until a good dark brown, the color of dark brown sugar. Add 4 cups brown stock and bring to a boil. Into container of an electric blender put white wine, carrot, onion, leek and garlic. Cover and blend on high speed for 5 seconds, or until vegetables are chopped. Add vegetables and liquid to skillet and bring to boil. Add tomato puree, thyme and bay leaf. Simmer for 30 minutes, stirring occasionally. Skim off the fat that rises to surface. Blend 2 cups at a time in container of electric blender until smooth. Correct seasoning of sauce with a little salt and pepper and stir in 1/2 cup sherry or Madeira.

Note: In blending thin sauces, it is best to begin on low speed with container covered. When the blades have gained full momentum, switch motor to high. This technique prevents any surge of the sauce out of the container.

CHICKEN VELOUTE

Can do ahead
Can freeze
Yields: 2-1/2 cups
Preparation: 20 minutes

4 Tablespoons butter
6 Tablespoons flour
1/2 teaspoon salt
1/4 teaspoon white pepper
1/2 cup cream
2 cups hot chicken stock
   (see index)

Into container of an electric blender put butter, flour, salt, white pepper, cream, and hot chicken stock. Cover container and turn motor on low speed. When blades have reached full momentum, switch motor to high speed and blend for 30 seconds. Pour into double boiler and cook over simmering water for 15 minutes, stirring occasionally.

Supreme Sauce: To 1 cup hot Chicken Veloute, stir in 1/4 cup cream.

Fish Veloute: Make as above, using fish stock instead of chicken stock.

BLENDER HOLLANDAISE SAUCE

Can do ahead
Can freeze
Yield: 1-1/4 cups
Preparation: 15 minutes

4 egg yolks
2 Tablespoons lemon juice
1/4 teaspoon salt
1/4 teaspoon Tabasco
1 cup butter

In a small saucepan, heat 1 cup butter until very hot, but not brown. Into container of an electric blender put egg yolks, lemon juice, salt and Tabasco. Cover container and turn motor on low speed. Immediately remove cover and pour in the hot butter in a steady stream. When all butter is added, turn off motor.

Serve immediately or keep warm by setting container into a saucepan containing 2 inches of hot water. If the sauce becomes too thick to pour when ready to use, return container to blender, add 1 tablespoon hot water and blend briefly.

HOLLANDAISE SAUCE

Can do a little ahead,
but best served at once
Yield: 1-1/2 cups
Preparation: 20 minutes

3 large egg yolks
3/4 cup butter (divided into
    3 equal parts)
4 teaspoons lemon juice
Dash cayenne
Salt, to taste

Combine egg yolks and lemon juice in top of double boiler, over slow heat, stirring constantly until it begins to thicken. Add 1/4 cup butter (cut into 3 or 4 small pieces); add another 1/4 cup butter (cut into small pieces), continue stirring. Add last 1/4 cup butter (small pieces). Add cayenne (and salt, if desired); stir until thickens. The sauce will be thick enough when the whisk leaves an indentation in the sauce and the surface will be shiny.

Hints for a good Hollandaise Sauce: It is best to undercook a bit if not serving immediately.

Don't try to make Hollandaise or Bearnaise on a very humid day, unless you use clarified butter.

Remove the cords from the egg yolks as they make the sauce lumpy.

Grainy appearance to the sauce means to remove it from the heat.

Hot eggs can cause sauce to separate.

Thais Wiener

MUSHROOM SAUCE

Can do ahead
Serves: 12-14 people
Preparation: 25 minutes

1/4 cup butter
1 pint chicken broth
   (see index)
2 egg yolks
1/4 cup flour
1/4 cup cream (or milk)
1 teaspoon lemon juice
1 teaspoon parsley, chopped
1/2 lb. mushrooms, sliced
Salt and pepper

Brown mushrooms in butter. Make a smooth paste of broth and flour. Add to mushrooms. Stir. Mix beaten egg yolks with cream. Gently add 2 or 3 tablespoons of warm mushroom mixture to yolks and cream. Then add yolk mixture to the mushroom mixture and stir. Cook gently until egg yolks are cooked.

Helen King Turner (Mrs. Franklin H., Jr.)

TOMATO SAUCE

Can do ahead
Can freeze
Yield: 3 quarts
Preparation: 2 to 2-1/2 hours

5 Tablespoons diced salt pork
2 Tablespoons butter
5 Tablespoons flour
1 carrot, coarsely cut
1 medium onion, coarsely cut
1 clove garlic
1 cup chicken stock (see index)
1 bay leaf
1/4 teaspoon thyme
5 lbs. ripe tomatoes, quartered
   (or two quarts canned
   tomatoes)
3 cups chicken stock
1 teaspoon salt
1/2 teaspoon pepper
2 Tablespoons butter

Saute diced salt pork in butter until salt pork is rendered and crisp. Remove salt pork. Stir in flour and cook until flour begins to brown. Into container of an electric blender put carrot, onion, garlic and 1 cup chicken stock. Cover and blend on high for 5 seconds, or until vegetables are chopped. Empty vegetables and liquid into flour mixture, and stir.

Add bay leaf, thyme, tomatoes and 3 cups chicken stock. Bring to a boil, stirring; cover and cook over low heat for one and a half hours. Blend 2 cups at a time in the electric blender and return to heat. Correct seasoning with salt and pepper, or to taste, and stir in two tablespoons of butter.

Hint:
Soup, sauce or gravy too salty? Place a peeled raw potato in the liquid and it will absorb the extra salt.

CLARIFIED BUTTER

Can do ahead
Can freeze
Yield: Depends on quality of butter used
Preparation: 25 minutes

1 lb. butter

Clarified butter can be another frozen convenience. It's great for sauteing fish and chicken. The food doesn't stick to the pan, for clarified butter doesn't burn as easily as regular butter. Melt 1 lb. butter over low heat. Skim off foam from surface and pour the clear oil carefully off the milky sediment which settles to the bottom of the saucepan. The clear oil, or butter fat, is the clarified drawn butter ready to use for storage. Pour into crock or bowl. Cool, cover and freeze.

SWEET BUTTER

Must do ahead
Yield: 3/4 cup
Preparation: 15 minutes

1 cup cream
1/2 cup water
2 cracked ice cubes

Into container of an electric blender put 1 cup cream. (Cream that has been refrigerated for a couple of days turns to butter faster than fresh cream.)
Cover and turn motor on high speed. Remove cover and blend until cream is whipped. Add one-half cup of water and 2 cracked ice cubes. Cover and blend on high speed for 1 or 2 minutes. The time depends on the age of the cream. The water increases the amount of liquid in the container so that when the butter particles form they rise above the blades. The ice chills the butter so that it is fairly firm. Pour butter particles and liquid into a small sieve to drain. Knead butter with back of a wooden spoon. Spoon into small crock, cover tightly, and chill.
Garlic Butter: Add 1 clove garlic along with the water and ice cubes.

ROUX

Can do ahead
Can freeze
Yield: 1-1/3 cups
Preparation: 10 minutes (after butter softens)

1/2 cup butter
1 cup flour

For the roux, let one-half cup butter soften at room temperature, then mix this to a smooth paste with 1 cup flour. This can be frozen in a small pot or bowl, covered with aluminum foil. When a recipe specifies "to stir in 1 tablespoon flour mixed to a smooth paste with 1 tablespoon butter," simply stir in 1 rounded tablespoon of the frozen roux.

COCKTAIL SAUCE
Excellent for boiled shrimp or crabmeat

Can do ahead
Yield: 1/2 cup
Preparation: 5 minutes

1/3 cup catsup
1 Tablespoon lemon juice
2 Tablespoons Worcestershire
   sauce
1 Tablespoon prepared
   horseradish
Salt/pepper

Combine all ingredients and chill.

Celine Hanan Lurey (Mrs. Michael F.)

FOOD PROCESSOR MAYONNAISE

Can do ahead
Yield: 1 cup
Preparation: 5 minutes

1 egg
1/4 teaspoon dry mustard
1/2 teaspoon salt
1 Tablespoon lemon juice
   or vinegar
1 cup vegetable oil
1/4 teaspoon red pepper
A little onion juice

Using plastic blade, put whole egg with mustard and salt in work bowl and process 20 seconds. Pour in lemon juice and process; pour oil slowly through feed tube until mixture starts to thicken.

Alice Ward Griffin (Mrs. William R., III)

SPICY HOMEMADE MAYONNAISE

Can do ahead
Yield: 1-1/3 cups
Preparation: 10 minutes

2 Tablespoons lemon juice or
vinegar (or 1 Tablespoon
of each)
1 cup of salad oil
1 egg
1 teaspoon dry mustard
1/4 teaspoon cayenne pepper
1/4 teaspoon ground
black pepper
1/4 teaspoon ground
chili powder

In blender or processor, put the lemon juice and/
or vinegar, 1/4 cup of salad oil, egg, dry mustard,
cayenne pepper, black pepper and chili powder.
Cover the container and blend at high speed.
Gradually, by drops or a thin stream, add the
rest of the oil through the hole in the top of the
container cover while the machine is still running.

Sandy Farnam Sellers (Mrs. Danny)

E'S BARBECUE SAUCE
It is hot!

Can do ahead
Yield: 1 quart
Preparation: 45 minutes

1/4 cup Worcestershire
sauce
Tabasco—hit bottle 6 times
1/2 cup prepared mustard
1 16-oz. bottle cider vinegar
1/2 cup chili sauce
1/2 cup ketchup
1 Tablespoon salt
1 Tablespoon pepper

Put all ingredients in saucepan. Stir until mustard dissolves. Bring to a boil and simmer 30
minutes. Good as barbecue on pork and chicken.
I use it to baste while it cooks, and serve it with
the meat as extra sauce. It's *HOT!* for a milder
sauce, cut down Tabasco, and pepper to taste.)

Marian Richards Atwater (Mrs. J. S.)

JEZEBEL SAUCE
Hot and spicy! Interesting flavor!

Can do ahead
Yield: 1 quart
Preparation: 3 minutes

1 8-oz. jar pineapple preserves
1 8-oz. jar apple jelly
1 6-oz. jar French's mustard
1 6-oz. jar horseradish

Blend the 4 ingredients together in blender. Store
in quart jar in refrigerator. Keeps indefinitely.
Divine with ham; also good with roast beef.

Cornelia Stephens (Mrs. F. Irby)

MUSTARD
Good on ham, roast beef, even turkey sandwiches

Must do ahead
Yield: 2 cups
Preparation: 20 minutes

2 cans (2 oz. each) Coleman's
    dry mustard
1 cup dark apple cider vinegar
2 eggs
1 cup sugar
Pinch of salt

Mix mustard and apple cider vinegar in bowl. Let stand overnight. Beat eggs and add sugar and salt to mustard and vinegar mixture. Cook until thick in double boiler over boiling water 5 to 10 minutes. Ladle into small jars. Refrigerate.

Nancy Sauer Crosby (Mrs. E. Brown)

ANN'S MUSTARD SAUCE

Can do ahead
Yield: About 2 cups
Preparation: 20 minutes

2-1/2 Tablespoons dry mustard
1/2 cup sugar
2 egg yolks
1 cup heavy cream
1/4 cup white vinegar

Mix first 4 ingredients in top of double boiler and heat. When it begins to thicken, *slowly* add the vinegar. Continue stirring over medium heat until nice sauce consistency. Great with ham— also good cold as spread on ham sandwiches.

Betsy Rawleigh Simons (Mrs. William J.)

SAVORY SAUCE FOR POTATOES

Can do ahead—just add lemon juice when reheating
Yield: 3/4 cup
Preparation: 30 minutes

1/8 lb. butter (1/2 stick)
3 teaspoons olive oil
Juice and grated rind
    of 1 lemon
Handful of chopped parsley
Chopped chives, to taste
Dash nutmeg
Pinch of flour
    (1/8 to 1/4 teaspoon)
Salt and pepper, to taste

Melt butter in pan. Add olive oil and lemon rind. Add remaining ingredients, except lemon juice. Simmer for 10 minutes. Add lemon juice just before serving. Pour over boiled new potatoes.

Robyn Frankel Leslie (Mrs. William H.)

Bread

TIPS ON BREAD MAKING

INGREDIENTS

Yeast
One cake of compressed yeast equals one package of dry yeast.

Cake yeast is perishable and must be refrigerated.

Dry yeast will keep for several weeks on the shelf or indefinitely under refrigeration.

When you wish to use dry yeast in a recipe calling for compressed yeast, remove 1/4 cup of liquid from the ingredients to dissolve the dry yeast.

Liquids
Milk, water or potato water may be used in making bread. Milk or potato water must always be scalded and cooled before using, to prevent souring.

Skim milk powder may be used in place of regular milk. To provide greater nutrition, double the amount of milk powder necessary: in a recipe calling for 2 cups of milk, use 2 cups water and 1/2 cup milk powder (the amount needed to make one quart of milk). For convenience in mixing, stir the milk powder in with the sifted dry ingredients and then use the water for the liquid.

Flour
Bread flour that is unbleached makes the best yeast dough. All-purpose flour may be used, but won't give the same results.

It is important to use good flour. If you buy it at the health food store, it will require refrigeration.

Different brands of flour, or the same brand at different times, will absorb varying amounts of liquids. The usual proportion is one cup liquid to three to four cups flour.

Sugar
Sugar helps to brown the crust and also helps the yeast to work properly.

Salt
Salt gives flavor and stabilizes fermentation. The usual proportion is one teaspoon salt to each two cups of flour.

Shortening
When butter is called for, margarine, shortening or lard may be substituted. When a small amount of shortening is called for, a liquid shortening may be substituted.

TECHNIQUES

Kneading

Except when otherwise specified, kneading is essential to a good loaf of bread. In general, turn the dough onto a lightly-floured surface and knead with the hands, approximately 7 to 10 minutes until the dough is smooth and elastic.

Rising

When the dough has been kneaded, it should be placed in a lightly-greased bowl and covered with plastic wrap or a damp cloth. Place in a warm, draft-free location. Rising times given in recipes are approximate times only, dependent upon room temperature and humidity.

Shaping

To make loaves, divide the dough into desired number of pieces, one for each loaf. Roll out into a rectangle, then roll the rectangle up in jelly-roll style to make a loaf. To make rolls, roll dough out and cut into desired shapes, or form into small balls and place in greased muffin tins.

Pans

Grease with shortening, butter or margarine—do not grease with oil unless the recipe specifically tells you to use oil.

Baking

Follow the recipe for baking times and temperatures. Your oven may vary slightly so always check before the suggested baking time is up. When bread is done, it will be an even rich brown color. To test to see if it is done, turn the loaf onto a bread board and tap the bottom lightly with a knuckle. If done, there will be a distinctly hollow sound. If you do not hear this, turn bread back into the pans and bake a short time longer.

Freezing

Cool breads to room temperature; wrap tightly in foil or place in freezer bags and freeze. Can thaw, then reheat in a warm oven. Always cool thoroughly before wrapping to freeze, to prevent ice from forming in the bread.

CROISSANTS

Yield: 32 medium
or 60-64 small
May be frozen
Baking Time: 12-15 minutes

2 pkg. active dry yeast
1/3 cup warm water
2 Tablespoons sugar
1 Tablespoon salt
1-1/3 cup cold milk
1/4 cup salad oil
4-1/2 cups flour, divided
3 sticks sweet butter

EGG GLAZE:

1 egg beaten with
   1 teaspoon water

Dissolve yeast in warm water in a large bowl of an electric mixer. Add the sugar, salt, cold milk and salad oil. Add 2-1/4 cups of flour. Beat until smooth, then stir in the other 2-1/4 cups of flour. Turn out onto a floured board and let rest a few minutes. Knead very briefly, just enough to make the dough hold together. Wrap in plastic wrap and refrigerate.

Beat cold butter with a rolling pin, then knead until it is a solid, pliable mass. Keep cold. Roll the butter between sheets of waxed paper to make a 6-1/2x13-1/2" rectangle. Remove the dough from the refrigerator and roll it into a 7x 21" rectangle. Place the butter one-half inch from one end of the dough. Fold the unbuttered dough over the middle third of the dough, then fold the remaining third over the unbuttered top, fold as if folding a letter in thirds. There will be one side of the fold which is a single fold with no loose ends, rather like the back of a book. Place dough with this side to your left in front of you. Pinch the edges to seal securely. Dough will be a 7" square. This completes one "turn." Roll out the dough to its original 7x21" rectangle. Fold the dough in thirds as before. Carefully wrap in plastic wrap and refrigerate. You have now completed two "turns." After one and a half to two hours of refrigeration, make two more "turns" —always keeping the single fold side to your left. At the end of these turns you will have 81 layers of butter. Wrap again and chill for another 2 hours or even overnight. Dough may be frozen at this point. Roll out dough into your original 7x21" rectangle. Cut in half crosswise and refrigerate one half. Roll the other half into a 16" square. Cut into 4" squares. Cut each square into 4 triangles. For small rolls, cut each triangle in half again. Flatten each triangle with a rolling pin into an even triangle shape. Roll up, starting with the wide 2 points, roll over jelly-roll fashion to the other point. Place on a lightly-greased pan with the point of the triangle underneath. Bend the 2 ends inward to make the crescent shape.

Continued...

Form all rolls in the same manner. Keep all un-formed dough refrigerated to make handling easier. Allow to rise slowly until fully doubled. Risen croissants may be frozen, then baked while still frozen. Preheat oven to 450°. Carefully brush croissants with an egg glaze. Do not allow the glaze to drip on the baking sheet. Cover bottom rack of the oven with heavy foil to prevent burned bottoms. Bake 12-15 minutes in the middle of oven until nicely light brown. Cool on a rack 10-15 minutes. Baked and cooled crois-sants may be frozen—to reheat bake in 400° oven for 5 minutes.

BRIOCHE BRAID

Must do ahead
Yield: 1 braid
Baking Time: 20-30 minutes

1-3/4 to 2-1/4 cup regular
all-purpose flour
1/4 cup sugar
1/4 teaspoon salt
1 pkg. active dry yeast
1/4 cup milk
1/4 cup water
1/3 cup butter
2 eggs
1/2 teaspoon vanilla
Melted butter

In a large bowl, mix 3/4 cup flour, sugar, salt and yeast. Combine milk, water and butter in sauce-pan. Heat over low heat until liquids are warm and butter is melted. Gradually add to dry ingre-dients and beat for 2 minutes on medium speed of electric mixer, scraping bowl occasionally. Add eggs, vanilla and 1/2 cup flour, to make a thick batter. Beat on high speed 2 minutes. Add enough additional flour to make a stiff batter. Beat by hand for 5 minutes. Brush with melt-ed butter. Cover, let rise in warm place until doubled in bulk (about 1 hour). Stir batter down, cover tightly with foil and refrigerate overnight. Turn out onto a heavily-floured board. Divide into 3 pieces. Roll each piece into a roll 20" long. Braid the rolls together. Pinch ends to seal. Place on a large greased baking sheet. Cover lightly, let rise in a warm place until doubled in size (1 hour). Bake at 350° 20-30 minutes. Remove from baking sheet and place on a rack to cool. Best served warm, either plain or frosted with a sugar glaze: 3/4 cup powdered sugar, 1 Table-spoon milk, 1/2 teaspoon vanilla; beat until smooth.

Candace Lincoln

TWO-WAY BRIOCHE

Baking Time: 30-35 minutes

2 pkgs. dry yeast
1/3 cup warm milk
1/4 cup sugar
7 large eggs
7 cups bread flour
1 Tablespoon salt
1 cup sweet butter,
    softened
1/2 cup cold butter

Dissolve yeast in milk in bowl of electric mixer. Beat in sugar, eggs, salt, soft butter and about half the flour. Beat well. Beat in the rest of the flour by hand. Remove a little less than half the dough and let rise in a covered bowl. Beat the hard cold butter with a rolling pin, and smear it with the heel of your hand until it is smooth. Knead it into the remaining dough 3 Tablespoons at a time. Use one hand and hold a spatula in the other to help you scrape up bits. Knead rapidly until the butter is absorbed. If dough turns oily, refrigerate for 15-20 minutes before proceeding. Dough is ready when it is elastic enough to draw back into shape when pushed out. Put this dough in another buttered bowl and let rise separately. Note on rising: This dough should not rise in a very warm place, or it will get oily. Let it take several hours to rise, but do not let it rise too much or it will taste bitter and "yeasty." (To be sure it rises to exactly double, measure you bowl with cups of water and mark each cup on the outside of the bowl with a pencil or tape. Then if you have 3 cups of dough, you will let it rise to the 6-cup mark.) Deflate the dough and refrigerate overnight. This will enable you to shape the dough more easily. Butter a 6-cup fluted mold for this dough that has the extra butter in it. Form 2/3 of the dough into a large ball and set it in the pan. With your fingers, hollow out a large hole in the center of the dough which goes almost to the bottom of the pan. Form the remaining 1/3 dough into a cone shape and insert it into the hole. This is traditional. Take the dough *without* the extra butter that was just kneaded and allowed to rise in a separate bowl, lightly butter a 9″ round cake pan and form the dough to fit it on a lightly-floured board. This will be the shortcake brioche.

Continued...

Allow both brioches to rise until double. Mix 1 egg with 1 teaspoon water and paint both brioches. With scissors, clip around the "ball" on the traditional brioche to insure its separation. Bake in 400° oven for 20 minutes *or until they begin to brown.* Lower heat to 350° and bake an additional 10-15 minutes, or until each has a hollow sound when tapped with the knuckles. You may have to cover lightly with foil if they brown too fast.

Brioche dough may turn stale in 12 hours. Freeze and defrost at room temperature or for 45 minutes in a 300° oven.

Celine Hanan Lurey (Mrs. Michael)

WHITE BREAD

Eating while warm can be habit forming and detrimental to your weight!

Baking Time: 40 minutes

1 pkg. active dry yeast
1/2 cup lukewarm water
1 Tablespoon sugar
1 egg
2 cups lukewarm water
1 stick margarine,
    or butter, melted
1-1/2 teaspoons salt
1/2 cup sugar
8 cups all-purpose flour,
    sifted

Dissolve one pack of dry yeast in 1/2 cup of lukewarm water and sugar in a large bowl. Let stand in a warm place for about 45 minutes. The yeast will foam up to almost 2 cups. Beat in 1 egg, the melted butter, 2 cups lukewarm water, the salt and sugar. Sift the flour. Begin to add flour on medium speed and add slowly until mixture begins to ride up the beaters or strain the mixer. Remove to a floured surface and knead in the remaining flour (or most of it). Knead folding toward the center, flatten and fold toward the center again and again for about 10 minutes until dough is elastic and doesn't stick to surface. Ball the mixture and put in well-greased, large mixing bowl. Place, covered with a cloth, in a warm place until double in bulk. Punch down center, knead in edges and let stand until double in bulk, covered with a cloth. Cut the dough into three pieces, shape into loaves and place in well greased loaf pans. Cover, let rise until double in bulk. Preheat oven to 400°. Bake for 15 minutes then reduce heat to 375° and bake 25 minutes longer. Top should be brown and sound hollow when tapped. Turn loaves onto wire rack and brush with melted margarine. Let cool and then wrap for storage.

Ralph Morris

FRENCH BREAD

Can do ahead
Freezes well
Yield: 4 loaves
Preparation: 4 hours
Baking Time: 35-45 minutes

2-1/2 cups warm water
  (105°-115°)
1 pkg. active dry yeast
2 Tablespoons sugar
1 Tablespoons salt
7 cups all-purpose flour

In a large bowl, sprinkle yeast over water, add the salt and sugar. Stir until all is dissolved. Stir in 5 cups of flour, beat with wooden spoon until it is mostly mixed. Add another cup of flour. Dough will be quite sticky at this point, but will leave sides of bowl. Turn dough onto lightly floured board. Knead until smooth and elastic, adding more flour as needed to prevent sticking. (One more cup of flour probably needed to knead into the dough). Knead about 10 minutes. Dough will be stiff. Place in lightly greased bowl, turn the dough over to bring up the greased side. Cover with damp tea towel. Set in a warm, draft-free place; allow to rise until double in bulk (about 2 to 2-1/2 hours). Lightly grease a very large cookie sheet. Dust with cornmeal. Punch dough down and knead 3 or 4 times to remove air. Divide into 4 equal pieces. On a very lightly floured board, with very lightly floured rolling pin, roll each into 14x8" rectangle. Roll tightly as for a jelly roll starting from the wide end. Taper the ends. Pinch the edges to seal. Place the rolls on the greased pan so that they do not touch. Brush each with cold water. With a sharp knife slash 3 diagonal slashes across each loaf. Let rise again until double in bulk. *Do Not Cover.* Let rise about 1 to 1-1/2 hours. Preheat oven to 400°. Place a shallow pan of water on bottom shelf of oven. Bake loaves in middle of oven 35-45 minutes. Brush with cold water before placing in oven. With a plant sprayer, spray water on loaves after 15 minutes of baking, 20 minutes of baking and 25 minutes. This gives a hard, brown crust similar to the type eaten in France.

Jo-Ann McGowan Grimes (Mrs. Charles W.)
Molly Riggins Sandridge (Mrs. David A.)

WHOLE WHEAT MOLASSES BREAD

Can do ahead
Freezes well
Yield: 2 loaves
Preparation: 4-5 hours
Baking Time: 45 minutes

1-1/2 cup lukewarm water
1 pkg. active dry yeast
1 Tablespoon salt
2 Tablespoons molasses
2 cups white flour
3 Tablespoons shortening
1/2 cup molasses
1/2 cup boiling water
4 cups (or more)
    whole wheat flour

In a large bowl mix well 1-1/2 cup lukewarm water, the yeast, salt and 2 tablespoons molasses. Add 2 cups white flour. Cover and let rise in a warm place until double in bulk. In another bowl, mix together the shortening, one-half cup molasses and 1/2 cup boiling water. When this is cooled to lukewarm point, add to first mixture. Stir in 4 cups whole wheat flour. Add a little more if needed. Turn out onto a floured board and knead until smooth. Put back into the greased bowl. Grease the top with corn oil; let rise until double in bulk. Cut in half, knead until smooth and shape into loaves. Cover with the well-greased loaf pan. Let stand 15 minutes. Place in loaf pan, cover with your bread cloth, let rise until oval top of loaf is at the top of pan or near top. Preheat oven to 350°, bake 45 minutes or less depending on your oven. Place on wire rack, right side up. Brush with margarine.

Tina McArdle McGuire (Mrs. John O.)

EASY WHITE BREAD

Can do ahead
Can freeze
Baking Time: 30 minutes

1 pkg. active dry yeast
1-1/2 cup warm water
    (105-115°), divided
5 or less Tablespoons sugar
2 teaspoons salt
4 cups flour (all-purpose)

Dissolve the yeast in 3/4 cups of the water. Mix the dry ingredients with the yeast mixture; add the other 3/4 cup of water. Allow to rise in a warm place (warm, turned off oven) until doubled in bulk (about 1 to 1-1/2 hours). Punch down, put into buttered bread pans. Allow to rise to size for bread (30-40 minutes). Put into a cold oven; turn to 400°. Bake for 30 minutes; remove from oven and cool on rack.
Variations: Substitute 2 cups whole wheat flour. Add wheat germ or dill weed or cinnamon to dry ingredients before the first rising.

Sara Hill Lavelle (Mrs. B.F.D.)

SWEDISH LIMPA RYE BREAD

Baking Time: 30-35 minutes

1 pkg. active dry yeast
1-1/2 cups warm water
1/4 cup molasses
1/3 cup sugar
1 Tablespoon salt
2 Tablespoons shortening
Grated peel of one-half orange
2-1/2 cups rye flour
2-1/4 to 2-3/4 cups white flour

Dissolve the yeast in the warm water. Stir in molasses, sugar, salt, shortening, orange peel and rye flour. Beat until smooth; then mix in the white flour, one-half cup at a time until dough leaves the sides of the bowl. Knead as much of remaining flour as is possible until dough is smooth and elastic (7-10 minutes). Put in a greased bowl. Cover and let rise until double in bulk. Punch down. Cover and let rise until double in bulk again—then shape into round loaves. Cover and let rise until double in bulk. Bake in 375° oven for 30-35 minutes.

Variation: Substitute honey for molasses and whole wheat for rye flour for honey whole wheat bread.

Molly Riggins Sandridge (Mrs. David A.)

WHOLE WHEAT BRAN BREAD

Can do ahead
Can freeze
Yield: 2 loaves
Preparation: 4-5 hours
Baking Time: 60 minutes

1 cup water
3/4 cup milk
1 cup whole bran cereal
4 teaspoons salt
4 Tablespoons honey
4 Tablespoons molasses
4 Tablespoons margarine
1/2 cup warm water
   (105-115°)
2 pkg. active dry yeast
1 Tablespoon sugar
3 cups whole wheat flour,
   unsifted
2-1/2 to 3 cups white flour,
   unsifted

Combine 1 cup water and milk in saucepan; bring to a boil. Stir in cereal, salt, honey, molasses and margarine until dissolved. Cool to lukewarm. Measure 1/2 cup water into a large, warm bowl. Sprinkle in yeast. Stir until dissolved. Add 1 tablespoon sugar. (Sugar will enable the yeast to foam up unless the water was too hot and killed the yeast.) Add lukewarm cereal mixture and whole wheat flour, beat until smooth. Add enough white flour to make a stiff dough. Turn out onto lightly floured board. Knead until smooth and elastic (about 8-10 minutes); dough will be slightly sticky. Place in a greased bowl, turning to grease the top. Cover, let rise in a warm place, free from draft, until doubled in bulk (about 1 hour). (If you have a gas oven, that is the perfect place to let you bread rise due to the pilot.)

Continued...

Punch dough down. Turn out onto a lightly floured board; divide in half. Roll each half into a 12x8″ rectangle. Shape into loaves. Place in 2 greased 8-1/2x4-1/2x2-1/2-inch loaf pans. Let rise in a warm place free from draft until doubled in bulk (about 1 hour). Bake at 350° for 45 minutes to 1 hour. Remove from pans and cool on wire rack.

Linda Downing Eubanks (Mrs. Reavis)

HERB WHEAT BREAD

Can do ahead
Can freeze
Yield: 2 loaves
Baking Time: 35-45 minutes

5-1/2 to 6-1/2 cups
    unsifted all-purpose flour
2 pkgs. active dry yeast
1/3 cup sugar
1 teaspoon salt
1 teaspoon thyme leaves,
    crushed
1 teaspoon marjoram leaves,
    crushed
1-1/2 cups milk
1/2 cup water
1/2 cup butter or margarine
2 eggs + 1 egg yolk
1-1/3 cups honey wheat germ
1 egg white
1 Tablespoon wheat germ

Combine 3 cups flour, yeast, sugar, salt, herbs in a large bowl. Stir well to blend. Heat milk, water and butter together until warm to the touch (butter need not be melted completely). Add warm liquid to ingredients in bowl. Stir to combine. Add 2 whole eggs and 1 egg yolk. Beat at high speed on electric mixer 3 minutes. Stir in 1-1/3 cup wheat germ. Then stir in just enough of remaining flour to make a soft dough, which leaves the side of the bowl. Turn out on a floured board. Knead about 10 minutes until smooth and elastic. Place in large, greased bowl, turning to coat all sides. Cover with damp cloth. Let rise in warm, draft-free place about 1 hour until doubled in bulk. Punch down. Divide dough in half. Roll each half into a 12 x 18″ rectangle. Cut each rectangle into three 12″ strips. With strips make 2 braids. Place each braid in well-greased loaf pan. Cover and let rise 1 hour. Brush tops with beaten egg white and sprinkle with wheat germ. Bake at 350° 35-45 minutes until done. Cover loosely with foil the last 10 minutes if crust is getting too brown. Cool on racks.

Mary Bruce Rhodes Woody (Mrs. S. W.)

ONION HERB BREAD

Can do ahead
Can freeze
Yield: 1 loaf
Preparation: 3 hours
Baking Time: 50-55 minutes

2 cups warm water
2 pkgs. active dry yeast
2 Tablespoons sugar
2 teaspoons salt
2 Tablespoons butter
4 cups flour
   (regular all-purpose)
1/2 cup grated fresh onion
1 Tablespoon caraway seeds

Measure water in large bowl. Sprinkle in yeast and stir until dissolved. Stir in sugar, salt and butter. Add 2 cups of flour; beat until smooth. Stir in onion and caraway seeds. Blend in remaining flour. Cover and let rise in a warm place until doubled in bulk (about 45 minutes). Stir batter down. Beat vigorously one-half minute. Turn into a greased 1-1/2 quart casserole. Bake at 350° for 50-55 minutes. Makes 1 loaf. Quick easy recipe because requires no kneading and only 1 rising.
Variations: Use 1 tablespoon basil instead of caraway seeds; or 1 tablespoon dried dill (2 tablespoons fresh dill) or any other favorite herb.

Candace Lincoln

MONKEY BREAD

Must do ahead
Baking Time: 45 minutes

2 pkg. active dry yeast
1 teaspoon sugar
1/4 cup warm water
1/2 cup butter
1/3 cup sugar
1 teaspoon salt
3/4 cup scalded milk
5 cups flour
3 large eggs
1/2 lb. or more melted butter
   for dipping

Dissolve the yeast and 1 teaspoon sugar in warm water. Combine 1/2 cup butter, 1/3 cup sugar and salt. Add scalded milk. Stir to melt the butter. Cool then add the yeast, half of the flour and eggs. Beat thoroughly. Stir in the rest of the flour to make a soft but not sticky dough. Turn out onto a floured surface, knead until smooth and satiny (8 to 10 minutes). Place in a buttered bowl, cover and let rise in a warm draft-free place until doubled—about 1 hour. Punch down, turn out onto a floured surface. Pinch off small pieces about the size of golf balls, dipping each piece into melted butter and arranging in a buttered 10" tube pan. Cover and let rise again until almost doubled. Bake in 375° oven for 45 minutes, or until browned and done. Serve warm. Guests just pull off the individual pieces.

Emily Caddell Gordon (Mrs. Alan F.)

GERMAN DARK RYE BREAD

Can do ahead
Can freeze
Yield: 2 loaves
Preparation: 3 hours
Baking Time: 25-30 minutes

3 cups all-purpose flour
2 pkgs. active dry yeast
1/4 cup cocoa powder
   (baking cocoa)
1 Tablespoon caraway seeds
2 cups water
1/3 cup molasses
2 Tablespoons butter
1 Tablespoon sugar
1 Tablespoon salt
3 to 3-1/2 cups rye flour

Combine white flour, yeast, cocoa and caraway seeds. In a saucepan, combine water, molasses, butter, sugar and salt. Heat until just warm and butter is melted. Add dry ingredients in bowl. Beat at low speed on electric mixer for one-half minute, scraping bowl. Beat at high speed for 3 minutes. By hand, stir in enough rye flour to make a soft dough. Turn out onto floured board and knead until smooth (about 5 minutes). Cover, let rest about 20 minutes. Punch down and divide dough in half. Shape each loaf round and place on a greased sheet. Brush surfaces of loaves with oil and slash tops. Let rise until double (45-60 minutes). Bake in 400° oven for 25-30 minutes or until done; cool on racks.

Candace Lincoln

OATMEAL MOLASSES BREAD

Can do ahead
Can freeze
Yield: 2 loaves
Preparation: 4-5 hours
Baking Time: 30 minutes

1 cup rolled oats (Quick)
2 cups boiling water
1/2 cup molasses
2 Tablespoons shortening
2-1/2 teaspoons salt
2 pkg. dry yeast
1/3 cup warm water
6 cups flour

Put oats and boiling water in large bowl and soak 30 minutes. Add molasses, shortening and salt to mixture while warm but not hot. Add yeast dissolved in 1/3 cup water. Blend in 2 cups flour using beater; add 2 more cups flour. Knead in last 2 cups flour; continue kneading until dough is elastic. Put in a greased bowl and turn to grease the top. Cover and set in a warm place to rise until doubled in size. Punch down and knead lightly. Shape into 2 loaves. Place in greased loaf pans and rise until double. Bake at 400° for 15 minutes, then turn down for 15 minutes at 350°.

Candace Lincoln

PITA BREAD

Can do ahead
Freezes well
Yield: 6-7 loaves
Preparation: 2 hours
Baking Time: 8-10 minutes

1 pkg. active dry yeast
1 to 1-1/4 cups warm water
Pinch of sugar
3-1/2 cups pre-sifted flour
1 teaspoon salt
2 Tablespoons oil
Cornmeal

In a large bowl, dissolve the yeast and sugar in 1/4 cup of water; let stand for 10 minutes then add the remaining water, salt and oil. Stir in one cup of flour at a time, forming a sticky dough. (More flour may be added if the dough is too sticky). Knead the dough on a lightly-floured surface for about 10 minutes. Shape the dough into a ball, coat lightly with oil, place in a bowl. Cover and let rise until double in bulk (about 1 to 1-1/2 hours). Punch down the dough and form 6 or 7 balls. On a lightly-floured surface, roll or press out the dough with the hands into 6 inch circles that are 1/4 inch thick. Dust lightly with flour. Place on lightly-oiled baking sheets that have been dusted with cornmeal. Cover and let rise for 15 minutes. Bake at 500° for 8-10 minutes until puffy and slightly golden. Wrap pitas in foil immediately after removing from the oven to preserve moistness.

Jean Trainer Veach (Mrs. John B., Jr.)

HOMEMADE ROLLS

Must do ahead
Can freeze after baking
Yield: 4 dozen
Baking Time: 12-15 minutes

1 cup boiling water
1 cup shortening
    (1/2 margarine, 1/2 Crisco)
1 cup sugar
1-1/2 teaspoons salt
2 eggs
2 pkg. yeast
1 cup warm water
6 cups unsifted flour,
    approximately

Pour boiling water over shortening, sugar and salt. Blend and cool. Add eggs. Dissolve yeast in 1 cup warm water and stir. Add to liquid mixture. Add flour one cup at a time and blend well. Cover and place in the refrigerator at least 4 hours. Knead on a well-floured board and roll out. Cut and brush with melted butter. Fold over. Place on a greased baking sheet. Let rise 1-1/2 to 3 hours before baking. Bake at 400° for 12-15 minutes.

Bitsy Murphee Powell (Mrs. James)

BRAN REFRIGERATOR ROLLS

Can do ahead
Can freeze
Yield: 4 dozen—can be doubled
Preparation: 2-3 hours
Baking Time: 20 minutes

1 pkg. active dry yeast
1/2 cup warm water
2/3 cup soft margarine
3/4 cup sugar
1-1/2 teaspoons salt
1 cup mashed potatoes
1 cup hot potato water
2 medium eggs
4-5 cups flour
1 cup bran flakes

Dissolve the yeast in warm water. Add margarine, sugar, salt and mashed potatoes to the hot potato water. When cooled, stir in yeast and the eggs. Add bran flakes and enough flour to make the dough stiff (about 4-5 cups). Turn onto a lightly floured board and knead well 7-10 utes. Put into a greased bowl, cover and refrigerate. When ready to use, remove the amount needed, let it warm to room temperature. Shape into rolls and place on greased cookie sheets or in muffin tins. Cover, and let rise until doubled. Bake in 400° oven until browned (about 20 minutes).

Variations: Substitute 1 cup sharp Cheddar cheese for the bran flakes or 1 teaspoon of any favorite herb.

Pat Harvard Godbold (Mrs. Ronald L.)

BUTTERFLAKE ROLLS

Must do ahead of time
Baking Time: 10 minutes

2 pkg. active dry yeast
1/2 cup warm water
1/2 cup sugar
1/2 cup butter
1/4 cup warm water
3 eggs beaten
4-1/2 cups sifted flour
2 teaspoons salt
Melted butter

One day in advance, soften yeast in 1/2 cup warm water. Stir in 1 Tablespoon of sugar. Set aside for 10 mintues. In another bowl, combine butter or margarine and remaining sugar. Stir in 1/4 cup warm water, beaten eggs and yeast mixture. Stir in flour and salt. Cover and refrigerate overnight. Divide dough in half. Roll out to 1/4" thick rectangle. Brush with melted butter. Starting at the wide side, roll jellyroll fashion. Pinch seams to seal. Cut in 1" slices. Dip in melted butter and put butter side up in buttered muffin tins. Let rise until double in bulk, about 1 hour. Bake in 400° oven for 10 minutes or until lightly brown.

Elaine Newman Schulman (Mrs. Dick)

SHORT BISCUITS FOR SMITHFIELD HAM

Can do ahead
Can freeze

BISCUIT MIX

Yield: 4-1/2 cups

3 cups self-rising flour
1-1/2 Tablespoons
baking powder
1 Tablespoon sugar
1 cup shortening
Milk
Melted butter

Sift dry ingredients in mixing bowl. Cut in shortening with a pastry blender until the mixture resembles cornmeal. Store in covered cannister in refrigerator. Will keep 4-6 weeks. For 18 1-inch biscuits, combine 1 cup mix with enough milk to moisten. Knead lightly on a floured surface 5 or 6 times. Roll out to 1/4 inch thickness. Cut with a 1 inch round cutter. Place on greased cookie sheets. Brush tops with melted butter. Prick tops with a fork. Bake in a preheated 450° oven 10 minutes (split open while still warm). Butter and fill with paper-thin slices of Smithfield Ham.

Mary Bruce Rhodes Woody (Mrs. Stephen W.)

SAUSAGE BISCUITS

Baking Time: 12-15 minutes

2 cups flour
1-1/4 teaspoon baking powder
1-1/4 teaspoon sugar
1/2 teaspoon salt
3/4 cup buttermilk
4 Tablespoons Crisco
shortening

Sift dry ingredients. Cut in shortening with pastry blender, until mixture is the consistency of coarse corn meal. Make a deep well in center of these ingredients. Pour all the buttermilk in at once. Stir cautiously until there is no danger of spilling; then stir vigorously until the dough is fairly free from sides of bowl (the time should be a scant one-half minute). Knead the dough gently and quickly for another scant one-half minute. Roll gently with a lightly-floured rolling pin or pat gently with palm of hand to 1/4" inch thickness. Cut with lightly-floured biscuit cutter. Place on ungreased pan. Bake in preheated 450° oven for 12-15 minutes. Serve with cooked sausage.

David A. Sandridge

ANGEL FLAKE BISCUITS
Easy and delicious!

Must do ahead
Can freeze
Yield: 2 dozen
Preparation: 1-1/2 hours
Baking Time: 15 minutes

1 pkg. yeast
2 Tablespoons warm water
5 cups flour
4 Tablespoons sugar
1 Tablespoon baking powder
1 teaspoon salt
1 teaspoon soda
1 cup shortening
2 cups buttermilk

Dissolv yeast in warm water. Sift dry ingredients and cut in shortening with a pastry blender (or knives). Stir buttermilk and yeast into flour/shortening mixture. Roll out on floured board, cut into biscuits. Brush with melted butter. Let rise, covered, in a warm place approximately 1 hour. Bake at 400° for 15 minutes.

Mrs. Vicki Hyde

EASY SOUTHERN BISCUITS

Yield: 12-14 biscuits
Baking Time: 10 minutes

2 cups self-rising flour
2 teaspoons of baking powder
1 teaspoon sugar
1/3 cup shortening
2/3 cup of milk

Put dry ingredients into bowl of food processor, using the metal knife blade. Add shortening and process in an on-off motion until the mixture resembles coarse meal. Add milk slowly while the processor is running. Mix only long enough for the dough to roll itself into a ball on top of the blade. Pat gently on floured surface until one-half inch thick. Cut with a floured biscuit cutter. Bake at 475° for 10 minutes.

Barrie Muilenburg Sneed (Mrs. A. L.)

Hint:
Your butter or cream cheese too hard to spread? Fill a bowl with hot water, empty, invert over butter a couple of minutes...it will be just right.

ENGLISH MUFFINS

Can do ahead
Freeze well
Yield: 24
Preparation: 3 hours
Baking Time: 8-10 minutes

YEAST-FLOUR MIXTURE:

2 cups all-purpose flour
2 Tablespoons sugar, or honey
2 teaspoons salt
1 pkg. active dry yeast

LIQUID MIXTURE:

1-3/4 cups milk
1/4 cup water
1 Tablespoon butter

1 egg
4 cups all-purpose flour
  (approximately)
1/2 cup cornmeal
  (approximately)

In a large bowl, stir together the yeast-flour mixture; set aside. Heat liquid mixture until very warm (120-130°). Add gradually to yeast-flour mixture and beat at medium speed 2 minutes. Add egg and 1 cup flour; beat at high speed 2 minutes. Stir in just enough remaining flour to make a soft dough. Knead on lightly floured surface until smooth and elastic, adding more remaining flour if dough is sticky. Cover with plastic wrap and let rise until double in bulk (about 1 hour). Cover and let rise again until double, about 45 minutes; punch down. On a lightly-floured surface, roll out 1/2 inch thick with a 3-1/4 inch round cutter (or a clean tuna can opened at both ends), cut out muffins. Sprinkle cookie sheets with cornmeal. Place the muffins on cookie sheet about 1" apart. Sprinkle muffins with more cornmeal. Cover; let rise until double, about 45 minutes. Slip a wide spatula under the risen muffins taking care not to compress or puncture the dough or they will collapse. Using a low heat, warm a lightly-greased griddle. Place the muffins on the griddle and bake 8-10 minutes on each side until light brown. Muffins should sound hollow. Cool on racks. These can also be baked in the oven at 375° for 12-15 minutes or until they sound hollow.

Jean Trainker Veach (Mrs. John B., Jr.)

BRAN MUFFINS

Can do ahead
Yield: 6 dozen
Preparation: 20 minutes
Baking Time: 15-20 minutes

15 oz. box Raisin Bran
* or Bran Flakes*
3 cups sugar
5 cups sifted flour
5 teaspoons baking soda
2 teaspoons salt
1 cup corn oil
4 beaten eggs
1 quart buttermilk

Mix bran, sugar, flour, baking soda and salt in a large bowl. Mix together and then add to the Bran mixture, the corn oil, eggs and buttermilk. Stir all well. Fill greased muffin tins 3/4 full. Bake in 400° oven for 15-20 minutes. (The dough can be refrigerated for up to six weeks.)

Jaime Porter Armstrong (Mrs. Jeff)

PLUM MUFFINS

Yield: 18
Preparation: 20 minutes
Baking Time: 20-25 minutes

3/4 lbs. (about 1-3/4 cups)
* red plums, finely chopped*
2-1/2 cups unsifted
* all-purpose flour*
2 teaspoons baking soda
1/2 teaspoon salt
1 cup, plus 1 Tablespoon sugar
1/4 cup butter or margarine,
* melted*
2 eggs, slightly beaten
1 teaspoon vanilla extract
1/2 cup milk
1/2 cup chopped walnuts

Preheat oven to 400°. Grease 18 muffin pan cups or line with paper liners. Sprinkle plums with 1 Tablespoon flour and toss lightly. In a large bowl, combine remaining flour, baking soda and salt with 1 cup sugar. In another bowl, combine melted butter or margarine, eggs, vanilla and milk. Stir until smooth. Add the liquid ingredients to dry ingredient mixture. Stir just until mixture is moistened. Fold in plums and walnuts. Spoon batter into muffin cups. Bake 20-25 minutes until a toothpick comes out clean. Cool on wire rack.

Millicent Bitter Elmore (Mrs. Miles)

SOUR CREAM MUFFINS

Can do ahead
Can freeze
Yield: 24 tiny rolls
Baking Time: 15 minutes

2 cups self-rising flour
1 cup sour cream
1-1/2 sticks butter,
* melted*

Combine all ingredients in bowl and stir until well mixed. Bake in tiny, lightly-greased muffin tins in 450° oven for 15 minutes.

Barrie Muilenburg Sneed (Mrs. A. L.)

BLUEBERRY OATMEAL MUFFINS

Yield: 16-18 muffins
Baking Time: 20-25 minutes

2 cups blueberries
2 Tablespoons flour
3/4 cup old-fashioned oatmeal
1-1/2 cups flour
1 cup sugar
2 teaspoons baking powder
1 teaspoon salt
3/4 teaspoon lemon peel
1/2 cup cold butter
2/3 cup buttermilk
1 egg
1-1/2 Tablespoons sugar
2 teaspoons cinnamon

In a bowl toss blueberries with 2 tablespoons flour. In a blender grind the oatmeal to a coarse powder and transfer it to a large bowl. Into this bowl, sift the flour, sugar, baking powder and salt. Combine the mixture well. With a pastry blender, cut in the butter until mixture resembles corn meal. Fold in the blueberries and lemon peel. Combine the buttermilk and egg and add to the flour mixture. Stir batter until just combined. Spoon the batter into greased 1/2 cup muffin tins filling them 2/3 full. Mix the cinnamon and sugar together and sprinkle over the muffins. Bake at 400° for 20-25 minutes until puffed and golden. Serve warm with butter.

Mary Bruce Rhodes Woody (Mrs. S. W.)

GOUGERE

Baking Time: 35 minutes

1/2 cup water
1/4 cup butter,
   cut into 4 pieces
1/4 teaspoon salt
1/2 cup all-purpose flour
2 eggs, at room temperature
1/4 cup grated
   Monterey Jack cheese
1/4 cup grated Cheddar cheese

Heat oven to 375°. Place water, butter and salt in heavy medium saucepan. Heat on medium, stirring until butter melts and mixture boils. Add flour all at once, stirring with wooden spoon until mixture forms a ball. Remove from heat. Beat about 1 minute until slightly cooled.
Add eggs, one at a time to flour mixture beating with electric mixer until it reaches dull, satiny sheen (about 1 minute per egg). Stir in cheese. Butter and flour baking sheet. Drop warm paste by heaping Tablespoonful onto sheet, placing 2 inches apart. Bake 35 minutes. Remove from oven. Transfer immediately to wire rack. Cut slit in side of each puff to allow steam to escape.

Dianna Blackwell Goodman (Mrs. J. V.)

MILLIE'S MUFFINS
Very good!

Baking Time: 25 minutes

1/4 cup Crisco
1/4 cup sugar
1 egg
2 cups regular flour
4 good teaspoons baking
    powder
1/4 teaspoon salt
1 cup milk
Optional: 1 cup berries, nuts
    or dates

Cream Crisco and add sugar gradually, creaming while adding. Add well-beaten egg. Sift flour, baking powder and salt together; add them alternately with milk to the butter/sugar mixture. Bake in greased muffin tins 25 minutes in 400° oven.

Emmie Spencer Field (Mrs. Arthur)

YORKSHIRE PUDDING

Serves: 4-6
Preparation: 5 minutes
Baking Time: 30-40 minutes

1 cup flour
1/2 teaspoon salt
2 eggs
1-1/8 cup milk
3/8 cup water
2 Tablespoons beef drippings
    or oil

Mix milk and water together. Sift flour with salt into a bowl. Make a well in the center and add eggs with 3/4 cup of the milk-water mixture. With a wisk stir carefully, drawing in all the flour to form a smooth batter. Add half the remaining liquid and beat for 3 minutes. Add the rest of the liquid, mix quickly, cover and let stand in a cool place (not the refrigerator) for 1 hour before cooking. Heat drippings or oil in 11-1/4x7-1/2" pan until very hot. Stir batter and pour into pan. Bake in a very hot oven (425-450°) until puffed and brown—about 30-40 minutes. Cut into squares and serve with roast beef or roast chicken.

Patricia Stancil Smith (Mrs. Phillip J.)

ONION BREAD

Baking Time: 30-35 minutes

3 cups flour
1 teaspoon salt
1/2 teaspoon baking powder
1/2 teaspoon baking soda
2-1/2 to 3 Tablespoons Crisco
1/2 cup onions, chopped
1-1/4 cup buttermilk
2 Tablespoons butter,
    melted
2 Tablespoons finely
    minced onion
Caraway or poppy seeds

Sift flour into a bowl and add salt, baking powder and soda. Mix well. Add the chopped onions and Crisco. Make a well in the center and pour in the buttermilk; stirring quickly with a spoon, mix in the buttermilk, mixing it first with the dry ingredients in the center of the bowl, then working in the outside ingredients. Knead lightly on a board. Shape into a 4x12" buttered bread pan. Make a depression down the length of the bread. Mix the melted butter and the remaining minced onions and spoon into the depression. Sprinkle with seeds. Bake 30-35 minutes in 425° oven or until light brown. Cool 5-10 minutes and then turn onto a rack.

Elaine Newman Schulman (Mrs. Dick)

DILL BREAD

Serve with barbeque dishes or pork roasts, etc.

Can do ahead
Can freeze
Yield: 1 loaf
Preparation: 2 hours
Baking Time: 30-40 minutes

1 pkg. dry yeast dissolved in
    1/4 cup warm water
1 cup creamed cottage cheese
1/3 stick butter
2 Tablespoons sugar
1 Tablespoon instant
    minced onion
2 teaspoons dill seed
1 teaspoon salt
1/4 teaspoon soda
1 egg, unbeaten
2-1/4 to 2-1/2 cups
    plain flour

Heat cottage cheese and butter to lukewarm. Combine all ingredients except flour in large bowl. Mix, add flour gradually to form a stiff dough. Cover and let rise for 50-60 minutes in a warm place. Then stir down dough and turn into a well-greased loaf pan or 8" round casserole (1-1/2 to 2 qt. size). Let rise for 30-40 minutes until again doubled in size. Bake at 350° for 40-50 minutes until golden brown.

Sandra Tucker Holt (Mrs. S. E.)

CORN OYSTERS

Yield: 12
Preparation: 20 minutes

2 ears corn on the cob or
8-3/4 oz. can whole kernel
   corn, drained
1 egg, beaten
1/4 cup all-purpose flour
3 Tablespoons light cream
   or milk
1 Tablespoon butter
   or margarine (melted)
1/4 teaspoon salt
Pepper to taste
Cooking oil for frying

Scrape corn from each row of corn, scrape cob. Or, coarsely chop whole kernel corn. In a bowl, combine the beaten egg, corn, flour, cream, butter, salt and pepper. In a heavy skillet, pour cooking oil to a depth of 1/2 inch. Heat oil to 365°. Carefully drop corn mixture by tablespoons into hot oil. Fry fritters 2 minutes or until golden, turning once. Serve hot.

Jean Trainer Veach (Mrs. John B. Jr.)

ZUCCHINI BREAD
Serve buttered and heated for breakfast

Can do ahead
Can freeze
Yield: 2 loaves
Preparation: 20 minutes
Baking Time: 60-70 minutes

3 cups flour, sifted
1 Tablespoon cinnamon
1 teaspoon salt
1 teaspoon baking soda
1/4 teaspoon baking powder
3 eggs, beaten
1 cup sugar
1 cup packed brown sugar
1 cup vegetable oil
1 Tablespoon vanilla
2 cups zucchini, grated
Optional: 1/2 cup nuts,
   chopped

Sift flour, cinnamon, salt, baking soda and baking powder. Set aside. In a large bowl, thoroughly beat eggs, sugar, brown sugar, vegetable oil and vanilla. Stir in sifted ingredients. Blend in grated zucchini and nuts. Pour into 2 greased and lightly floured 4-1/2 x 8-1/2″ loaf tins. Bake at 325° for 60-70 minutes.

Jeanne Forsythe Powell (Mrs. B. G.)

PUMPKIN BREAD

Can do ahead
Freezes well
Yield: 2 loaves
Preparation: 15 minutes
Baking Time: 60 minutes

3 eggs
1-1/2 cups sugar
1-1/2 cups pumpkin,
   cooked or canned
1 cup plus 2 Tablespoons
   salad oil
1-1/2 teaspoon vanilla
2-1/4 cups flour
1-1/2 teaspoon baking soda
1-1/2 teaspoon baking powder
1-1/2 teaspoon salt
1-1/2 teaspoon cinnamon
1/2 teaspoon cloves
1/2 teaspoon nutmeg
1/4 teaspoon ginger
3/4 cup chopped pecans

Beat eggs and sugar together well. Add pumpkin, oil, and vanilla, mixing well. Sift flour, soda, baking powder, salt and spices. Add to pumpkin mixture and beat. Add pecans. Bake at 350° for one hour in two well-greased loaf pans. (Baking time may vary.)

Jamie Porter Armstrong (Mrs. J.)

BANANA BREAD

Yield: 1 loaf
Baking Time: 50-60 minutes

2 cups flour
2 teaspoons baking powder
1 teaspoon baking soda
1/4 teaspoon salt
1 stick, plus 2 Tablespoons
   butter
1/2 cup walnuts, chopped
1/4 cup brown sugar,
   firmly packed
3 teaspoons vanilla
1 cup white sugar
2 eggs, slightly beaten
1 cup overripe bananas,
   mashed
1/2 cup sour cream

Sift flour, baking powder, soda and salt together and set aside. Mix 2 tablespoons butter, brown sugar, walnuts and one teaspoon vanilla and set aside. Cream remaining stick of butter and white sugar until lighty and fluffy. Mix eggs, sour cream, bananas and 2 teaspoons vanilla. Blend into butter-sugar mixture. Blend in flour until just mixed. Reserve one-quarter cup nut mixture to sprinkle on top. Pack rest into bottom of well greased 9x5x3 loaf pan. Pour batter on top and top batter with remaining nut mixture.
Bake at 350° for 50-60 minutes or until done. Cool 10 minutes before turning out of pan. Cool completely before cutting.

Susan Murray Daniel (Mrs. J. N., Jr.)

MEXICAN CORN BREAD

Baking Time: 35-45 minutes

2 eggs
2/3 cup cooking oil
1-1/4 cup milk
1 cup cream style corn
2 cups yellow corn meal
3 teaspoons baking powder
1 teaspoon salt
3 chopped jalapenas
    green peppers
    (can use green chilies)
1 cup grated sharp cheese

Beat eggs, oil and milk until mixed. Stir in corn, corn meal, baking powder and salt. Then add peppers. Pour half of the mixture into a hot, greased iron skillet, add half of the cheese and repeat. Bake in 350° oven 35-45 minutes or until done.

Nancy Young Hunnicutt (Mrs. Thomas B.)

CORN SPOONBREAD

Delicious—easy!
Can be served as a vegetable; has a very delicate, fine texture

Can do ahead
Can freeze
Serves: 8
Preparation: 10 minutes
Baking Time: 30-40 minutes

1 cup white or yellow cornmeal
1 cup commercial sour cream
1 lb. can cream-style corn
2 eggs
1-1/2 teaspoons salt
2 teaspoons baking powder
1/2 cup corn oil

Combine all ingredients except oil and mix only until blended. Heat oil in large pan or skillet and stir into batter when smoking. Turn into still hot casserole and bake at 375° for 30 to 40 minutes. Serve immediately.

Carol Ingram Matthews (Mrs. W. H.)

CHERRY NUT APPLE FROST BREAD
Very good and different!

Can freeze
Preparation: 30 minutes
Baking Time: 60 minutes

2 cups flour
3 teaspoons baking powder
1 teaspoon salt
3/4 cup sugar
1 egg
1 cup pecans, chopped
1 8-oz. jar chopped maraschino
    cherries and juice
1 cup apple sauce
2 Tablespoons salad oil

Combine ingredients and bake in 9x5x3" loaf pan at 350° for one hour. Cool 10 minutes and remove from pan. Cool thoroughly. Can be served with cream cheese, if desired. (Nice change from pumpkin bread, etc.)

Gay Woolard Coleman (Mrs. S. B.)

APRICOT TEA LOAF

Baking Time: 55-60 minutes

1 cup dried apricots
1-1/2 cup warm water
2 cups flour
2 teaspoons baking soda
1 teaspoon salt
1/2 cup chopped nuts
1 cup sugar
2 Tablespoons melted butter
1 large egg
1/4 cup water
1/2 cup orange juice

Soak apricots in warm water 1/2 hour. Drain and cut. Grease and flour small loaf pan. Sift dry ingredients. Mix sugar, butter, egg, water and juice. Add dry ingredients, apricots and nuts. Mix to dampen. Pour into pan. Bake at 350° for 55-60 minutes (cover with foil if top gets too brown.)

Linda Hinson Adams (Mrs. A. G.)

STRAWBERRY BREAD

Yield: 2 loaves
Baking Time: 45-50 minutes

2 cups frozen unsweetened
    whole strawberries
Sugar
3 cups plus 2 Tablespoons
    all-purpose flour
2 cups sugar
1 Tablespoon cinnamon
1 teaspoon salt
1 teaspoon baking soda
1-1/4 cups oil
4 eggs, beaten
1-1/4 cups chopped pecans

Place strawberries in a medium bowl. Sprinkle lightly with sugar. Let berries stand until thawed, then slice. Combine flour, sugar, salt, cinnamon, and baking soda in a large bowl and mix well. Blend oil and eggs into strawberries. Add to flour mixture. Stir in pecans, blending until dry ingredients are just moistened. Divide batter between two 9x5" loaf pans which have been buttered and floured. Bake in 350° oven for 45-50 minutes or until a tester inserted in center comes out clean. Let cool in pans for 10 minutes. Turn loaves out and cool completely.

Rebecka Tartain Blalock (Mrs. Barry)

MORAVIAN SUGAR CAKE

Must do ahead
Freezes well
Yield: 2 cakes
Baking Time: 15-20 minutes

1 cup milk
1/2 cup sugar
1/2 teaspoon salt
1/2 cup margarine
1 pkg. active dry yeast
1/4 cup warm water
1 egg, well beaten
4 cups unsifted
    all-purpose flour
1-1/2 sticks butter
    or margarine
3/4 lbs. brown sugar
Cinnamon

Scald milk. Add sugar, salt, margarine. Cool to lukewarm. Dissolve yeast in 1/4 cup warm water. Add to the milk mixture. Add egg plus 2 cups flour. Beat until smooth. Stir in remaining flour. Cover and refrigerate 2 hours or up to 2 days. Spread in 2 greased jelly roll pans. Cover with waxed paper and a towel until dough rises to double in bulk. Dot every 3/4 inch with butter, making little wells or indentations with the butter in the dough. Fill each "well" with brown sugar. Sprinkle all over with cinnamon. Bake at 375° about 15-20 minutes until lightly browned. The secret of this cake is to place the dots of butter quite close together.

Linda Hinson Adams (Mrs. Alfred G.)

RAISIN BREAD

Can do ahead
Yield: 4 loaves
Baking Time: 40 minutes

2 pkgs. active dry yeast
1/2 cup warm water
1/3 cup plus 2 teaspoons sugar
1/3 cup shortening
4 teaspoons salt
2 cups, scalded milk
1-1/2 cup cold water
2 cups raisins
4 teaspoons cinnamon
10-12 cups (about 3 lbs.
    all-purpose flour)

Soften yeast in warm water. In a large bowl, blend sugar, shortening, salt and milk until shortening has melted. Add cold water, raisins and cinnamon. Cool to lukewarm. Stir in yeast. Gradually add flour to form a stiff dough. Knead on a floured surface until smooth and satiny. Place in greased bowl. Cover with a damp towel. Let rise until doubled in size. Punch dough down and let rise again for 30 minutes. Place on a floured surface and divide into 4 portions. Mold into loaves and place in greased loaf pans. Let rise again for 1-1/2 hours. Bake at 375° for about 40 minutes until golden brown. Remove from pans immediately. Cool on wire racks.

Robbie Peters Hendon (Mrs. William)

CINNAMON ROLLS

Can do ahead
Can freeze
Yield: 4 or 5 dozen
Preparation: 2 hours
Baking Time: 20 minutes

2 pkgs. active dry yeast
1/4 cup warm water
1-3/4 cups milk
1/4 cup sugar
1/2 cup butter (1 stick)
1/2 teaspoon salt
4 eggs, beaten
8 cups regular all-purpose flour

FILLING:

2 cups brown sugar
1/2 lb. (2 sticks)
    softened butter
2 Tablespoons cinnamon
Optional: chopped nuts
Optional: raisins

Soften yeast in water. Scald milk, add sugar and butter, stirring until butter melts. Cool to luke-warm, stir in softened yeast and salt. Beat the milk mixture into the eggs and blend well. Place flour in large bowl, mix in the egg and milk mixture, stirring until the liquid is well blended into the flour and the mixture forms a ball. Knead the dough on a floured board for 5 minutes, kneading in 1/4 cup more flour as necessary until dough is smooth and elastic. Place dough in a greased bowl, cover and let rise in a warm place until doubled in bulk, about 1 hour. Punch down. Dough can be used immediately, but it is better and easier to work with if it is chiled for several hours, or overnight. Roll out 1/2 of the dough recipe to a large rectangle. Spread one stick of softened butter over all. Sprinkle with 1 cup brown sugar, 1 tablespoon cinnamon, and nuts or raisins, if desired. Starting with the long

Continued...

side, roll up dough, jelly-roll fashion. With a sharp knife, slice through the dough at 1-1/2" intervals. Place each section in a buttered muffin tin. Cover lightly and let rise until nearly doubled. Repeat procedure with second half of dough. Bake in 350° oven for 20 minutes or until lightly browned. Turn out of pans while warm onto a cooling rack. Glaze cooled rolls with powdered sugar and warm water mixture. Makes 4-5 dozen.

Candace Lincoln

SOUR CREAM BREAD

Must do ahead
Can freeze
Yield: 4 loaves
Preparation: 2 hours
Baking Time: 12-15 minutes

1 cup sour cream
1/2 cup melted butter
1/2 cup sugar
1/2 cup warm water
2 pkgs. active dry yeast
2 eggs
5 cups flour
1/2 teaspoon salt

FILLING:

3/4 cup sugar
1 lb. cream cheese, softened
to room temperature
1 egg
1/8 teaspoon salt
2 teaspoons vanilla

ICING:

2 cups powdered sugar
2 teaspoons vanilla
4 Tablespoons milk

Scald sour cream. Stir in sugar and salt and butter. Set aside to cool to lukewarm. In a separate, large bowl, dissolve yeast in warm water (105°-115°). Add eggs to sour cream mixture. Add sour cream mixture to yeast. Blend in 5 cups flour. Dough will be sticky. Cover tightly and refrigerate. Next day...mix filling ingredients in either food processor or with hand mixer. Set aside. Divide the dough mixture into 4 equal parts. Roll out each piece on a lightly-floured surface to measure 8x12." Spread each 8x12" piece of dough with one-quarter of filling, taking care not to go to outer edges. Starting with the longest side, roll up the dough, jelly-roll fashion. Pinch edges to seal. Transfer each loaf onto a greased foil-lined cookie sheet. With a sharp, floured knife, cut through top layers of the roll. Set aside until loaves are almost doubled in bulk (1 to 1-1/2 hours). Bake loaves 12-15 minutes at 375° until slightly browned. Cool and frost with icing or with an apricot or other fruit preserve icing. Good cold from the refrigerator, room temperature or slightly warmed. Doesn't keep well at room temperature after 48 hours.

Alice Henderson Myer (Mrs. T. G.)

SOUR CREAM COFFEE CAKE

Baking Time: 35-45 minutes

2 sticks butter
1-1/4 cup sugar
2 eggs
1 cup sour cream
1/2 teaspoon baking soda
2 teaspoons vanilla
2 cups sifted flour
1 teaspoon baking powder

TOPPING:

1 cup brown sugar
2 teaspoons cinnamon
1/2 cup pecans

Cream butter and sugar. Add eggs, sour cream, flour, baking soda, baking powder and vanilla. Mix well. Pour one-half of the batter into a well-greased and floured 9x13″ pan. Cover with half the topping and add remaining batter and cover with topping. Bake 35-45 minutes in a 350° oven.

*Melanie Huntsman Hudgins
(Mrs. Roderick M., Jr.)*

QUICK RUM BUNS

*Can do ahead and refrigerate until baking time
Yield: 32
Baking Time: 15-20 minutes*

2 pkg. refrigerator
    crescent rolls
Melted butter

TOPPING:

2 teaspoons cinnamon
1/4 cup raisins
1/4 cup sugar
1 teaspoon dark rum

GLAZE:

1/2 cup confectioners' sugar
2 Tablespoons dark rum

Roll out the 8 sections of rolls to make 4 rectangles. Brush the rectangles with melted butter. Combine the topping ingredients and sprinkle on each section. Roll each rectangle up as a jelly roll. Cut each roll into fourths and place in greased small muffin tins. Brush with melted butter. Bake in 375° oven for 15-20 minutes. Combine the glaze ingredients and pour over the hot rolls in the muffin tins. Remove quickly from the pans. Serve warm with butter.

Mary Bruce Rhodes Woody (Mrs. Stephen W.)

OATMEAL BUTTERMILK PANCAKES

Yield: 14-16 pancakes

2 cups quick oats, uncooked
1/2 teaspoon soda
2-1/2 cups buttermilk
1 cup all-purpose flour
2 teaspoons baking powder
1 teaspoon salt
2 Tablespoons sugar
1/3 cup salad oil
2 eggs, beaten

Combine oats, soda and buttermilk. Combine flour, baking powder, salt and sugar. Add to oat mixture, along with oil and eggs. Stir until blended. Bake on hot, lightly-greased griddle until golden brown. Serve hot with butter and warm syrup. Yield 14-16 pancakes.

Mary Bruce Rhodes Woody (Mrs. S.W.)

HIGH ENERGY PANCAKES

Yield: 12-16 pancakes

1 cup flour, sifted
1/2 teaspoon salt
1 Tablespoon baking powder
1 Tablespoon sugar
1 egg
1 cup milk
2 Tablespoons cottage cheese
2 Tablespoons sour cream
2 Tablespoons melted butter
    or shortening

Sift dry ingredients into bowl. Add egg, milk, cottage cheese and sour cream. Stir until smooth and add shortening. Drop by heaping table-spoons on a hot griddle. If too thick, add a little more milk. Can be doubled.

JoAnn McGowan Grimes (Mrs. Charles W.)

QUICK AND EASY SOUR CREAM PANCAKES

Yield: 16 small pancakes

1 cup Bisquick
1 teaspoon baking powder
1 egg, slightly beaten
8 oz. sour cream
3-5 teaspoons of milk

Mix together the Bisquick, baking powder, egg and sour cream. Add milk gradually. Cook as for regular pancakes, on a griddle.
Variation #1—use plain yogurt for sour cream (lower calorie)
Variation #2—use fruit flavored yogurt—orange or peach—for the sour cream.

Lelia Kincaid Cort (Mrs. John)

119

OVERNIGHT FRENCH TOAST

Must do ahead
Yield: 8 slices
Preparation: 10 minutes
Baking Time: 15 minutes

8 thick slices French bread
(3/4")
4 eggs
1 cup half and half
1 Tablespoon sugar
1/8 teaspoon salt
2 Tablespoons orange juice
or 1 Tablespoon
Grand Marnier
1/4 cup butter or margarine,
divided

Place bread slices in a 9x13" dish. Beat the rest of the ingredients together except the butter. Pour over bread and refrigerate overnight covered. Saute in butter about 4 minutes on each side. Serve with your choice: honey, syrup, powdered sugar, etc.

Gail Northen Rogers (Mrs. George H., Jr.)

WAFFLES

Serves: 4
Preparation: 10 minutes
Baking Time: 3-4 minutes each

1 cup Bisquick
1 cup all-purpose flour
3 Tablespoons sugar
Pinch of salt
5 eggs
2 cups milk
1 teaspoon vanilla

Mix all ingredients in order listed. Whisk to remove lumps. Bake in waffle iron.

Pat Stancil Smith (Mrs. Philip J.)

Hint:
A little butter on the tip of the spout will keep a pitcher from dripping.

FOOD PROCESSOR-WHOLE WHEAT BUTTERMILK BREAD

Makes 2 baquettes

GLAZE:
1 large egg
1/2 teaspoon salt

BREAD:

1 envelope dry yeast
1 Tablespoon sugar
1/2 cup plus
*   2 Tablespoons warm water*
2-1/3 cups bread flour
2/3 cup whole wheat flour
1 Tablespoon salt
1/2 cup plus 1 Tablespoon
*   warm buttermilk*
2 Tablespoons (1/4 stick)
*   butter, room temperature*
Cornmeal

For glaze: Insert steel knife and mix egg with salt 2 seconds; remove and set aside. Do not clean work bowl.

For bread: Oil large mixing bowl and set aside. Combine yeast and sugar with warm water in small bowl and let stand until foamy, about 10 minutes.

Steel Knife: Combine 2 cups bread flour with whole wheat flour and salt in work bowl. With machine running, pour yeast mixture and buttermilk through feed tube and mix until dough forms ball. Add butter and mix until dough works away from sides of bowl and is smooth and elastic, about 40 seconds. If dough is too wet, add remaining 1/3 cup bread flour, one tablespoon at a time, and mix. Transfer to oiled bowl, turning to coat all surfaces. Cover bowl with damp towel. Let stand in warm, draft-free area until dough has doubled in volume, about one hour. Meanwhile, grease 1 double French bread pan or baking sheet and sprinkle lightly with cornmeal. Transfer dough to lightly-floured surface and divide in half. Roll one piece into rectangle, then roll up lengthwise, pinching ends and seam tightly. Arrange loaf seam side down in half of prepared pan or sheet. Repeat with remaining dough. Cover loaves with damp towel. Let stand in warm, draft-free area until doubled, approximately 45 minutes. Position rack in center of oven and preheat to 425°. Brush tops of loaves with glaze, being careful not to drip on to pan. Bake until bread is golden brown and sounds hollow when tapped on bottom (25 to 30 minutes). Remove from pan and let cool on rack.

Emily Caddell Gordon (Mrs. Alan F.)

FOOD PROCESSOR BISCUITS

Can freeze, but better if you don't
Preparation: 10 minutes
Baking Time: 425° for 8 to 10 minutes

2 cups self-rising flour
2/3 stick of butter
2/3 to 3/4 cup buttermilk

Put flour in processor bowl, fitted with steel blade. Cut butter into 4 or 5 chunks and blend with flour until consistency of coarse meal. Pour buttermilk into a 1 cup measure, then with motor running, pour buttermilk through the feed tube just until a ball forms. Turn onto floured board. Pat to about 3/4 inch thick and cut with biscuit cutter. Bake at 425° for 8 to 10 minutes.

Alice Ward Griffin (Mrs. William R., III)

CORN BREAD LOAF
This is different cornbread—moist and a little sweet

Serves: 8-10
Preparation: 30 minutes
Baking Time: 30-35 minutes

1-1/2 cups corn meal,
   yellow or white
1 cup all-purpose flour
1/3 cup sugar
1 teaspoon salt
1 Tablespoon baking powder
2 eggs
6 Tablespoons melted
   and cooled margarine
8 Tablespoons melted and
   cooled vegetable shortening
3/4 cup milk
3/4 cup half and half

Preheat oven to 400°. Sift cornmeal, flour, sugar, salt and baking powder into a large mixing bowl. Beat eggs lightly, add melted margarine and shortening. Stir in milk, and half and half. Pour over dry ingredients and beat for approximately one minute, or until smooth. Do not overbeat. Pour into lightly-greased 9x5x3″ loaf pan. Bake in the center of the oven for 30-35 minutes or until bread comes slightly away from the sides of the pan. Serve hot with butter, or slice for toast when cold.

Elizabeth Glenn Biggers (Mrs. Carl)

Fish & Seafood

We are very lucky here in Asheville, a mountain town: we have a fresh fishmarket with regular deliveries from the coast. If they don't have on hand what is needed, they can usually get it on short notice.

Few people know how to handle fish and shellfish properly. One of the most common errors made is to overcook fish. When buying fish or shellfish, select fresh smelling fish. Stay away from anything smelling "fishy." Fish or shellfish is a very perishable form of food and, therefore, should be kept refrigerated until ready to use.

It is also good to know the bone structure since that will help in both filleting your own fish, and in eating whole sole or trout. Most fish are easy to fillet. They fall generally into two families—the flat family like flounder and the oval shaped family such as trout and salmon. Exceptions are shad, pike and herring.

If you are budget minded, costs can be reduced by filleting your own fish. All that is needed is a sharp knife and a cutting board. Place the fish on the cutting board. Cut down the back of the fish from tail to head on its "upper" side. Then cut just behind the gills down to the backbone. Holding the knife at a slight angle against the bone, cut with sliding motion along the bone, pulling back the fillet with the other hand until the flesh is removed down to the tail. Then, turn the fish over and repeat the cutting process for the other fillet.

To skin, place the fillet on the cutting board, skin side down. Starting from the tail end, cut through the flesh to the skin (but not through the skin) and, holding the knife at an almost flat angle against the skin, cut and slide the blade under the flesh toward the wide end.

Crab

Fresh and pasteurized crab meat is sold usually in 8 oz., 12 oz. and one pound cans in fishmarkets or supermarkets.

Backfin: Whole pieces of white meat from the large body muscles that operate the swimming legs of the crab.

Regular: small bits of whole meat from the body.

Special: a mixture of backfin and regular.

Claw: the brownish-tinted meat from the claws.

Crab Fingers: the large biting claws of the crab with the shell partially removed.

One pound of crabmeat yields approximately 3 cups of cooked meat.

Shrimp

Shrimp may be cooked in the shell or unshelled. The shell adds to the flavor of the shrimp. Shelling is easy—either before or after cooking. A slight tug releases the body shell from the tail. Using a small, pointed knife or the end of a toothpick deveins the shrimp before or after cooking. This is an essential step. If using canned shrimp rinse briefly in cold water to remove excess salt.

124

Scallops

Scallops, like clams and oysters, are mollusks having two shells. Sea scallops sometimes have an eye reaching up to two inches in diameter. Bay scallops are the smaller variety of scallops and are excellent for use in seafood casseroles, etc. Fresh scallops are either a light creamy color or sometimes a light pink. One pound of fresh scallops yields approximately 2 cups of cooked meat.

Oysters

Oysters are found in the waters from Maine to Florida. The flavor in oysters depends on the location from which they are harvested. Oysters taken from water with a high salt content have the most distinctive flavor and are generally eaten raw on the half shell. Oysters sold in the shell must be alive when purchased and used. If alive, the oyster shell will be tightly closed. If not tightly closed, they should be discarded. Shucked oysters have been removed from the shell and are sold by the half-pint, pint, quart and so on. Shucked oysters should be plump and have a natural creamy color. Oysters are graded and sold in the following sizes:
Standard—30 to 40 oysters to a pint. Select—26 to 30 oysters to a pint.

Tuna

In our diet-conscious society, we now mostly use canned tuna in "spring-water" but, a real connoisseur of tuna prefers it in oil for better flavor.

WILD RICE AND SHRIMP CASSEROLE

Can do ahead
Can freeze
Serves: 4
Baking Time: 35-45 minutes

1 can cream of mushroom soup
2 Tablespoons chopped
    green pepper
2 Tablespoons chopped onion
2 Tablespoons melted butter
1 Tablespoon lemon juice
2 cups cooked wild rice (4 oz.
    box) (not a blend)
1/2 teaspoon Worcestershire
    sauce
1/2 teaspoon dry mustard
1/4 teaspoon pepper
1/2 cup cubed Cheddar cheese
1/2 lb. uncooked shrimp

Mix all ingredients together thoroughly. Pour into greased one and a half quart casserole. Bake in 375° oven 35-45 minutes. If frozen, uncooked shrimp is used, thaw it in several layers of paper towels to remove excess moisture.

June Stroupe Baker (Mrs. Henry L.)

WHOLE TROUT SAUTEED IN BUTTER

Living in the mountains one may have chance to catch trout in a mountain stream with a lean and delicate taste, although cultivated ones from the fishmarket are not bad at all.

Serves: 4

4 1/2-lb. each, cleaned
    trout (with heads on)
Salt and pepper
Flour
3/4 cup clarified butter
Juice of 1/2 lemon
1/4 cup chopped parsley
Lemon wedges for garnish

Just before cooking the trout, sprinkle them inside and out with salt and pepper, and dust both sides with flour. Pour 1/2 cup clarified butter (butter melted, skimmed and clear liquid poured off milky residue) into a frying pan large enough to hold fish. Heat until bubbling hot. Put trout in pan and maintain heat so that butter is always very hot, but not browning. After 5 to 6 minutes, turn fish over and saute 5 to 6 minutes on other side. Trout will be done when you peer inside and there is no trace of reddish raw color at backbone; meat should be cooked through and juicy. Remove to hot plates, squeeze lemon juice over the fish and sprinkle parsley. Pour the rest of the hot butter over trout. Garnish with lemon wedges and serve immediately. Pass additional butter around.

BURNED BUTTER FLOUNDER

Serves: 4
Preparation: 10 minutes
Baking time: 20-25 minutes

4 large bottom side (dark) of
    flounder fillets
Salt and pepper
1 stick of butter
2 Tablespoons lemon juice
2 Tablespoons vermouth
Parmesan cheese
Paprika

Melt butter on a large foil-lined baking sheet. Scorch butter at 400-500° until brown. Place fish, flesh side down, in butter. Cook 10-15 minutes. Turn fish over and baste with butter. Sprinkle with lemon juice, vermouth, Parmesan cheese and paprika. Return to oven about 5 minutes. Run under broiler quickly and serve at once.

Ruth Bowles Carson (Mrs. Philip G.)

FLOUNDER WITH ALMONDS AND SHRIMP TOAST

Serves: 6-8
Preparation: 45-60 minutes

4 Tablespoons butter
4 oz. slivered almonds
12 slices good white bread
3/4 lb. jumbo shrimp
6 thin slices Swiss cheese
Melted butter
3 lb. flounder fillets
8 Tablespoons butter, melted
6 Tablespoons heavy cream
6 lemon slices

Lightly toast almonds in butter. Keep warm or reheat later. Cut crusts from bread and toast on one side. Cook shrimp in a court bouillon. (Bring to a boil water with lemon slices, onion, celery tops, parsley, and salt added. Add shrimp, return to boil, remove from heat, let sit 5 minutes, cool rapidly in cold water and peel.) Cover the toasted side of 6 slices of bread with cheese and shrimp, slicing shrimp lengthwise if necessary to cover bread. Cover with waxed paper and weight down slightly. About 20 minutes before serving, brush both sides of toast with melted butter and place on cookie sheet in a 350° oven. Bake until golden brown. Heat cream and set aside. Melt 8 tablespoons butter and pour half into an oven-proof casserole which will hold fish in a single layer. Add fish and pour remaining butter over. Season. Place under broiler and brown. Pour cream over fish and keep casserole warm. Cut shrimp toast diagonally to make four small triangles of each. To present, garnish fish with toast triangles and a few slices of lemon, sprinkle with almonds.

Helen King Turner (Mrs. Franklin H., Jr.)

COQUILLES OF FLOUNDER

Serves: 8-10

2-3 lbs. flounder
Butter
Salt and pepper
2/3 cup dry Vermouth
2/3 cup heavy cream
2/3 cup chicken broth
Pinch of thyme
4 Tablespoons butter
4 Tablespoons flour
2 teaspoons lemon juice
1/2 teaspoon Worcestershire
    sauce
Salt and pepper
1/4 cup chopped parsley
Optional: 1/2 cup sauteed
    sliced mushrooms

Brush flounder with butter, salt and pepper. Broil on a buttered surface until fish flakes easily, just a few minutes. Cool, remove bones, and separate into small pieces.
Bring vermouth, cream, chicken broth and thyme to a boil. In a separate pan, melt butter and stir in flour. Cook for a minute or two, then stir in boiling liquid. Stir until thickened. Stir in parsley, mushrooms (if desired) and fish. Divide among shells or small oven-proof dishes. Heat shells under the broiler.

Celine Hanan Lurey (Mrs. Michael)

BEER BATTER FRIED FISH

Serves: 6
Preparation: 10 minutes
Cooking Time: Few minutes

1-1/2 to 2 lbs. fish fillets
   (any kind; Blue fish
   especially good) cut into
   3/4 inch strips or bite-size
   pieces
Peanut oil

BATTER:

1 cup Bisquick
1 egg
1/2 can beer (regular)
Salt and pepper

Mix batter ingredients thoroughly with a fork and let stand for a few mintues. Pat fish fillet strips dry with paper towels. Dip fish in batter and fry in deep, hot peanut oil until golden brown. Strained peanut oil can be reused.

James E. Chapman

FISH RATATOUILLE

Can do ahead
Serves: 6
Preparation: 45 minutes

1-1/2 lbs. fish fillets
   (may use 2-3 kinds)
3 onions
4 Tablespoons olive oil
1 can (16 oz.) tomatoes or the
   same amount freshly
   peeled tomatoes
3 oz. olives, preferably black
1 bay leaf
Salt
Pepper
Thyme
Parsley

Peel onions and cut them into wedges. Let onions, tomatoes and olives slowly simmer in olive oil together with herbs, covered, for about 25-30 minutes. Cut fish in large cubes and put them in the pot with the rest. Let simmer for about 10 more minutes until the fish is done. Sprinkle with minced parsley and serve with rice. Any leftover ratatouille is delicious served cold with lemon wedges.

Yvonne Eriksson Day (Mrs. James K. M.)

SEAFOOD MOUSSE

Must do ahead
Serves: 8

1-1/2 cups cooked shrimp or
  crabmeat or lobster
1/2 cup finely chopped green
  pepper
1 cup finely chopped celery
2 Tablespoons grated onions
1 teasp. salt
3 Tablespoons Worcestershire
  sauce
1 dash pepper sauce
1 can tomato soup
1 (8 oz.) pkg. cream cheese
3 envelopes unflavored gelatin
1 cup cold water
1 cup mayonnaise

Combine first seven ingredients. Combine soup and cheese in double boiler and stir until cheese melts. Soften gelatin in water; add to soup mix and stir until dissolved. Cool. Add mayonnaise and fish mixture. Turn into 1-1/2 quart mold and place in refrigerator to congeal.

May use a fish mold and decorate with slices of egg and black olives.

Lee Tickle Mynatt (Mrs. William)

CRAB MEAT CASSEROLE I

Serve with: salad (Romaine, mandarine orange, almonds). French bread and Pinot Chardonnay wine

Can do ahead
Serves: 6
Preparation: 1 hour
Baking Time: 30 minutes

2 Tablespoons flour
2 Tablespoons butter
1-1/4 cup half and half cream
Salt
White pepper
4 Tablespoons sherry
1 (8-1/2 oz.) can artichoke
  hearts
1 lb. fresh mushrooms, sauteed
  in butter
1/2 lb. lump crab meat
Paprika
Parmesan cheese

Melt butter and whisk in flour. Slowly stir in half and half, salt and pepper. When sauce thickens, remove from heat and add sherry. Put artichoke hearts, sauteed mushrooms, and crab meat in buttered casserole dish. Cover with white sauce and sprinkle with paprika and Parmesan cheese. Bake at 350° for 20-30 minutes until heated thoroughly.

Candy Stell Shivers (Mrs. James A.)

CRAB MEAT CASSEROLE II

Serves: 4-6
Baking time: 30 minutes

6-1/2 oz. can crab meat,
    drained
6-1/2 oz. can shrimp,
    drained
1 medium chopped green
    pepper
1 medium chopped onion
1 cup chopped celery
1 cup mayonnaise
1/2 teaspoon salt
Dash of pepper
1 cup buttered bread cubes

Combine all of the above ingredients, except the bread cubes which you sprinkle on top. Bake for 30 minutes in 350° oven.

MENU SUGGESTIONS:

Hot fresh bread
Pineapple tidbits (well drained)
    and white seedless grapes
    tossed with sour cream
Dry white wine

Diana Roscoe Bilbrey (Mrs. George M., Jr.)

CRAB CASSEROLE III

Serves: 10-12
Baking time: 30 minutes

2 cans (7-1/2 oz.) crab meat
    (washed and checked for
    any shell)
1 cup chopped celery
1 medium onion, chopped
1 medium green pepper,
    chopped
1 cup mayonnaise
1/2 teaspoon pepper
1 teaspoon Worcestershire
    sauce
4 hard-boiled eggs, chopped
1 stack pack Waverly wafers
1 stick butter, melted

Mix all ingredients, except butter and crackers. Crumble crackers and toss with melted butter. Put on top of casserole.
Bake in 350° oven for 30 minutes.

Susan Murray Daniel (Mrs. John N., Jr.)

MEETING STREET CRAB MEAT

Can do ahead
Cannot freeze
Serves: 4
Bake: 450°

1 lb. white crab meat
4 Tablespoons butter
4 Tablespoons flour
1/2 pint cream
4 Tablespoons sherry
3/4 cup sharp cheese, grated
Salt and pepper to taste

Make a cream sauce with the butter, flour and cream. Add salt, pepper and sherry. Remove from heat and add crab meat. Pour the mixture into a buttered casserole or individual baking dishes. Sprinkle with grated cheese and bake in a hot oven until cheese melts. Do not overcook! (1-1/2 lbs. shrimp may be substituted for the crab)

Mrs. Thomas A. Huguenin
Charleston, South Carolina
From: CHARLESTON RECEIPTS

SHRIMP SCAMPI

Serves: 4-6

2 lbs. raw shrimp, shelled
    and deveined
2 cups butter
2 garlic cloves, chopped
1 large onion, chopped
Salt and pepper to taste

Melt butter in a saucepan. Add onion, garlic, salt and pepper. Cook until onions are soft. Place shrimp in a shallow pan. Pour butter mixture over the shrimp. Broil for 7 minutes, turning shrimp once.

Louise Ready Hanks (Mrs. W. Neal)

CRAB CAKES

Yield: 6 cakes or 6 servings

1 lb. crab meat
1 egg
1/4 cup finely chopped green
    pepper
2-4 Tablespoons mayonnaise
1 teaspoon Worcestershire
    sauce
1 teaspoon dry mustard
1 teaspoon lemon juice
Salt and pepper to taste
1 slice white bread, cubed

Remove cartilage from crab meat. In a medium bowl, beat egg slightly, and mix thoroughly with all ingredients, except crab meat and bread cubes. Pour mixture over crab meat and bread cubes and fold gently. Form into six cakes. Cook cakes in frying pan, in just enough butter or oil to prevent sticking, until browned; about 5 minutes on each side.

Yvonne Eriksson Day (Mrs. James K. M.)

SHRIMP CASSEROLE
Serve with marinated green bean salad and hot fruit casserole

Can do ahead
Can freeze
Serves: 6
Preparation: 30 minutes
Baking Time: 30 minutes

1 lb. large shrimp
2 chicken bouillon cubes
1 cup hot water
1 cup minute rice
1/2 cup butter
3 Tablespoons flour
1-1/2 cups milk
1 teaspoon dillweed
1 Tablespoon wine vinegar
1 teaspoon seasoned salt
1-1/2 cup shredded, sharp,
  Cheddar cheese
Paprika

Dissolve bouillon cubes in hot water, bring to a boil, and add rice. Turn heat to low or off until rice is done. In another pan, melt butter; stir in flour, add milk and cook over medium heat until thick and smooth, stirring constantly. Stir in dillweed, vinegar and seasoned salt. Add shrimp and simmer for 10 minutes. Spoon rice into baking dish, top with shrimp mixture, add cheese on top and sprinkle with paprika. Bake at 350° for 25-30 minutes. (If casserole has been made ahead and is cold when you start to bake it, bake for 45 minutes or until hot through and through.)

Sandra Tucker Holt (Mrs. Stanley E.)

CHARCOAL BROILED SHRIMP
Serve with salad and garlic bread.

Must do ahead
Allow 6-8 shrimp per serving

Large shrimp (10-12 to a pound)

MARINADE:

1/3 cup oil
1/3 cup sherry
1/3 cup soy sauce
1 peeled garlic clove, crushed

Wash shrimp but do not shell. Split shrimp up the back with scissors and devein. For each pound of shrimp, mix one recipe of the marinade. Place shrimp in plastic bag; add marinade. Keep airtight and marinate overnight in refrigerator. Drain before cooking and save sauce. String shrimp on skewers and cook over hot coals at medium height for about 10 minutes. Baste with sauce. Serve with melted butter.

Fran R. Wilson

SHRIMP AND CHICKEN CASSEROLE

Baking Time: 35-45 minutes

2 Tablespoons butter
1/2 cup chopped onions
3 Tablespoons flour
Salt and pepper to taste
1 can (4 oz.) sliced mushrooms
1/2 cup sherry
Milk
2 cups cooked chicken breast,
    diced
2 cups cooked shrimp
1 can (5 oz.) water chestnuts,
    drained and sliced
1/4 cup diced pimento
3/4 cup grated Muenster cheese
1-1/2 cups soft bread crumbs,
    buttered

Melt butter in skillet. Add onions. Cook until softened. Stir in flour, salt and pepper. Drain mushrooms reserving liquid. Combine mushroom liquid, sherry and enough milk to make one and a half cups. Add to flour and onions. Cook until smooth, stirring constantly. Fold in mushrooms, chicken, water chestnuts, shrimp and pimento. Do not stir. Turn into a greased 2 quart casserole. Sprinkle with cheese and buttered crumbs. Bake in 350° oven for 30-45 minutes.

Lynn Mernin Salley (Mrs. Alfred N.)

SHRIMP COQUILLE
Serve as first course or main meal with rice.

Can do ahead
Serves: 6
Preparation: 20 minutes
Baking Time: 15 minutes

1 lb. peeled and deveined
    shrimp (raw)
1 bunch green onions
1/2 lb. mushrooms
6 Tablespoons butter
2 Tablespoons white vermouth
1 Tablespoon flour
1-1/2 cup sour cream

Ahead of time, prepare shrimp, chop green onions and wash mushrooms and refrigerate all. Up to one and a half hours before serving, melt butter, toss shrimp in butter until they turn pink, then remove. Add green onions and sliced mushrooms. Saute 5 minutes.
Stir vermouth in pan and boil until it evaporates. Stir in flour, salt and pepper; stir until well distributed and heated. Stir in sour cream and shrimp; heat gently. Do not boil. Serve in individual shells or ramekins. If done ahead, reheat on low heat.

Celine Hanan Lurey (Mrs. Michael)

R's JAPANESE FRIED SHRIMP
This is heaven—especially if someone will fix it for you!

Serves: 4
Preparation: 15 minutes

1 lb. jumbo fresh shrimp,
   cleaned and deveined,
   butterflied
1 cup flour
1 cup water
1 egg
1/4 cup sugar

Mix all ingredients except shrimp. Batter will be lumpy. Dip shrimp in batter and fry until brown at 375.°

Mern Richards Atwater (Mrs. J. S.)

CASSEROLE SAINT JACQUES
Excellent!

Can do ahead
Serves: 6
Baking time: 25 minutes

16 oz. scallops
1 cup dry white wine
1 small onion, sliced
2 teaspoons lemon juice
1/2 teaspoon salt
4 Tablespoons margarine,
   or butter
4 Tablespoons flour
1 cup evaporated milk
2 oz. or more Gruyere
   cheese, grated
7-1/2 oz. can crab meat,
   drained and flaked
4-1/2 oz. can shrimp, drained
3 oz. can sliced mushrooms
1-1/2 cups soft bread crumbs
1 Tablespoon melted butter

Combine scallops, wine, onion, lemon juice and salt. Bring to a boil, simmer 5 minutes. Drain, reserving 1 cup liquid. In a saucepan, melt butter; stir in flour. Add evaporated milk and reserved scallop liquid. Cook and stir over medium heat until mixture thickens and bubbles. Remove from heat; add cheese and dash of pepper. When cheese melts, add scallops, crab, shrimp and mushrooms. Spoon into individual casseroles. Combine bread crumbs and melted butter and sprinkle over casseroles. Bake at 350° for 25 minutes.

Jeannie Renick Davis (Mrs. John N., Jr.)

SEAFOOD EN CASSEROLE

Can be made ahead
Serves: 6-8
Preparation: 30 minutes
Baking Time: 20-30 minutes

1 9-oz. pkg. frozen lobster tails, cooked
1 lb. pkg. frozen shrimp, cooked
1 can crab meat, drained
1 can button mushrooms, drained
6 slices fresh bread
1 cup melted butter, divided
1/2 cup flour
1-1/2 cups light cream
1-1/2 cups milk
1/4 cup white wine
1/2 cup grated Swiss or Gruyere cheese
Pinch cayenne

Cook lobster and shrimp as directed on package. Drain crab and mushrooms. Crumb bread in blender and mix with 1/2 cup melted butter. Make a sauce by melting remaining 1/2 cup butter in a large saucepan over medium heat. Add flour; cook several minutes, stirring with a wire whisk. Do not let mixture brown. Stir in milk and cream; stir constantly until sauce boils. Add white wine and cheese; stir until cheese melts. Combine mushrooms, seafood and sauce. Turn into 9 x 13 baking dish. Top with buttered crumbs. Bake at 400° until bubbly and crumbs are brown, 20-30 minutes. Can be made the day before and refrigerated. Bring to room temperature before baking.

Helen King Turner (Mrs. Franklin H., Jr.)

BROILED SEA SCALLOPS

Must do ahead
Serves: 2-3
Preparation: 10 minutes

1/2 cup dry vermouth
1 Tablespoon salad oil
1 small, crushed garlic clove
3/4 teaspoon salt
2 Tablespoons parsley
1 lb. scallops
1 Tablespoon melted butter
1/2 cup bread crumbs
Paprika

Mix vermouth, oil, garlic, salt and parsley. Add scallops and stir. Marinate for 1 hour. Preheat broiler. Toss melted butter with crumbs. Spoon scallops and marinade into shallow dish. Place 2" from broiler. Broil 3 minutes. Turn, sprinkle with crumbs and paprika. Broil 3 minutes more. Serve hot.

Gail Southwood Golding (Mrs. James N.)

COQUILLE ST. JACQUES

Serves: 6-8
Baking time: 5 minutes

1 lb. scallops (or more)
2 shallots or 1/2 bunch
  green onions
Salt and pepper
1/2 cup dry vermouth
1 cup heavy cream
3 Tablespoons butter
1 Tablespoon flour
Chopped parsley

Chop shallots or white part of green onion. Place scallops, shallot or onion, about one-half teaspoon salt, a dash of white pepper and the vermouth in a saucepan. Bring to a boil and simmer for 2 minutes. Lift scallops from sauce into 6-8 serving shells or dishes. Add cream to sauce and boil rapidly until it thickens to the consistency of a light cream sauce. Combine butter and flour; stir into sauce. Let boil again and pour over the scallops. Bake in a 450° oven for 5 minutes or until sizzling. Sprinkle with parsley and serve.

Celine Hanan Lurey (Mrs. Michael)

CRAB, SHRIMP AND WILD RICE CASSEROLE
This recipe was brought back from France by a nun and is an excellent cook-ahead recipe.

Best when done ahead at least 1 day
Serves: 8
Preparation: 1 hour, 15 minutes
Baking time: 1 hour

1 pkg. wild/tame rice
  mixture, cooked
1/2 cup celery, chopped
1/2 cup green pepper, chopped
1 cup onions, chopped
1 lb. mushrooms, sliced
Oregano, garlic salt, salt and
  pepper to taste
1 lb. shrimp, cooked
6 to 12 oz. Alaskan king crab,
  frozen or canned
1 can cream of mushroom soup
8 oz. sharp Cheddar cheese,
  cubed
1 cup thick white sauce (made
  of 2 Tablespoons butter,
  2 Tablespoons flour,
  1 cup milk)
1 cup slivered almonds

Prepare rice according to directions on package. Meanwhile, saute in butter green pepper, onions, celery; add mushrooms. Cook until soft, but not brown. Take off heat and add spices to taste. Stir in shrimp, crab meat and then combine with mushroom soup and rice mixture, put into casserole dish. Cube Cheddar cheese and place at random on top. (Do not stir.) Make a thick white sauce and spread a thin layer evenly over top. Saute slivered almonds in butter and arrange over casserole dish. Bake covered for 1 hour at 350° or refrigerate at this point for 2-3 days. Serve with a salad, French bread and wine.

Christine Longoria

SEAFOOD CASSEROLE

Baking Time: 15-20 minutes

1 can condensed chicken broth
1 pkg. frozen chopped spinach
1 pkg. frozen corn
1 13-oz. can evaporated milk
1/3 cup flour
Salt and pepper to taste
1/4 cup white wine
Pinch of tarragon
1 can or 1 cup of shrimp
1 can or 1 cup crab meat
1 lb. scallops
1 small box corn bread mix

Heat chicken broth in large dutch oven. Add spinach and corn; cook for a few minutes until spinach and corn are separated. Mix together flour and evaporated milk; add to broth and vegetables. Salt and pepper to taste; add tarragon and white wine. Simmer until thickened, stirring constantly. (You may add pimentos for color if you wish.) Add seafood, stir well and pour into a large casserole dish. Sprinkle the small box of corn bread mix over top. Bake at 400° until topping is golden brown about 15-20 minutes.

Kay Ramsey Saenger (Mrs. George W.)

SAILING STEW

Serve with tossed green salad, buttered French bread

Can do ahead
Serves: 6
Preparation: 10 minutes

1 stick butter or margarine
2 lbs. shrimp, cleaned, deveined
2 8-oz. cans of minced clams
   and juice
1 10-oz. can of She Crab Soup
2 10-oz. cans Manhattan style
   clam chowder
Lots of fresh, snipped parsley
Pepper
1/2 teaspoon oregano
Vermouth to taste

Melt butter in large saucepan. Add all ingredients and simmer 10 minutes.

Katherine Rorison (Mrs. Brainerd)

TUDIE GLEASON'S SPINACH AND OYSTER CASSEROLE
Delicious with steak and salad

Serves: 4-6
Preparation: 30 minutes

2 pkg. frozen spinach
2-3 cloves crushed garlic
1 pint oysters, drained
1 cup sour cream
Swiss cheese, grated

Cook the spinach and garlic together, drain well. Place drained oysters under broiler just to curl. Put oysters in the bottom of a casserole. Add sour cream to spinach mixture; blend well. Pour over oysters. Cover with grated Swiss cheese and bake at 400° for 10 minutes.

Elizabeth Carpenter Boys (Mrs. G. Waring, Jr.)

TULU'S ESCALLOPED OYSTERS
An integral part of every family Thanksgiving and Christmas celebration when I was growing up.

Can do ahead early in the day
Serves: 6-8
Preparation: 20 minutes
Baking Time: 20-30 minutes

1 pint standard size oysters
1 stick **real** butter
3/4 box oysterette crackers
   (coarsely broken)
1/2 pint half and half cream
Salt and pepper to taste

In a medium casserole, put a layer of coarsely broken crackers. Dot generously with butter. Snip oysters in half and place one layer in casserole. Salt and pepper lightly. Repeat crackers, butter, oysters, salt and pepper. Finish with a layer of cracker crumbs dotted with butter. Just before baking, pour half and half around the edges. Bake at 350° for 20 minutes or until golden brown. Do not pack casserole down; it must be kept very light.

Lelia Kincaid Cort (Mrs. John)

NEW ORLEANS OYSTER DRESSING

Serve with Christmas or Thanksgiving Turkey Dinner. Not meant to take the place of turkey stuffing—just a tasty morsel on the side.

Serves: 6-8
Baking time: 10-15 minutes

1 pint oysters, chopped
   (save juice)
5 to 6 stalks celery, chopped
1 green pepper, chopped
1 large onion, chopped
1 Tablespoon parsley, chopped
1 egg
5 to 7 slices bread, cubed and
   soaked in water to cover
Cracker crumbs to cover

Fry vegetables in 2 to 3 tablespoons of bacon fat. Add oyster juice and cook until it thickens. Add oysters, salt and pepper to taste. Beat in the egg; cook until the edges curl on the oysters. Squeeze water out of the bread and add to the oyster mixture. Transfer to a buttered 9" pie pan. Top with cracker crumbs. Bake at 350° for 10-15 minutes or until the top browns.

Nell Cundiff Staples (Mrs. Lawrence H.)

EASY TUNA-BROCCOLI CASSEROLE

Can do ahead
Serves: 4
Preparation: 15 minutes
Baking Time: 30 minutes

1 pkg. frozen broccoli spears or
   chopped broccoli, cooked
1 can tuna
1 can cream of mushroom soup
Potato chips

Combine cooked broccoli with drained tuna and cream of mushroom soup. Top with crushed potato chips and bake in 350° oven for 30 minutes.

Margaret Farrington Baumann

CHINESE TUNA

Serves: 6

2 7-oz. cans tuna
2 cups celery slices
2 cups mushroom slices
1 cup coarsely chopped
   sweet onions
1 cup chopped green pepper
1 (15-1/2-oz.) can pineapple
   chunks, drained
3 bouillon cubes
1 cup hot water
1/4 cup soy sauce
2 teaspoons Accent

Place tuna, celery, mushrooms, onions, green peppers and pineapple in a covered skillet. Dissolve bouillon cubes in hot water, add soy sauce and Accent. Pour over all. Cover tightly and steam until vegetables are tender crisp—about 15 minutes. Serve with rice.

Gail Southwood Golding (Mrs. James N.)

SHRIMP SALAD
Side dish with roast beef sandwiches or fried chicken

Must do ahead
Serves: 8
Preparation: 60 minutes

1/2 cup mayonnaise or salad
    dressing
1/2 cup sour cream
3 Tablespoons vinegar
3/4 teaspoon salt
Dash of hot pepper sauce
1 lb. shrimp; shelled, cooked
    and cut into 3-4 pieces each
1-1/2 cups macaroni shells,
    cooked and drained
4 oz. processed American
    cheese, cubed (1 cup)
1/2 cup chopped celery
1/4 cup chopped green pepper
2 Tablespoons chopped onion
Green pepper rings for garnish

Blend mayonnaise, sour cream, vinegar, salt and pepper sauce. Toss with all the other ingredients. Cover and chill several hours. At serving time, stir salad. Turn into lettuce-lined salad bowl and top with green pepper rings.

Pat Harvard Godbold (Mrs. Ronald)

GARDEN OF THE SEA SPAGHETTI

Serves: 6

1 can cream of celery soup
1 cup milk
1/2 teaspoon onion salt
1 can tuna, drained and flaked
    (7 oz.)
1/3 cup pimento
2 cups (8 oz.) Cheddar cheese,
    grated
1/3 cup slivered almonds or
    water chestnuts, sliced
Hot buttered spaghetti
Parmesan cheese

In a large skillet, place soup; while stirring, gradually add milk. Heat over low heat 15-20 minutes. Stir in onion salt, tuna, pimento, cheese and water chestnuts or almonds. Keep stirring until cheese melts; pour over spaghetti. Sprinkle with Parmesan cheese.

Gail Southwood Golding (Mrs. James N.)

HERRING SALAD
This is a must for a festive Swedish smorgasbord!

Must do ahead
Serves: 6-8

1 salt herring
1-1/2 cups diced boiled
   potatoes
1-1/2 cups diced pickled beets
1/3 cup diced dill pickles
1/2 cup diced apple
1/4 cup finely chopped onion
4 Tablespoons vinegar or liquid
   from pickled beets
2 Tablespoons water
Dash of pepper
2 hard-boiled eggs
Chopped parsley
Sour cream

Clean fish, removing head. Soak fish 10-12 hours, changing water a few times so fish will not be too salty. If you wish, start soaking fish 3 or 4 hours before you go to bed, change the water a few times and soak overnight. Bone and fillet. Dice fillets. Mix all diced ingredients together thoroughly but carefully; they should not be mashed. Combine vinegar, water and pepper; blend well. Gently stir into the fish mixture. Pack into a 5-cup mold that has been rinsed with cold water and brushed lightly with salad oil. Chill in refrigerator for a few hours. Unmold onto serving platter and garnish with hard-boiled eggs and chopped parsley; serve with sour cream.

Yvonne Eriksson Day (Mrs. J.K.M.)

SHRIMP AND CRAB MEAT SALAD
Nice luncheon dish

2 lbs. medium shrimp, cooked,
   shelled and deveined
1 lb. frozen crab meat
1 small onion, chopped
1 celery heart (do not use
   outer stalks), diced
1 green pepper, diced
1 teaspoon lemon juice
Dash of Worcestershire sauce
1 small jar pimentos, diced
Mayonnaise
Salt and pepper, to taste

Cut shrimp into pieces. Drain crab meat and add to shrimp. Add all the other ingredients. Add mayonnaise until desired consistency is reached. With lots of mayonnaise, it makes a delicious spread with crackers. With less mayonnaise, it is a nice luncheon dish which could be served in an avocado half or on a bed of lettuce.

Ellie Obiel Daniels (Mrs. James)

PAELLA

After experimenting with several versions of this Spanish dish,
this is our favorite combination.

Must do ahead
Serves: 8
Preparation: 3 hours
Baking Time: 30 minutes

1/4 cup olive oil
3-1/2 lbs. good chicken pieces,
* cut small*
1 onion, chopped
1 large green pepper, chopped
2 to 3 cloves garlic, minced
1-1/2 teaspoons salt
1/2 teaspoon pepper
1-1/4 lbs. Spanish chorizo
* sausage (or your favorite*
* smoked sausage; can use*
* 1/2 sausage, 1/2 cut*
* up pork)*
2-1/2 cups long-grain rice
5 cups hot chicken stock
1 teaspoon saffron
1-1/4 lbs. shrimp
1 lb. scallops
18 clams (or up to 2 doz. clams
* and mussels combined)*
* and shells*
1 10-oz. pkg. frozen peas
1 small jar chopped pimento
1 cup wine

Preparation time is 3 hours, but chicken stock needs to have been prepared ahead as well as cleaning of shellfish. Brown chicken in olive oil; transfer to a plate. Add to skillet onion, green pepper, garlic, salt and pepper; cook over moderate heat, stirring for 5 minutes or until the vegetables are softened. Add sausage, cut in 1/2" slices; saute. Add rice and saute for 5 minutes or until rice is coated in oil. Add chicken stock and saffron; bring to boil. Lower heat; let cook for 20 minutes or until rice begins to look dry. Add peas; cook for 10 minutes. Add pimento. Put mixture in a large serving dish; mix in shrimp, scallops and clams. (First, clean clams under cold, running water and discard any suspicious, heavy or half-opened shells. Put in a large bowl of salty water. Add 2 handfuls of flour. Set bowl in refrigerator for as long as possible. Rinse in cold water.) Put 1 cup wine in medium-sized soup pot. Bring to a rolling boil; add clams and mussels. Continue to cook for 5 minutes at high temperatures. As the shells open, remove the clam shell. When all are opened, dig meat out of shells and add with the shrimps and scallops (as above). Save one-half dozen of the best shells for decoration. Embed some chicken pieces and a few clam shells on top. Bake in 350° oven at least 30 minutes.

Thorunn Kjerulf Ivey (Mrs. David P.)

Poultry & Game

Cooks love poultry due to the great variety it offers in preparation and the ease with which vegetables and other side dishes accompany it. Most poultry may be roasted, broiled, grilled, fried, stewed, braised, microwaved or slow cooked in a crock pot. It may be served whole, in pieces, in casseroles—the possibilities are limited only by the imagination of the cook.

POULTRY HINTS

1. In purchasing chicken to be used cooked in casseroles, two whole chicken breasts (about 10 oz. each) yield about 2 cups cubed or chopped, cooked chicken; a 2-1/2 to 3 lb. broiler/fryer yields about 2-/2 cups chopped cooked meat and a 3-1/2 lb. roasting chicken yields about 3 cups chopped cooked meat.

2. In purchasing chicken to be used whole or in pieces, allow 1 lb. per serving.

3. To defrost chicken, do not use hot water as this toughens the flesh. Do soak it in cold water that has been heavily salted as this draws out the blood and ensures breast meat that will be pure white.

4. Marinate chicken breasts in milk or buttermilk for 3 hours in refrigerator before frying or baking to ensure tenderness.

5. It is easier to bone chicken breasts if the pieces have been placed in the freezer for 30 minutes to 1 hour.

6. After flouring chicken for frying, chill for 1 hour. The coating will adhere better.

7. Dark meat takes longer to cook than white. When you saute chicken pieces, cook the drumsticks and thighs for about 5 minutes longer.

8. To ensure completely cooked grilled chicken, try one of the following:
   A. Boil chicken for 15 minutes; drain and marinate in barbecue sauce for 30 minutes before putting on hot grill. (Also helps to tenderize chicken.)
   B. Precook 1 layer of chicken pieces in a 10 x 6 x 2 covered dish for 15 minutes in microwave oven. You will only need to grill for 10-15 minutes to have tender, barbecued chicken.
   C. Season chicken with salt and pepper. Do not add barbecue sauce. Bake in conventional oven at 350° for 30 minutes. Grill outside for an additional 30 minutes, basting with the barbecue sauce. (Also good technique to use with spareribs.)

9. Before roasting chicken, rub well with a good brandy—then season as desired.

10. If you desire a crisp, brown crust on roasted or broiled chicken, rub the skin well with mayonnaise before cooking.

11. When making chicken gravy, use flour as thickening agent. When making turkey gravy, use cornstarch as thickening agent.

CHICKEN EXTRAORDINAIRE

Yummy—men will adore. Easy to prepare and perfect for company

Can partially do ahead
Serves: 6
Preparation: 30 minutes

3 whole chicken breasts, halved,
    skinned and boned
1 teaspoon Accent
1/2 cup flour
1/4 cup cooking oil
6 slices French bread
    (approx. 1/2")
6 slices Swiss cheese
1 Tablespoon butter
1/2 lb. mushrooms
2/3 cup white wine
1 teaspoon salt
1/4 teaspoon pepper

Sprinkle chicken with Accent; roll in flour. Heat oil in frying pan; add chicken and brown. Reduce heat; cover and cook 15 minutes or until fork can be easily inserted. Place bread slices topped with cheese on baking sheet. Heat in 200° oven while preparing mushrooms. Remove chicken. Add butter and mushrooms to pan; cook about 3 minutes. Push mushrooms aside; add wine, salt and pepper. Return chicken to pan; simmer until sauce is slightly thickened. Place chicken piece on each bread slice; spoon mushrooms and sauce over chicken.

Pat Stancil Smith (Mrs. P. J.)

CHICKEN BREASTS IN CHAMPAGNE

Can partially do ahead
Serves: 6
Cooking time: 25 minutes

4 whole chicken breasts,
    skinned and boned
1/3 cup all-purpose flour
1 teaspoon salt
1/8 teaspoon freshly ground
    pepper
4 Tablespoons butter
1-1/2 cups champagne
1 cup heavy cream
Optional: sauteed mushrooms

Combine the flour, salt and pepper and dust breasts on both sides. Saute, full side down in butter and oil for 5 minutes, shaking pan to prevent sticking. Turn the chicken and add champagne. Cook another 15 minutes until liquid is reduced by half. (Can be done ahead to this point). Remove chicken to a serving platter, add cream to the pan juices and cook until thickened. Add sauteed mushrooms, if desired. Pour sauce over chicken and serve.

Barrie Muilenburg Sneed (Mrs. A. L.)

BREAST OF CHICKEN WITH SPINACH AND MUSHROOMS
A really good recipe—looks attractive and is different

Serves: 6
Preparation: About an hour
Cooking Time: 25 minutes

6 chicken breasts, skinned
   and boned
1/2 cup flour
1/2 teaspoon salt
2 eggs, slightly beaten
1/2 cup cream
1 cup bread crumbs
3 Tablespoons butter
2 Tablespoons salad oil
1 cup fresh mushrooms, sliced
2 Tablespoons butter
Juice of 1/2 lemon
2 Tablespoons chopped, fresh
   parsley
2 cups cooked spinach (hot)
3 cups cooked rice (hot)

Pound chicken breasts lightly to flatten. Dip them in flour mixed with salt. Combine eggs and cream and dip floured breasts in this mixture, then in bread crumbs. Heat the 3 tablespoons butter with 2 tablespoons oil in a large, deep skillet. Brown the chicken breasts on both sides. Cook over low heat for 25 minutes or until meat is cooked. In separate saucepan, saute mushrooms in 2 tablespoons butter for 2 minutes; add lemon juice and parsley.

To serve: Place a portion of hot cooked spinach on each plate, cover with chicken breast, top with mushrooms, and serve with hot cooked and buttered rice.

Sue Small Durham (Mrs. C. J., Jr.)

CORONATION CHICKEN

1 (4-1/2 lb.) chicken, broiled or
   roasted with butter in oven

CURRIED MAYONNAISE:

1 Tablespoon olive oil
1 small onion, peeled
   and chopped
1 Tablespoon curry powder
1/4 pint chicken stock
1 teaspoon tomato puree
Juice of one-half lemon
2 Tablespoons apricot,
   gooseberry jam or sweet
   chutney
1/2 pint mayonnaise
3 Tablespoons cream

Cool chicken. Heat oil in skillet—saute onion until soft (about 5 minutes). Stir in curry powder. Add stock, tomato puree, lemon juice and jam or chutney. Bring to boil and then simmer 5 minutes. Strain sauce into bowl—cool. Then add mayonnaise and cream. Remove meat from bone in chunks and place in serving dish. Spoon curried sauce over chicken and serve with boiled cold rice tossed in vinaigrette dressing.

Beatrice Michael Smith (Mrs. F. S., Jr.)

CHICKEN IN DUCK SAUCE

Must do ahead
Baking Time: 35-40 minutes

8 chicken breasts, boned
*   and skinned*
1 cup Italian salad dressing
2 jars currant jelly
2 cans dark pitted cherries
1 6-oz. can frozen concentrated
*   orange juice*

Marinate chicken in salad dressing for 3-4 hours, turning once. Drain. Bake in 375° oven for 20 minutes; then turn on broiler and broil for 5 minutes. Combine jelly, cherries, and orange juice in saucepan and cook until melted. Take chicken out of pan and pour off drippings. Place in 9 x 13x2" pan, and pour cherry sauce over chicken and continue baking for 10-15 minutes. Good with herbed rice.

Joyce Lichtenfels Cole

QUICK AND DELICIOUS CHICKEN CORDON BLEU
Tasty and elegant!

Can do partially ahead
Serves: 4
Preparation: 20 minutes
Cooking Time: 25 minutes

4 boneless chicken breasts
Salt, pepper and parsley
*   to taste*
4 strips Mozzarella cheese
4 strips ham (or cooked bacon)
3 Tablespoons vegetable oil or
*   1/2 cup butter*
2 cans condensed cream of
*   chicken soup*

Pound chicken breast with mallet until about 1/8" thick. Salt, pepper and parsley to taste. Place on top of each chicken breast 1 slice of cheese and 1 slice of ham (or bacon). Roll up jelly roll style and secure with toothpick. Brown chicken roll-ups in oil or butter, until golden. Thin the soup with milk; pour over chicken. Bring to a boil over medium heat, then simmer covered for 25 minutes. (Option: to the chicken soup mixture add some white wine.)

Sarah Ann Raynor Lamm (Mrs. R. M., Jr.)

CHICKEN L'ORANGE

Baking Time: 1 hour, 30 minutes

4 breasts of chicken
3 Tablespoons butter or
   margarine
Minced onion
Tarragon
Paprika
1 can frozen orange juice

Melt butter or margarine in a flat pan. Coat meat sides of chicken with butter and arrange in pan meat up. Cover with minced onion, tarragon and paprika. Bake in 400° oven for one hour, basting every 15 minutes. Drain butter or margarine off. Spoon frozen orange juice over chicken using whole can (about 2 heaping spoonfuls on each piece). Bake another 30 minutes in 400° oven basting every 10 minutes with orange juice.
Serve with wild rice with mushrooms.

Mrs. Raymond F. Moran
Hendersonville, North Carolina

CHICKEN STRATA

Must do ahead
Serves: 6-8
Baking Time: 45 minutes

8 slices day-old bread,
   cubed into 1" pieces
2 cups cooked chicken
1/2 cup mayonnaise
Salt and pepper
Celery
Green olives
Almonds or water chestnuts
2 eggs, beaten
1-1/2 cups milk
1 can cream of chicken soup
Buttered crumbs
1/2 cup shredded cheese

Place one half of bread in baking dish. Place 2 cups cooked chicken, 1/2 cup mayonnaise, salt and pepper on bread. Top with rest of bread. Combine celery, green olives, almonds, beaten eggs and milk; pour over chicken. Let set one hour to one day. Top with soup (undiluted). Top with crumbs. Bake in 325° oven for 45 minutes Before removing from oven, top with cheese.

Lynell Bell (Mrs. C. R., Jr.)

CHICKEN BREAST PARMESAN

Serves: 4-6
Baking Time: 60 minutes

1 cup crushed Pepperidge
  Farm Herb Stuffing
1/2 cup Parmesan cheese
1/8 cup parsley
1 teaspoon salt
1/8 teaspoon pepper
1 teaspoon garlic salt
1/2 stick butter
4 chicken breasts, deboned

Mix all dry ingredients. Melt butter; dip chicken breasts in butter, then cover with dry mixture. Bake in 350° oven for one hour. Menu suggestion: good with tomatoes/spinach.

Beverly M. Bagley (Mrs. Carter S.)

CHICKEN SOUFFLE SANDWICH

Must do ahead
Baking Time: 1-1/2 hours

9 slices white bread
4 cups diced, cooked chicken
  (about 5 medium breasts)
1/2 lb. mushrooms, sliced
1/4 cup butter
2 (5-oz.) cans water chestnuts,
  drained and sliced
1/2 cup mayonnaise
9 slices sharp cheese
4 eggs
2 cups milk
1 teaspoon salt
1 can cream of celery soup
1 can mushroom soup
2 oz. jar pimentos, drained
  and chopped

Remove crusts from bread and lay bread in 9x 13 baking dish which has been buttered. Top with 4 cups diced, cooked chicken. Cook 1/2 lb. mushrooms, sliced, in 1/4 cup butter for 5 minutes. Place over chicken together with 2 (5-oz.) cans water chestnuts, drained and sliced. Dot with 1/2 cup mayonnaise and top with 9 slices sharp cheese. Beat 4 eggs, add 2 cups milk and a teaspoon of salt. Pour over the chicken.
Mix 1 can cream of celery soup, 1 can mushroom soup and a 2 oz. jar of pimentos, drained and chopped. Spoon over all.
Cover with foil and store in refrigerator overnight. Bake uncovered in 325° oven for 1-1/2 hours. Sprinkle with one-half cup bread crumbs for the last 15 minutes of baking.

Mrs. Howard W. Poe
Hendersonville, North Carolina

COQ AU VIN
Very good—yet simple version of a classic

Can do ahead
Can freeze
Serves 4-6
Preparation: 30 minutes
Cooking time: 1 hour, 30 minutes

1 cut-up chicken
1 teaspoon salt
Dash pepper
1/2 cup flour
3 Tablespoons salad oil
2 minced garlic cloves
3 sliced green onions
1/2 lb. sliced mushrooms,
     sauteed in butter
1 bay leaf
2 cups white wine (Chablis)
1/4 cup minced parsley

Dust chicken lightly with seasoned flour. Brown in oil in large frying pan, then remove chicken. Cook garlic and onions until tender. Add remaining ingredients and chicken. Cover and simmer 1-1/2 hours or until tender. May be frozen, then thawed and reheated in oven.

Celine Hanan Lurey (Mrs. B. M.)

KING RANCH CHICKEN
Spicy and colorful—easy to make and tasty!

Can do ahead
Can freeze
Serves: 6
Preparation: 1-1/2 to 2 hours
Baking Time: 30 minutes or
45-60 minutes if frozen

1 chicken cut up or 2 large
     breasts
1 (10-1/2 oz.) can cream
     of mushroom soup
1 (10-oz.) can tomatoes and
     green chiles
1 small green pepper; chopped
2 jalapeno peppers, seeded
     and chopped
1 small onion, chopped
1/2 lb. grated, Cheddar cheese
8 corn tortillas

Simmer chicken until tender, about 40 to 45 minutes. Bone chicken and combine with mushroom soup, tomatoes and green chiles, jalapeno peppers, onions and green pepper. Heat thoroughly and keep warm. Soften each tortilla in warm water. Cut each tortilla into quarters and line bottom of 2 quart baking dish. Add half of the chicken mixture and then top with half of the grated cheese. Repeat layer with remaining half of ingredients. Bake in 375° oven for 30 minutes or 45 minutes to 60 minutes, if frozen.

Jeanne Forsyth Powell (Mrs. B. P.)

CHICKEN IN RICE
Delicious—easy to prepare and could be used for company

Serves: 4-6
Preparation: 20 minutes
Baking Time: 1 hour

1 stick butter, melted
1 cup uncooked rice
1 medium onion, chopped
2 cans Campbell's beef
    consommé
4 to 6 chicken breasts

Layer: Melted butter in 9 x 13 casserole or pyrex dish, onion, rice and consommé. Place chicken breasts on top and push down gently. Bake uncovered in 350° oven for 1 hour.
Serve with broccoli, fruit salad and hot rolls.

Bettie Griffin Watts (Mrs. N. B.)

FANTASTIC FRIED CHICKEN
Crispy and can be partially done ahead

Baking Time: 60 minutes

Chicken pieces
Flour mixed with salt, pepper
    and paprika
Oil
Margarine

Flour chicken pieces by shaking in a paper bag. Brown in oil in frying pan. Place chicken pieces so they overlap in pyrex baking dish that has been lined with 2 or 3 layers of paper towels. Put about a teaspoon of margarine on top of each piece. *This can be done a day or so ahead and placed, covered, in refrigerator.* When ready to bake, bring to room temperature and bake in 350° oven, uncovered, for one hour.

Nancy Sauer Crosby (Mrs. E. Brown)

LAYERED CHICKEN

Baking Time: 1 hour

4 or 6 chicken breasts, skinned
1 medium onion, sliced thickly
3 medium zucchini squash,
    sliced
1 cup fresh mushrooms, sliced
1 large can tomato wedges,
    drained
Garlic salt
Seasoned salt

Place chicken in bottom of shallow, oblong baking dish that has been sprayed with PAM. Layer remaining ingredients on top of chicken in order listed. Sprinkle each layer with garlic salt and seasoned salt. Bake for one hour uncovered in 350° oven.

Susan Lee Drenning (Mrs. Dennis)

CHICKEN TETRAZZINI

Can do ahead
Can freeze
Serves: 8-10
Preparation: 1 hour
Baking Time: 30 minutes

2 large chickens, cooked
  and boned
2 chopped green peppers
1 large onion, chopped
1/2 lb. fresh mushrooms
1 pint cream
1-1/2 lbs. medium
  Cheddar cheese
1 lb. vermicelli
2 sticks butter
Flour to thicken
1 cup white wine
Parmesan cheese
Garlic salt
Pepper

Cook chicken in water to cover, with celery leaves and small onion. Save 2 cups of broth. Chop chicken into bite-size pieces and season with garlic salt and pepper. Set aside. Cover liberally with Parmesan cheese.

Saute green pepper and onion in 1/2 stick of butter until tender. Mix with the chicken. Slice mushrooms and add to chicken mixture. Sauce: Melt 1-1/2 sticks butter. Add flour to thicken. Mix well. Add cream, chicken broth and wine. Grate 1 lb. cheese and add to sauce. Sauce should be of medium thickness. Set aside. Break vermicelli into 3-inch pieces, cook according to package directions, and drain. Mix chicken mixture, sauce and vermicelli together. Pour into a greased casserole and sprinkle with remaining grated cheese. Cook in 375° oven until bubbly. Lightly brown top of casserole under broiler before serving.

Lauri C. Marlowe

ALMA'S CHICKEN

Can do ahead
Can freeze
Baking Time: 45 minutes

8 skinned chicken breasts
1 stick butter
1 large can mushrooms
  (1/2 lb. fresh)
1 large can artichoke hearts
2 Tablespoons flour
1 can beef bouillon soup
1/2 cup Sauterne wine
Paprika

Salt, pepper and paprika chicken and saute in butter until brown. Place in casserole dish. Briefly saute mushrooms and artichoke hearts. Place around chicken in casserole. Brown flour in drippings and add bouillon. Mix well. Add wine. Pour over chicken, mushrooms and artichoke hearts. Bake in 350° oven for 45 minutes (or until tender). Baste occasionally. Can be loosely covered with foil during cooking. Serve with hot noodles.

Janet Yarborough Kelly (Mrs. E. G.)

CHICKEN CASSEROLE DIVINE
Nice for a crowd

Serves: 8-10
Baking Time: 30-45 minutes

3 cups cooked chicken, diced
1/2 green pepper, chopped
1 cup celery
1 pimento, chopped
1 medium onion, chopped
2 Tablespoons Worcestershire
 sauce
Pepper to taste
1/2 teaspoon salt
1 cup mayonnaise
1 cup raw rice
1 4-oz. can mushrooms
1 cup light cream

Cook rice according to package directions. Combine all ingredients. Pour into large casserole, cover and bake in 375° oven for 30-45 minutes or until heated through and bubbly. Can be held over. Like the loaves and fishes, this will expand any number of times to feed a crowd. Original recipe will feed 8-10.

JoAnn McGowan Grimes (Mrs. Charles W.)

CHICKEN CASSEROLE DELUXE

Baking Time: 40 minutes

2 cups cooked regular rice
1 cup sour cream
1-1/2 cup cooked, diced chicken
1-1/4 cup shredded Monterey
 Jack cheese
1/4 cup chopped green pepper

Combine all ingredients and place in well-buttered deep 1 to 1-1/2 quart casserole. Top with Parmesan cheese and buttered breadcrumbs. Dot with additional butter. Bake uncovered for 40 minutes in a 350° oven.

Jaime Porter Armstrong (Mrs. J. R.)

CHICKEN MARINADE

Make ahead at least 6 to 8 hours

1/3 cup salad oil
1/3 cup grapefruit or
 orange juice
1 pkg. Italian dressing mix

Combine all ingredients. Pour over chicken pieces and marinate at least 6 to 8 hours. Bake in oven or grill over slow coals.

Libba Shuford

CURRIED CHICKEN SALAD
Perfect for a luncheon—served with rolls

Must do ahead
Serves: 12
Preparation: 20 minutes

2 quarts cooked chicken, cubed
1 can water chestnuts, sliced
    and drained
2 lbs. seedless grapes, halved
Can pineapple chunks, drained
2-3 cups celery, sliced
2-1/2 cups almonds, slivered
3 cups mayonnaise
1 Tablespoon curry powder
2 Tablespoons soy sauce
2 Tablespoons lemon juice

Combine chicken, water chestnuts, grapes, pineapple, celery and almonds. Mix all remaining ingredients; add to chicken and toss well. Chill several hours. Serve on lettuce bed.

Carol Abbott McCollum (Mrs. Hugh)

CHEESEY CHICKEN CASSEROLE
Very good! Cream cheese gives an unusual and different taste!

Can do ahead
Can freeze
Serves: 6-8
Preparation: 20 minutes
Baking Time: 30 minutes

2 pkgs. frozen broccoli
    (or 2 cans asparagus tips)
2 cups cooked chicken or 4
    whole chicken breasts, cut
    in large chunks
2 (8-oz.) pkgs. cream cheese
2 cups milk
1 cup Parmesan cheese
1 teaspoon salt, or less
3/4 teaspoon garlic salt

Cook broccoli. Place in buttered 2 quart casserole. Add chicken on top. Make sauce in double boiler. Cook remaining ingredients until creamy, and pour over chicken and broccoli. Bake in 350° oven for 30 minutes. Sprinkle top with paprika. Menu suggestion: Gelatin salad; white wine.

Nancy Sauer Crosby (Mrs. E. Brown)

Hint:
Thaw your turkey in a camping cooler. Faster than frige...safer than room temperature...and no turkey crowding your refrigerator.

HAYDEE'S CURRIED CHICKEN SALAD

Must do ahead
Serves: 8-10
Preparation: 30 minutes

4 cups diced, cooked chicken
2 Granny Smith apples, peeled,
    cored, cut into quarters and
    sliced crosswise
1 cup pecans, broken
1 can pineapple chunks,
    drained

DRESSING:

1/2 cup mayonnaise
1/4 cup vegetable oil
1 Tablespoon curry powder
1 Tablespoon chutney
2 Tablespoons cider vinegar

Put all dressing ingredients into processor and process until well combined. Put the chicken, apples, pecans and pineapple into bowl, pour dressing over it and mix well. Keep in refrigerator 30 minutes. Serve on Romaine with tomato and parsley to decorate.

Lelia Kincaid Cort (Mrs. J. E.)

FOOLPROOF CHICKEN CASSEROLE

Serves: 12
Baking Time: 30 minutes

2-1/2 cups diced chicken
2 cups diced celery
2 cups diced onion
1 pkg. almonds
2 cups cooked rice
    (melt 1 stick butter in this)
1 can cream of chicken soup
1 teaspoon salt
3 Tablespoons lemon juice
1/2 cup chicken broth
1 can water chestnuts, sliced
3/4 cup mayonnaise (mixed
    with broth)

Mix soup, mayonnaise and seasonings. Pour over rice while it is hot. Add chicken; mix well. Bake for 30 minutes in 350° oven. Cover with crushed cracker crumbs and dot with butter. Run under broiler. You can substitute shrimp for chicken and change the cream of chicken soup to cream of shrimp.

Beverly M. Bagley (Mrs. Carter S.)

HONEY FRENCH CHICKEN
This recipe won second prize in the North Carolina Chicken Cooking Contest

Can do ahead
Serves: 6
Preparation: 10 minutes
Baking Time: 35-40 minutes

6 chicken breasts, (Optional:
    skinned and boned)
1/2 cup corn oil
1/2 cup honey
1/4 cup cider vinegar
1 teaspoon flavor enhancer
1/4 cup chili sauce
1 Tablespoon Worcestershire
    sauce
1/2 envelope (1-3/8 oz.) onion
    soup mix
1/4 teaspoon salt

Sprinkle chicken with flavor enhancer. In a jar, place corn oil, honey, vinegar, chili sauce, Worcestershire sauce, soup mix and salt. Shake well. Place chicken in single layer in large shallow baking pan. Pour sauce over chicken. Bake, uncovered, in 350° oven about 35-40 minutes or until fork can be inserted with ease.
*Sauce can be made a week ahead. Keep in refrigerator and pour over chicken when ready to cook the chicken. Boning of chicken is optional. Serve with Oriental rice.

Sandra Tucker Holt (Mrs. S. E.)

SOUTHERN BARBECUED CHICKEN
Sinfully good—yet easy to make

Serves: 4
Prepartion: 30 minutes
Baking Time: 2-1/2 hours

1 chicken, quartered or cut up
    for frying
1/2 cup catsup
2 Tablespoons Heinz 57 sauce
1 teaspoon Texas Pete Hot
    Sauce (or more to taste)
1 Tablespoon vegetable oil
1 teaspoon Worcestershire
    sauce
1/4 cup brown sugar
1/4 teaspoon black pepper
6 Tablespoons vinegar
1 small onion

Clean and salt one chicken, quartered or cut up for frying. Mix catsup, Heinz 57 sauce, Texas Pete sauce, oil, Worcestershire sauce, brown sugar, pepper, vinegar and chopped onion. Process in blender. Place chicken in rectangular baking dish—single layer. Pour sauce over, coating chicken well. Cover with aluminum foil. Cook for 2-3 hours in 325° oven, basting regularly. Sauce is delicious over rice.

Pat Stancil Smith (Mrs. P. J.)

CHINESE CHICKEN WITH PINEAPPLE AND APRICOTS

Can do ahead partially
Serves: 6

3 whole chicken breasts
2 onions, sliced in wedges
3 stalks celery, sliced diagonally
1 can water chestnuts, halved
2 Tablespoons corn starch
4 Tablespoons soy sauce
1 cup white wine or sherry
2 cans whole apricots
1 can pineapple chunks (or 2
    cans mandarin oranges)

Bone and cut up chicken. Combine cornstarch, soy sauce and wine. Marinate uncooked chicken in this mixture for two or three hours. Saute onions, celery and water chestnuts briefly in 1-2 tablespoons oil; remove from pan. Drain chicken (reserve marinade); cook chicken in 1-2 tablespoons oil for 5-10 minutes, stirring frequently. Remove from heat and allow to cool. Add to chicken the sauted onion, celery and water chestnuts; apricots (drained) and pineapple (reserve juice). Pour over all of this the saved marinade, 6 tablespoons pineapple juice and 4 tablespoons chicken stock (I make up a little with instant bouillon). Can be prepared ahead to this point. Just before serving, heat 5-10 minutes. Serve over rice. A nice meal with the addition of a tossed salad and rolls.

Kathleen Fairburn Armstrong (Mrs. R. N.)

SOY SAUCE CHICKEN

Serves: 4
Preparation: 10 minutes
Cooking Time: About 45 minutes

1 whole fryer (2 to 2-1/2 lbs.)
    or fryer parts

SAUCE:

2/3 cup soy sauce
4 slices ginger
2 Tablespoons wine
1/2 to 2/3 cup sugar
2 cups water

GARNISH:

2 green onions, slivered

Combine sauce ingredients in wok and heat to boiling. Put chicken in wok, cover, and cook for 10 minutes. Remove cover, lower heat, turn and baste chicken. Add a few tablespoons of water, if necessary. Cook about 20 minutes per pound, basting occasionally. Sauce will be reduced to about 1 cup and will thicken.
Arrange chicken pieces on platter; garnish with green onion and pour sauce over chicken and onion. Serve hot or cold.

Nancy Reid Graham (Mrs. F. P.)

STIR-FRIED CHICKEN AND CASHEWS

Serves: 4-6

2 whole medium chicken
    breasts, skinned, boned
    and cut into 1/2" cubes
2 Tablespoons soy sauce
1 Tablespoon dry sherry
1 cup raw cashew nuts
    (available at health food
    stores)
2 Tablespoons cooking oil
1 Tablespoon hoisin sauce
    (available at gourmet
    stores)
Sliced green onion

In medium bowl, combine chicken, soy sauce, sherry; set aside. Stir fry cashews in hot oil in wok over high heat for 1-2 minutes or until browned. Lift out with slotted spoon and set aside. Add chicken mixture to wok and stir-fry over high heat 2-3 minutes until just done. Stir in hoisin sauce and cashews. Sprinkle with sliced green onions and serve at once over hot cooked rice.

Emily Caddell Gordon (Mrs. A. F.)

PENNY'S CHICKEN AND DUMPLINGS

Serves: 4-5
Preparation: 30 minutes
Cooking Time: 2-1/2 hours

1 whole chicken
2 heaping cups flour
1 teaspoon salt
1/2 teaspoon soda
1 teaspoon baking powder
4 Tablespoons Crisco
1/2 to 2/3 cup buttermilk
    (powdered buttermilk
    can be used)

Cook whole chicken in salt water on simmer until very done, about 2 hours. Remove chicken and bone it. *This dish uses only the dark meat; reserve the white meat for future use.*

Mix dry ingredients together; cut in shortening. Add buttermilk until mixture is thoroughly moistened, but not sticky. Knead about 5 times. Separate into two portions. Roll out each portion on an *extremely* well floured surface, as thin as possible. Cut into strips. Repeat with other portion. Keep strips well floured.

Add about 1 cup of water to chicken stock. Bring to a boil and pinch off pieces of dough into boiling stock. When all pieces are in liquid, give it a quick stir and lower the heat to simmer. Cover and cook about 20 minutes. Add pieces of chicken to stock and continue simmering until slightly thickened. Serve in bowls.

This recipe works best in a *non-stick* Dutch oven.

Jeannie Renick Davis (Mrs. J. N., Jr.)

COLD CHICKEN ENTREE
Easy to prepare—good even with leftover baked chicken.

Must do ahead
Serves: 4
Preparation: 30 minutes

8 boned and skinned, halved
    chicken breasts
1 can chicken broth
Grated rind of one lemon
Fresh dill (or dried dill)

SAUCE:

8 oz. cream cheese
4 Tablespoons mayonnaise
2 to 3 teaspoons lemon juice
1 teaspoon salt
Slivered almonds

Steam chicken in 1 can chicken broth. Cook covered. Refrigerate chicken in broth overnight. 30 minutes before serving, remove chicken from broth and dry with paper towels. Combine cream cheese, mayonnaise, lemon juice, lemon rind and salt. Pour over chicken. Top with fresh or dried chopped dill and toasted slivered almonds.

Elizabeth B. Thurlow

JEAN'S FAVORITE CHICKEN CASSEROLE
Great for after football game or golf—smells great while cooking!

Do ahead
Freeze cooked or uncooked
Serves: 8 generously
Baking Time: About 1 hour

1 8-oz. pkg. Pepperidge Farm
    stuffing mix, cornbread
    or plain
1 stick oleo, melted
1 cup undiluted chicken broth
3-1/2 or more cups cooked
    chicken, cut in bite size (7
    half breasts make 4 cups)
1/4 cup chopped green
    onion tops
1/2 cup chopped green onions
1/2 cup chopped celery
1/2 cup mayonnaise
2 eggs
1-1/2 cups milk
Grated cheese

Mix stuffing, oleo and broth. Put half in a shallow, buttered two-quart casserole. Mix chicken, onion, celery, and mayonnaise and spread it over stuffing. Add rest of stuffing mixture. Beat eggs in milk, pour over stuffing. Cover with foil and *refrigerate overnight*. Remove 1 hour before baking. Spread mushroom soup on top; bake in 325° oven about 40 minutes; sprinkle grated cheese on top, and bake 10 minutes longer.

Virginia C. Taylor (Mrs. William F.)

BRUNSWICK STEW

Preparation: 2-3 hours

1 large fryer
5 cans (28 oz.) tomatoes,
   mashed
4 cans (16 oz.) lima beans,
   drained
4 cans (16 oz.) white
   creamed corn
1 stick butter
2 Tablespoons bacon drippings
1 teaspoon red pepper
Salt and black pepper, to taste

Cook chicken in 2 quarts of water until very tender. Remove chicken from bones and cut in pieces. Add tomatoes and bacon fat to chicken stock, season and simmer uncovered until liquid is reduced (about 1 hour). Add chicken, beans, corn and butter; cook until thick, stirring often.

Sarah Greene Hensley (Mrs. Donald)

BUSY DAY CHICKEN PIE

Children love this—can be prepared ahead for those busy days.

Can do ahead
Serves: 4-6
Baking Time: 20-30 minutes

2 deep-dish piecrust shells
2 cups cooked, cut up chicken
1 stick butter, or margarine
1 cup chicken broth
1 can cream of chicken soup
2 hard-boiled eggs, sliced

Put chicken and hard-boiled eggs in pie shell. In saucepan, heat together butter, stock and soup until well blended. Pour sauce over chicken to fill pie shell (reserve remainder to use as gravy). Top with other piecrust shell. Cut slits for steam. Bake in 375° oven for 20-30 minutes or until the crust is golden brown.

Betsy Rawleigh Simons (Mrs. W. J.)

CHICKEN BONUS

1 to 2 whole frying hens
Salt, pepper, to taste
Celery salt
Garlic salt
Onion salt
Paprika

If you have a grill with a lid, and have leftover coals, have ready one or two whole frying hens. Season chickens with a sprinkling of salt, pepper, celery salt, garlic salt, onion salt and paprika. Wrap in foil and place over coals. Put lid of grill down. Let chickens cook overnight. You now have one or two "energy-saving" chickens!

Walter Watts

BRUNSWICK STEW À LA WEAVER

Serves: 20-25

2 lbs. fatback
5 lbs. boneless beef stew
3 roasting chickens
4 quarts peeled tomatoes
1 quart tomato juice
10 lbs. potatoes, cubed
4 quarts baby butter beans
2 quarts fresh corn
1 stick margarine
1 pod red pepper
1/2 cup sugar
Salt and pepper, to taste

Cook beef and chickens in water until tender. Remove skin and bones from chicken. Cook fatback in 10 gallon cast iron pot over a hardwood fire for 30 minutes. Do not burn fatback. Pour in beef and chicken with broth, potatoes, tomatoes, tomato juice, red pepper, salt, pepper and sugar. Remove fatback and feed to dog. Keep fire so as to create a low boil and stir constantly for 2 hours. Add butter beans and cook 1 more hour. Add corn and cook another hour. Add margarine and cook until desired consistency. Add water at intervals as needed for desired consistency. Stew needs to be stirred constantly during the entire cooking period with a large, wooden spoon. (This may also be cooked inside in a large pot.)

Bruce Weaver

FIRST PRESBYTERIAN NAZARETH CHICKEN

Baking Time: 2 hours

3 lb. chicken cut up
1 stick butter, or margarine
1/2 cup vinegar
3 Tablespoons water
1/3 cup Worcestershire sauce
2 Tablespoons sugar
1 onion, peeled and sliced
Salt and pepper

Wipe chicken thoroughly with cloth. Melt half the butter in large skillet and brown chicken lightly. Melt rest of butter, vinegar, water, sauce, sugar, salt and pepper; pour over chicken. Put in casserole. Top with onion slices and bake, covered, for 2 hours in 325° oven. Also cooks beautifully in crock pot for 6-8 hours on low heat.

Elizabeth Hudson McAnally (Mrs. L. W.)

STUFFED CORNISH HENS WITH ORANGE SAUCE

Serves: 4

4 Cornish game hens
1 recipe plain cornbread
    stuffing
1 recipe orange sauce

CORNBREAD STUFFING:

1 cup cornmeal
1/2 cup flour
2 teaspoons baking powder
Dash salt
2 Tablespoons shortening,
    melted
1 cup milk

ORANGE SAUCE:

1 teaspoon cornstarch
1 cup dripping from hens
2 Tablespoons vinegar
2 Tablespoons sugar
1-2 Tablespoons chopped
    orange rind
1/2 cup hot orange juice
1 teaspoon lemon juice
2 Tablespoons white wine

Thaw birds; remove gizzards, etc. Heat greased baking dish or skillet. Stir dry ingredients for stuffing together, add milk and shortening. Pour into heated pan. Bake 20-25 minutes in 425° oven. Cool. Crumble cooked cornbread. Add 1 small chopped onion, 1 cup chopped ripe olives, dash of salt and pepper, dash of sage. Moisten to damp consistency with melted butter and a little water. Stuff birds with mixture. Tie legs. Bake hens at 375° for one hour, basting with melted butter at intervals. (If birds are over 1 lb. 6 oz., bake 15 to 30 minutes longer.) Place on heated platter, garnish with orange slices and pour orange sauce over all. Thicken drippings with cornstarch. In another saucepan, cook vinegar and sugar until sugar is dissolved. Add cornstarch mixture, cook 3-4 minutes. Add orange rind, orange juice, lemon juice and wine. Cook until blended and thickened.

Pour over hens immediately before serving. Serve with brown rice.

Jane Perry Hildebrand (Mrs. R. D., Jr.)

DEE-LICIOUS DOVES

Tastes very gourmet; men love this!

Can do ahead
Serves: 4
Preparation: 10 minutes
Baking Time: 20 minutes

10-12 doves
1 stick melted butter
1 can cream of mushroom soup
Salt and pepper, to taste

Parboil doves 1 hour; remove from bone and cut in quarters. Place in casserole with other ingredients. Bake in casserole 20 minutes uncovered in 350° oven. Can be served over rice (wild or plain).

Bam Kelly Coleman (Mrs. R. L., Jr.)

TENDER WILD DUCKS

Serves: 4-5
Preparation: 10 minutes
Cooking Time: 2-1/2 hours

2 ducks
Salt and pepper
Orange, quartered
Apple, quartered
Several stalks celery
1 Tablespoon flour
3 Tablespoons orange juice
Optional: white wine

Have husband clean the ducks! Stuff cavity with the quartered orange, apple and celery. Salt and pepper the ducks, inside and out. Place ducks in brown-in-bag after adding flour, orange juice and wine. Put holes in bag, place in roasting pan and cook at 350° for two and a half hours.
Have sharp knife to carve duck breasts.
Menu Suggestion: Tossed salad, rolls, squash and tart orange marmalade.

Jean Fitzhenry Coughlin (Mrs. J. D.)

BEAR ROAST

Must do ahead
Baking Time: 4 hours

THE MARINADE:

2-3 cups dry red wine
1/4 cup vegetable oil (optional depending on leaness of roast)
1/4 cup vinegar
1/4 cup Worcestershire sauce
3 Tablespoons soy sauce
6-8 bay leaves
1/4 cup chopped red peppers
2 Tablespoons thyme
3-4 large onions, sliced

Roast must marinate for 24 to 36 hours to insure tenderness and to make it less strong. It should be turned often to allow marinade to work.
Place roast in pot (Dutch oven, large frying pan, etc.) for marinating and cooking. After marinating time, preheat oven to 325.° cook roast, uncovered, for about 4 hours. Baste every 15 minutes with marinade.
Optional: If meat is still too strong for your taste, add the following ingredients to desired results: 2 Tablespoons oregano; 1 Tablespoon curry, 1 cup chopped celery, 1 cup catsup and/or 2 Tablespoons Allspice.

Pearce Weaver

Hint:
Wild ducks are easier to pluck if dipped in melted parafin. When it's cool, pull the paraffin off; the feathers come right off.

VENISON STEW

Better if done ahead
Serves: 10-12

3-5 lbs. venison
2 cups dry red wine
6-8 medium potatoes, cubed
6-8 carrots, sliced
4-5 medium onions, quartered
1 cup sliced mushrooms
2 Tablespoons Worcestershire
     sauce
Salt, pepper, to taste

Cut venison into 1 inch cubes and saute in olive oil until tender and brown in Dutch oven. Add wine, potatoes, carrots, onions, Worcestershire sauce, salt and pepper. Add enough water to cover and simmer for 2 hours. Add mushrooms and continue simmering until vegetables are tender.

Bruce Weaver

Meat

PERFECT TENDERLOIN OF BEEF
Easy, elegant and impressive!!

Can do ahead
Baking Time: 30 minutes

Tenderloin
Bacon
Rosemary
3/4 cup burgundy
Salt and pepper

Wrap tenderloin in bacon; sprinkle generously with rosemary. Broil 4″ from heat for 30 minutes (15 minutes each side). Place in foil, add 3/4 cup burgundy, salt and pepper. Wrap and bake in 350° oven for 30 minutes. Serve hot.

Candy Stell Shivers (Mrs. James A.)

BEEF AND MUSHROOM VINAIGRETTE
A good summertime entree.

Can do ahead
Serves: 4-6

1 large white Bermuda onion
15 large mushrooms
Salt and lemon juice
1-1/2 lbs. beef sliced thin
    (medium rare tenderloin)
1/4 cup red wine vinegar
1 teaspoon brown
    prepared mustard
Pinch marjoram and chervil
Ground pepper
1/2 cup salad oil
2 teaspoons parsley

Slice onion thinly and separate. Drop mushrooms into boiling water with pinch of salt and a few drops of lemon juice. Remove immediately. Blot dry; slice lengthwise. Do same with onions. Arrange mushrooms, meat, and onions on platter. Blend vinegar into mustard; stir in herbs, salt and pepper to taste. Gradually blend in oil. Pour over meat, mushrooms and onion. Chill several hours. Bast occasionally. Arrange on platter. Top with watercress.

Ruth Bowles Carson (Mrs. Phillip)

SCOTCH STEAK

Must do some ahead
Serves: 6

1 teaspoon whole black peppers,
    crushed in mortar
3 lbs. steak with bone or 2 lbs.
    flank steak
2 Tablespoons olive oil
2 Tablespoons vinegar
1 teaspoon sugar
2-3 Tablespoons Scotch
    whiskey

Rub crushed pepper over steak and place in marinade of oil and vinegar for 3-4 hours at room temperature. Grill steak to medium rare. (Be especially careful not to overcook if using flank steak.) Remove to hot platter. Sprinkle with sugar, pour on Scotch and flame. Spoon liquid over steak until fire dies. Salt to taste.

Barbara Thompson (Ann Arbor, Michigan)

FILLET OF BEEF BENEDICT

Serves: 4
Preparation: 15 minutes
Baking Time: 15 minutes

4 thick beef fillets
4 pieces cooked ham, cut into
    round shape
4 eggs, poached
Fresh asparagus, cooked
    (keep warm)
Hollandaise sauce (add 2
    tablespoons horseradish
    to sauce before serving,
    or to taste)

Put a platter in oven to get hot. Grill fillets to medium rare. While grilling, poach eggs. Remove platter from oven and place ham (at room temperature) on it; top with fillets, then eggs.
Place asparagus around edge of platter. Cover all with the hollandaise-horseradish mixture. Serve at once. (The hot platter and fillets on top heats the ham.)
Serve with tossed salad, rolls or bread and wine.

Renie Fridy (Mrs. Wallace)

FIVE FLIES BEEF STEW

Can partially do ahead
Can freeze (before addition of sour cream)
Serves: 6
Preparation: 15 minutes
Cooking Time: Depends on type of meat used—up to 2 hours if using round steak

1-1/2 lbs. steak, cut 1" thick
    (sirloin or round)
1/3 cup flour
1/4 teaspoon ground cloves
1/4 teaspoon ground ginger
1/4 teaspoon curry powder
1/4 teaspoon garlic salt
1/4 teaspoon black pepper
1/2 teaspoon salt
1/4 cup salad oil
2 beef bouillon cubes
2 cups hot water
2 Tablespoons butter
1/4 cup slivered almonds
1 4-oz. can mushrooms (or use
    equal amount fresh
    mushrooms)
1 cup drained <u>sour</u> red cherries
1 cup sour cream

Cut the steak into one-inch cubes. Combine the flour with the cloves, ginger, curry powder, garlic salt, pepper and salt. Dip the pieces in the seasoned flour. Heat the salad oil in a heavy frying pan. Brown the meat in the hot oil. When the meat is well browned, sprinkle it with any remaining seasoned flour. Stir until the flour is well browned. Dissolve the bouillon cubes in hot water and pour over the browned meat.
Cover and simmer over low heat for about 2 hours or until the meat is tender. Meanwhile, melt the butter in a small saucepan. Add the almonds and cook until dark brown.
At serving time stir the almonds into stew along with the mushrooms and their liquid and the drained cherries. Simmer about 10 minutes or until bubbling hot. Blend in sour cream and serve at once.
Serve with: buttered noodles or steamed rice with chopped parsley; green salad.

Linda Cogdill Winner (Mrs. Dennis)

FLANK STEAK DERVISH

Must do ahead
Serves: 8

2 to 2-1/2 lbs. flank steak
1/2 cup soy sauce
2-1/2 Tablespoons brown sugar
2 Tablespoons lemon juice
1 teaspoon ground ginger
1/2 teaspoon garlic salt

Trim all fat from 2 to 2-1/2 lbs. flank steak; score the steak on both sides with a sharp knife. Put in a shallow baking pan; pour over it a mixture of 1/2 cup soy sauce, 2-1/2 tablespoons brown sugar, 2 tablespoons lemon juice, 1 teaspoon ground ginger and 1/2 teaspoon garlic salt. Chill the steak in the marinade overnight, turning occasionally. Drain the marinade from the meat and broil 5 minutes on each side for rare beef. Sprinkle the meat with salt and pepper to taste. Slice steaks diagonally across the grain. Serve.

Diana Roscoe Bilbrey (Mrs. George)

GROUND MEAT PIE

Serves: 4-6
Baking Time: 25 minutes

3-1/2 oz. butter or margarine
1 cup flour
3-1/2 oz. cottage cheese
1 lb. ground meat
1 Tablespoon butter or
    margarine
1 (16 oz.) can of tomatoes
1 Tablespoon tomato paste
Salt and pepper
1 teaspoon soy sauce
1/2 teaspoon basil
1/2 teaspoon oregano
3-4 tomatoes
8 slices of cheese

With a pastry cutter, cut together butter and flour; add cottage cheese and blend together. Let the dough rest in a plastic bag in the refrigerator for an hour. Saute ground meat in butter until brown; add soy sauce, tomato paste and the can of tomatoes. Salt and pepper to taste and let simmer for about 10 minutes. Stir in basil and oregano and let the meat filling cool off a bit. Turn oven on to 425° (200°-225°C.) Roll out the dough thin and a little bit bigger than the pie plate so that the dough can be folded over the filling a bit. Put the dough in pie plate and spread the meat filling. (I use a French-made pie plate that is 28 cm in diameter or 10-3/4.") Cover with a layer of cheese slices and on top of that a layer of tomatoes; put on the rest of cheese slices. Fold over dough edges and brush with a whipped egg if you wish and have one on hand. Bake about 25 minutes and serve with a salad.

Yvonne Eriksson Day (Mrs. James K. M.)

BEEF BROCCOLI PIE
Great!

Can do ahead
Can freeze
Serves: 6
Preparation: 30 minutes
Baking Time: 40 minutes

1 lb. ground beef
1/4 cup chopped onion
2 Tablespoons all-purpose flour
3/4 teaspoon salt
1/4 teaspoon garlic salt
1-1/4 cups milk
1 3-oz. pkg. cream cheese,
    softened
1 egg, beaten
1 10-oz. pkg. frozen chopped
    broccoli, cooked and well
    drained
2 pkgs. refrigerated crescent
    rolls
4 oz. Monterey Jack cheese
Milk

In skillet, brown beef and onion; drain off fat. Stir in flour, salt and garlic salt. Add milk and cream cheese; cook and stir until mixture is thickened and smooth. Add a moderate amount of hot mixture to beaten egg; return to mixture in skillet. Cook and stir over medium heat for 1-2 minutes or until thick. Stir in well-drained broccoli. Unroll one package of crescent rolls. On floured surface, place the 4 sections of dough together, forming a 12x7" rectangle. Seal edges and perforations together. Roll to a 12" square. Fit into 9" pie plate; trim. Spoon meat mixture into shell. Cut Monterey Jack cheese in slices; arrange atop meat mixture. Roll second package of rolls to 12" square as before. Place atop filling. Trim and seal edges with fork; cut slits for escape of steam. Brush top of pie with a little milk. Bake in 350° oven for 40 minutes. If pastry browns too quickly, cover with foil the last 20 minutes. Let stand 10 minutes before serving.

Ann McBride Gray (Mrs. Robert F.)

CHAMPINE'S CHOP SUEY

Can do ahead
Can freeze
Serves: 8

1-1/2 lbs. ground beef
1 medium onion, chopped
1 cup celery, chopped in
    1/4" pieces
1 No. 2-1/2 can tomatoes
1 8-oz. can tomato sauce
1 can kidney beans, partially
    drained
1 can mushroom pieces,
    drained
1 can water chestnuts, drained
    and sliced
Salt, pepper, garlic salt —
    to taste

Brown onion and ground beef in large skillet. Add celery, tomatoes, tomato sauce, salt, pepper and garlic salt; simmer 30 minutes. Add kidney beans, mushrooms and water chestnuts; simmer 10-15 minutes.
Serve with Chinese noodles or rice.

Suzanne Champine Byron (Mrs. Robert)

HOMEMADE SALAMI

Must do ahead
Can freeze
Yield: 5-6 1-1/2" round
Preparation: 4 days
Baking Time: 8 hours

5 lbs. raw hamburger (high
    fat content)
5 rounded teaspoons of curing
    salt (can also use regular
    table salt)
3-1/2 teaspoons mustard seed
1-1/2 teaspoons black pepper
3-1/2 teaspoons garlic salt
2 teaspoons hickory smoke salt

First Day: Mix all ingredients; cover and refrigerate.
Second Day: Mix well again; cover and refrigerate.
Third Day: Repeat.
Fourth Day: Mix and form into 1-1/2" round logs — about 6 inches long.
Place on broiler pan in oven. Bake 8 hours at 200° Turn every 2 hours.
Serve with crackers and cheese.

Carolyn Roberts Smith

LAMB EN BROCHETTE

Must do ahead

2-1/2 lbs. lean lamb, cut
   in 1" cubes
1 cup oil
1/2 cup lemon juice
1/2 cup dry Vermouth
2 teaspoons salt
Pepper
1 clove garlic, pressed
1 bay leaf
2 Tablespoons chopped parsley

Combine all ingredients and marinate overnight, or at least 6 hours. Thread lamb on skewers and broil for 10-15 minutes, basting frequently. Lamb should be pink in center.
Serve on a bed of rice, cooked according to package directions and buttered well.

Celine Hanan Lurey (Mrs. Michael)

BEST LAMB I EVER TASTED

Must do ahead
Baking Time: 20 minutes

Ask butcher to butterfly a 7 lb.
   leg of lamb which should
   serve up to 12 or 14
Marinate overnight in:
3-4 Tablespoons olive oil
2 Tablespoons soy sauce
Lemon juice
1/2 teaspoon rosemary
2 cloves garlic, pureed

Rub unboned side of lamb with olive oil and place oiled side down in a baking pan. Rub other side with marinade; cover.
Roast marinated lamb flat, boned side up in middle of pre-heated 375° oven for 20 minutes. Do not turn to other side. Push 2 skewers lengthwise through meat to secure; then baste with more olive oil and broil for 2 to 3 minutes under pre-heated broiler until browned. Allow to sit at least 10 minutes to reabsorb juices before carving. Serve with spiced onions, bernaise sauce or mint jelly, along with Pita triangles.
TO CARVE: Start at small ends and make longish slices, angling knife as you would for flank steak.

Henny Hohlt Steinfeld (Mrs. John R.)

CURRIED LAMB
A good way to use leftover leg of lamb

Serves: 4

2 cups cold cooked lamb
3 Tablespoons butter
1/2 medium onion, diced
1 clove garlic, pressed
1/2 apple, unpeeled
2 stalks celery
2 Tablespoons flour
1 teaspoon salt
2 Tablespoons curry powder
2 cups lamb stock (I use beef
    or chicken bouillon cubes)

Cut fat away from lamb. Melt butter in saucepan; add onion, garlic, apple and celery. Cook until yellowed. Add flour, salt and curry powder. Cook for 1-2 minutes. Add lamb stock or bouillon cubes. Stir until mixture boils and thickens slightly. (Can be done ahead to this point.)
Add lamb. Simmer 10 minutes. Serve over rice. Pass any or all of the following condiments: Chutney, crumbled bacon, chopped hard-boiled eggs, peanuts or almonds, coconut, diced celery, diced green pepper, mandarin orange slices, raisins.

Kathleen Fairburn Armstrong (Mrs. Robert)

VEAL ROLLS

Baking Time: 20-30 minutes

16 small scallions (with root
    ends and green stems
    removed, washed
    thoroughly)
2 lbs. veal cutlets cut into 16
    even slices
8 slices Prosciutto ham, very
    thin
2 6-oz. pkgs. meunster cheese
    cut into 16 pieces
1/2 lb. butter, clarified
1 2/3 cups sweet Vermouth
1 Tablespoon parsley, chopped

Spread cutlets out on wax paper—cover with another sheet of wax paper and pound until very thin. Place 1/2 slice Prosciutto on each cutlet piece. Top with cheese slice and one scallion. Roll up slice and tie with string. Place clarified butter in frying pan and heat to sizzling. Add rolls and brown quickly on all sides. Remove. Put rolls in baking dish. Add vermouth to pan drippings and stir to mix well. Pour liquid from pan over the veal rolls. Place in 350° oven and bake 20-30 minutes; baste occasionally. Remove string and sprinkle with parsley.
Serve with hot madrilene with lemon slice, zucchini with mustard hollandaise, beef and endive salad and lemon chiffon pie.

Jean Moffat Frady (Mrs. A. Hampton, Jr.)

SWEET AND SOUR PORK WITH VEGETABLES

Serves:4
Preparation: 30 minutes
Baking Time: 15-20 minutes

1 lb. pork, cut into 1" cubes

MARINADE:

1 Tablespoon wine
2 Tablespoons soy sauce
1 teaspoon minced ginger
1 clove garlic, mashed
1/2 teaspoon Accent

BATTER:

2 egg yolks or 1 egg
4 Tablespoons cornstarch

SAUCE:

6 Tablespoons sugar
2 Tablespoons soy sauce
1 Tablespoon wine
3 Tablespoons vinegar
1/2 cup pineapple juice
3 Tablespoons catsup
1/2 cup water
2 Tablespoons cornstarch

VEGETABLE MIXTURE:

1/2 cup green pepper in
1" squares
1/2 cup carrots, cut on diagonal
1/2 cup bamboo shoots
1/2 cup pineapple slices,
quartered
1/2 cup chopped onion
1/4 teaspoon Accent
1/4 teaspoon salt

Soak meat in marinade 2-3 hours or overnight. Mix egg yolks or egg and cornstarch well. Add additional cornstarch if necessary to achieve a stiff batter. Drain meat well and combine with batter. Deep fry at 420° in wok until crisp and golden brown. Turn out on platter.

Combine sugar, soy, wine, vinegar, pineapple juice, catsup and bring to boil. Mix cornstarch and water. Add to boiling ingredients and stir until thick.

Fry vegetable mixture in 6 tablespoons oil at 420° in wok for a few minutes or just until vegetables take on transparent appearance. Add sauce and blend. Add meat; combine well and serve.

Nancy Reid Graham (Mrs. Frank P.)

SWEET AND SPICY PORK ROAST

Serves: 8

*Have butcher bone, roll and tie
about a 5 lb. center cut pork
loin roast*

BASTING SAUCE:

*1/2 cup orange marmalade
1 14-oz. jar applesauce
1 teaspoon table mustard
1/2 teaspoon cinnamon*

Cook at 325° about 20-25 minutes per pound. Baste roast 2 or 3 times during last hour of baking. When meat thermometer reads 175° the pork is done. Allow to sit 20 minutes before carving.

Anne Hirzel Rector (Mrs. Frederick)

GLAZED PORK CHOPS

Serves: 4

*8 loin pork chops, 1" thick
1/4 teaspoon salt
1/8 teaspoon pepper
1/2 cup white wine*

GLAZE:

*4 oz. Guyere cheese, finely
grated
2 Tablespoons Dijon mustard
3 Tablespoons heavy cream*

Brown chops quickly on both sides; sprinkle with salt and pepper. Add wine; cover and simmer 40 minutes. Cream together glaze ingredients until smooth. Place chops in broiler pan. Spread tops with glaze and broil 3" from heat for 3 minutes until glaze is browned.

Henny Hohlt Steinfeld (Mrs. John R.)

HAM SALAD CASSEROLE

Serves: 6-8

*2 cups chopped ham
2 cups chopped celery
1/3 cup chopped green pepper
2 Tablespoons grated onion
1 cup almonds or pecans
1 cup mayonnaise
1 cup grated Cheddar cheese
Ritz crackers*

Mix first 6 ingredients and put in lightly-buttered casserole; top with cheese. Bake in 350° oven until cheese melts and casserole is bubbly. Crumble Ritz crackers on top. Return to oven 1 minute.

Susan Murray Daniel (Mrs. John)

174

HAM AND ARTICHOKE CASSEROLE

Can do ahead
Serves: 6
Preparation: 30 minutes
Baking Time: 25-30 minutes

4 Tablespoons butter
4 Tablespoons all-purpose flour
2 cups warm milk
Generous dash seasoned salt
Generous dash cayenne pepper
1/4 teaspoon nutmeg
Paprika
Pinch white pepper
2/3 cup shredded Swiss and
    Parmesan cheese mixed
4 Tablespoons dry Sherry
2 (1 lb.) cans artichoke hearts,
    drained
12 thin slices boiled or baked
    ham

TOPPING:

2/3 cup buttered bread crumbs
2/3 cup shredded Swiss and
    Parmesan cheese mixed

Melt butter in saucepan over medium heat; blend in flour. When smooth, remove from heat. Gradually stir in warm milk; when smooth, return to heat. Stir constantly until thickened. Add seasonings, then cheese. Stir over low heat until melted. Remove from heat; stir in sherry.

If artichoke hearts are large, cut in half and wrap 2 halves in a slice of ham, allowing 2 rolls per person. Arrange in buttered casserole with sides touching; pour sauce over all. Sprinkle with topping and bake at 350° for 25 to 30 minutes until brown and bubbly.

Carol Ingram Matthews (Mrs. William)

LIVER AND BACON BAKE

Serves: 4
Baking Time: 25 minutes

6 slices bacon, chopped
1 cup chopped onion
1/4 cup flour
1 teaspoon salt
Dash pepper
1 lb. beef liver, cut in serving
    pieces
1-1/2 cups milk
1/4 cup bread crumbs
1 Tablespoon melted butter

Combine bacon and onion in skillet—cook until bacon is crisp and onion tender. Remove. Reserve drippings in skillet. Combine flour, salt, pepper. Coat liver in flour mixture. Reserve remaining flour mixture. Brown liver in bacon drippings. Remove liver to baking dish. Blend flour mixture with drippings in skillet until smooth. Add milk. Cook and stir until thick and bubbly. Pour over liver. Sprinkle with bacon and onion. Combine crumbs and melted butter. Sprinkle on top. Bake uncovered in 350° oven for 25 minutes.

Bea Smolka Russell (Mrs. Jeffrey)

GOURMET CASSEROLE
Nice for brunch

Can do ahead
Can freeze
Serves: 6-8
Baking Time: 45-60 minutes

2 lbs. bulk pork sausage
1/2 cup onion, chopped
1/3 cup green pepper, chopped
1 can (10-1/2 oz.) cream of
   mushroom soup
3/4 cup milk
1/2 cup shredded American
   cheese
1 3-oz. can sliced mushrooms,
   undrained
1 2-oz. jar sliced pimento,
   drained
2 cups cooked wild rice
2 cups cooked white rice

Heat oven to 350.° Shape sausage into 1-1/2″
balls. Brown well on all sides in skillet. Cover
and cook 10 minutes. Remove balls and drain
on paper towels. Combine with remaining ingredients. Pour into two-quart casserole. Cover and
bake 45 minutes to one hour, or until center
bubbles. Stir before serving. Garnish casserole
with thin green pepper rings, if desired.
Serve with: tossed salad; white wine, peach
with chutney.

Nancy Sauer Crosby (Mrs. E. Brown)

SUNDAY SAUSAGE

Baking Time: 40 minutes

1 lb. mild sausage
1/2 lb. hot sausage
2 envelopes Lipton chicken
   noodle soup
1 cup minute rice
2 cups boiling water
1 bell pepper
2 cups celery, chopped
1/2 onion
1 small can pimentos
1/2 teaspoon salt
1 small can water chestnuts,
   sliced thin

Break the sausage and cook until the red is out.
Drain and keep 2 tablespoons of the grease;
saute vegetables. Mix both envelopes of the soup
and 1 cup rice in a bowl and pour the boiling
water over it. Let stand. In a few minutes when
the rice is ready, add the other ingredients to rice
mixture. Pour into casserole. Bake in 350° oven
about 40 minutes.

Susan Lee Drenning (Mrs. Dennis)

CORNED BEEF CASSEROLE

Can do ahead
Baking Time: 25-30 minutes

4 or 5 slices rye bread, spread
    with mustard and cubed
12 oz. corned beef, or about
    2 cups
1 16-oz. can sauerkraut,
    chopped
1 10-oz. can condensed tomato
    soup
1/4 cup water and 3 Table-
    spoons sweet pickle relish
5 slices Swiss cheese

Layer the bread cubes in a 9x9 casserole. Crumble corned beef over bread. Stir together sauerkraut, tomato soup, water and spread over corned beef. Bake uncovered for 25 minutes in 375° oven. Arrange Swiss cheese on top. Heat 5 minutes more and cut into squares.

Mrs. James H. Glenn

SAUSAGE CASSEROLE

Can be done ahead
Serves: 10-12
Preparation: 20-30 minutes
Baking Time: 60 minutes

2 pkgs. (1 lb. each) sausage,
    mild or hot
2 large onions
1 stalk celery
1 green pepper
2 cups uncooked rice
2 pkgs. Lipton dry chicken
    noodle soup
1-1/2 cups slivered almonds

Crumble and fry sausage until slightly brown. Drain on paper towels. Pour off 1/3 of the drippings. Add cut up onions, celery, pepper and rice. Brown slightly. Prepare soup as directed. Combine all ingredients and add slivered almonds last. Pour in large casserole and cook covered at 350° stirring 3 times while baking. Serve with crisp green salad or crisp green beans.

Jeanne Forsyth Powell (Mrs. Benjamin)

DINNER IN A CRUST

Freezes well
Yield: 2 9-inch pies

1-1/2 lbs. ground beef
3/4 cup chopped onion
1/3 cup chopped celery
1 Tablespoon melted shortening
1 (8 oz.) can tomato sauce
1/2 cup corn flake crumbs
2 teaspoons salt
1-1/2 teaspoons whole oregano
1 Tablespoon Worcestershire
    sauce
Dash of pepper
2 eggs, beaten
2 unbaked 9" pastry shells
6 slices American cheese
Optional: 12 tomato slices

Cook beef, onion and celery in shortening, stir-ring to crumble beef; drain off drippings. Stir in next 7 ingredients and spoon into pastry shells. Bake at 400° for 25 minutes. Cut cheese in half diagonally, and arrange 6 halves on each pie; return to oven 5 minutes or until cheese melts. Top pies with tomato slices.

Helen King Turner (Mrs. Frank)

BEEF TENDERLOIN MARINADE

Must do ahead
Serves: 6-8

1 stick butter
1/2 cup olive oil
1/4 cup vinegar
Juice of 2 lemons
2 heaping Tablespoons sugar
Salt and garlic powder
Crushed red pepper
3 Tablespoons dried parsley
    flakes
2 Tablespoons Worcestershire
    sauce

Combine marinade ingredients in saucepan and bring to boil. Pour over the tenderloin and marinate at least 2 hours but preferably 24 hours. Broil whole tenderloin about 10 minutes per side.

Elizabeth Glenn Biggers (Mrs. Carl)

Rice,
Pasta,
Eggs & Cheese

CHEESE PUDDING

Do ahead
Serves: 6-8
Baking Time: 20-30 minutes

3 cups or more grated cheese
(about 1 lb.)
(I prefer sharp)
9 slices white bread (crusts
removed, spread lightly
with softened butter)
4 eggs
2 cups milk
1 teaspoon salt
1 teaspoon dry mustard
Dash of Worcestershire
Dash of Tabasco

Butter casserole. Tear bread into small pieces, and place layer of bread, then layer of cheese (cheese should be on top.) Mix dry ingredients. (Make paste with a small amount of the milk.) Beat eggs, add milk and dry mustard, and mix well. Pour over cheese and bread. Cover and refrigerate for several hours (even overnight). Remove from refrigerator 1 hour before baking in 350° oven for 20-30 minutes until firm. Serve as soon as possible.

Adelene Barnett Watts (Mrs. Walter M., Jr.)

EASY EGGS FLORENTINE
Great for a bunch! Colorful

Serves: 8
Preparation: 30-40 minutes
Baking Time: 12 minutes

3 pkgs. frozen Stouffer's
Spinach Souffle (cooked
3/4 of time stated on
package)
16 3x3" slices of thinly sliced
baked ham
8 English muffins, halved
and buttered
16 eggs, poached
2 cans Cheddar cheese soup
1 can cream of mushroom soup
Small spinach leaves or
watercress leaves for garnish

Arrange sliced, buttered English muffins, halved, on an oven-proof baking platter. Brown the muffins very slightly. Add a slice of ham to each muffin half and a tablespoon of the partially-cooked spinach souffle. Poach eggs and place one on each prepared muffin. Add mixture of undiluted Cheddar cheese soup and mushroom soup over the egg and muffin arrangement. Bake in a preheated 250° oven for 12 minutes. Serve in the baking dish, undisturbed, garnished with spinach or watercess leaves and a grinding of fresh black pepper.

Carl Biggers

WILD RICE, SAUSAGE AND EGG CASSEROLE

Do ahead
Serves: 12
Baking time: 45 minutes

1 lb. hot sausage
1 box wild rice
1/4 lb. grated sharp cheese
8 eggs, well beaten
2 cups milk
1 teaspoon salt and pepper
Dash Worcestershire sauce

Fry sausage until done, not brown. Drain. Mix rice and seasonings, add to sausage. Place in bottom of lasagne dish or casserole. Sprinkle cheese over sausage mixture. Beat eggs, salt, pepper and Worcestershire sauce. Pour over mixture. Let stand overnight in refrigerator, covered. Bake uncovered in 300° oven for 45 minutes.

Sherry Snipes Harbin (Mrs. Thomas)

LAYERED CHEESE SOUFFLE

Must do ahead
Serves: 8-10
Baking Time: Approximately 60 minutes

10 slices slightly stale thin,
  white bread
6 eggs, beaten
2 cups milk
3/4 teaspoon salt
1 teaspoon dry mustard
1 teaspoon Worcestershire
2 cups sharp Cheddar cheese,
  grated
Optional: tuna, shrimp,
  crabmeat, or turkey slices
3 Tablespoons butter

Trim crusts off bread. Combine eggs, milk, salt, mustard and Worcestershire, beating well. Grease an 11x13" pan and alternate layers of bread and cheese, ending with bread. If seafood or poultry is used, add it to the cheese layer. Cover with the liquid mixture and refrigerate for 3-4 hours or overnight. Bring to room temperature; dot with butter and bake in a preheated 350° oven for about 1 hour.

Elaine Littlejohn Gennett (Mrs. Philip R.)

GRITS CASSEROLE

Serves: 6
Baking Time: 45 minutes

1 cup grits
1 stick butter
1 pkg. garlic cheese (or 8 oz.
  sharp Cheddar and 1
  teaspoon garlic powder)
2 beaten eggs
3/4 cup milk

Cook grits in 4-1/2 cups salted water. When done add butter, garlic cheese, eggs and milk. Stir until melted. Pour into greased casserole and sprinkle buttered bread crumbs on top. Bake 45 minutes (or until center is done) in 350° oven.

Nancy Young Hunnicutt (Mrs. Thomas B.)

GARLIC SPAGHETTI

Serves: 6-8

1 small box spaghetti, cooked
    and drained
1-1/2 cups mayonnaise, to
    which you add 2 garlic
    cloves, minced, salted
    and mashed
2 tomatoes, cut into
    small pieces
2 green peppers, cut into
    small pieces
1/3 cup chopped nuts
Generous sprinkling of
    Parmesan cheese
1 Tablespoon herb seasoning

Mix all ingedients. Keep warm in 200° oven until serving time, or serve at once.

Marlene Butcher Whitaker (Mrs. Gary)

SPAGHETTI CASSEROLE

Serves: 6-8
Baking Time: 25-30 minutes

8 oz. spaghetti, cooked al dente
1 lb. ground meat
1 Tablespoon butter or
    vegetable oil
1 onion, chopped
3/4 cup carrots, chopped
1/4 cup parsley, chopped
1 clove garlic, put through
    the garlic press
Salt and pepper
1 teaspoon oregano
2 Tablespoons tomato paste
1 can (16 oz.) whole tomatoes,
    reserve liquid
3/4 cup half and half cream
1/4 cup grated cheese

Cook spaghetti according to directions on the box. Saute ground meat in butter with onions, carrots, parsley and garlic. Add salt, pepper and oregano. When meat is browned, stir in tomato paste and the liquid from the tomatoes. Let simmer for about 5 minutes. Butter an oven-proof casserole dish with high sides and alternate layers of spaghetti and meat filling, making sure the last layer is spaghetti. Press down carefully the whole canned tomatoes into the dish. Salt and pepper and pour the cream over top and sprinkle with grated cheese. Put in a 400° oven until casserole has a nice brown color and is warm through...about 25-30 minutes.

Yvonne Eriksson Day (Mrs. James K. M.)

MEATLESS OR SPINACH LASAGNA

Baking Time: 30 minutes

TOMATO SAUCE:

1 (16-oz.) can whole tomatoes or
*   1 (8-oz.) can whole tomatoes*
*   and 1 (8-oz.) can tomato*
*   puree*
2 Tablespoons olive oil,
*   or butter*
1 cup chopped onion
1-1/2 cloves garlic, minced
1 bay leaf,
1 teaspoon Italian seasoning

CREAM OF WHEAT MIXTURE:

1-1/3 cups milk
1/8 teaspoon salt
2-1/2 teaspoons Cream of
*   Wheat (quick, not instant)*
1 egg, beaten
2 to 3 Tablespoons Parmesan
*   cheese*

SPINACH MIXTURE:

1 box frozen chopped spinach
*   (thawed and drained)*
2 Tablespoons butter, or olive oil
1/2 cup chopped onion
1/2 clove garlic, minced
1 egg, beaten
2 cups ricotta cheese

REMAINING INGREDIENTS:

9 cooked lasagna noodles
1 cup shredded mozzarella

For tomato sauce, saute the onions and garlic in oil or butter, and add remaining seasonings and tomatoes. Simmer.

For Cream of Wheat mixture: Heat milk and salt until boiling, gradually add Cream of Wheat after milk has begun to boil. Stir constantly to prevent sticking. Once mixture has returned to a boil, lower heat and cook for 2-1/2 minutes. Remove from heat, and add the beaten egg and Parmesan cheese. Stir until well blended.

For Spinach Mixture: Saute onion in butter or oil, and add garlic. Put spinach in pan with sauteed onion and heat slowly until spinach is dry. Remove from heat. Add beaten egg and ricotta cheese. Stir until well blended.

Preheat oven to 350°. Cover bottom of large casserole dish with 1/3 cup tomato mixture (just enough to cover bottom). Place 3 lasagna noodles over tomato mixture, cover with 1/2 spinach mixture and 1/3 cup mozzarella cheese. Cover with 3/4 cup tomato mixture, 3 noodles, cover with all of the farina mixture, 1/3 cup mozzarella cheese, 3/4 cup tomato mixture, 3 noodles, rest of spinach mixture, remaining tomato and cheese. Bake in a 350° oven for 30 minutes.

Margaret Alice Shaw

183

SPAGHETTI ROCKEFELLER

Serves: 4-6
Baking Time: 20 minutes

4 oz. cooked spaghetti
10-oz. pkg. frozen spinach,
   cooked and drained
1 beaten egg
1/2 cup sour cream
1/4 cup milk
2 Tablespoons grated
   Parmesan
2 teaspoons minced, dried onion
1/2 teaspoon salt
2 cups shredded Monterey
   Jack cheese

Combine egg, sour cream, milk, Parmesan cheese, minced onion, salt, and Monterey Jack cheese. Add spaghetti and spinach. Mix well. Sprinkle top with more grated Parmesan cheese. Bake 20 minutes in uncovered dish in 350° oven.

Marlene Butcher Whitaker (Mrs. Gary)

AMERICAN TOSTADAS

Many people have asked me for this recipe. It's very filling. Fun for large groups. Fun for two friends to do together for a group!

Must do ahead
Can freeze shells
Serves: 8-10

TOSTADA SHELLS:

3 cups all-purpose flour
2 Tablespoons paprika
3 heaping Tablespoons Crisco
Enough water to form a very
   stiff ball (1/4 to 1/2 cup)

TACO FILLING:

3 lbs. ground beef
1 large onion, chopped or
   1-1/2 cup
1 cup (1 pint) sliced green olives
1 can mushroom soup
1 can tomato sauce
1 can drained pinto beans
1 cup instant potato flakes

Mix all ingredients together for shells with hands until forms a stiff ball. Refrigerate 2 to 3 hours—up to 3 days—covered tightly. To make shells—roll out a portion of dough 3/8" thick. Cut with biscuit cutter on well-floured board. Roll small circles out as far as you can 4 to 5." They will be paper thin. Continue until all dough is rolled, frying some as you go so will not dry out.
Dry Fry First: Cook shell in ungreased skillet on medium high heat until puffed and brown lightly.
Deep Fry Second: In skillet in hot oil—turning to achieve a uniform golden brown. Drain and store in air-tight container. (May freeze up to one month.)
Note: Yield: 20-25 shells—these are also good with a la King and chipped beef. They are very light and fragile.

Continued...

Cook beef with onion until onion is tender and beef browned. Add olives. Add next 3 ingredients—stir occasionally; add potato flakes. Add 1 lb. of muenster or Monterey Jack cheese in chunks and stir until melted. Serve or refrigerate and heat on *low* later. Spoon over shells. Top with diced tomatoes, shredded lettuce tossed with vinegar.

Optional: More chopped onions, grated Cheddar; bottled taco sauce Texas Pete.

Serve with beer and margueritas and fresh fruit.

Karen Altizer Fields (Mrs. Jay, Jr.)

MANICOTTI AND MEAT TOMATO SAUCE

Serves: 6-8
Baking Time: 10-15 minutes

MEAT TOMATO SAUCE:

1 large onion, chopped
2 to 3 cloves garlic
Olive oil to cover bottom of pan
1 lb. chopped beef
2 (35-oz.) cans plum tomatoes
    (Italian style)
Salt and pepper, to taste
2 to 3 bay leaves
2 teaspoons basil
1 carrot

MANICOTTI SHELLS:

6 eggs
1-1/2 cups flour
1/4 teaspoon salt
1-1/2 cups water

FILLING:

2 eggs
2 lbs. ricotta
1 lb. mozzarella, cubed, grated
    or in slivers
1/2 to 3/4 cup grated Romano
    or Parmesan cheese
Salt and pepper
1 Tablespoon chopped parsley
    or basil

Saute the onion and garlic in oil until tender. Add chopped meat, saute until brown. Puree the tomatoes and add. Add salt, pepper, bay leaves, basil and scraped carrot. Simmer for about 3 hours.

Combine all ingredients for shells with electric beater, just until smooth. Let stand 30 minutes. Rub small frying pan with oil or put one drop of oil in pan. Pour about 2 tablespoons butter per shell into pan, tilting pan back and forth to spread evenly. Cook slowly one side (about 1 minute), flip and cook other side the same. Slide off pan onto workboard. Repeat procedure until batter is used. (Throw first crepe away). Allow shells to cool slightly before filling.

Blend all ingredients of filling together. Spread a tablespoon or two of filling on each shell, roll and close. Place manicotti side by side in a baking dish. Cover with meat tomato sauce and grated cheese. Bake in hot (400°) oven 10 to 15 minutes.

Molly Riggins Sandridge (Mrs. David A.)

PIZZA

Can do ahead
Yield: 3 12" pizzas or 4 10" (sauce)
1 12" crust

SAUCE: *(Make ahead*
if possible)

1 lb. bulk sausage
Cooking oil
1/2 green pepper, chopped
1 large onion, chopped
1 clove garlic, minced
1 large can tomatoes
Grated American cheese
Sliced mozzarella cheese
1 lb. ground beef
1 large can tomato paste
1 teaspoon oregano
1 teaspoon salt
1 teaspoon chili powder
1 teaspoon sweet basil
1 large can mushrooms,
    drained

CRUST FOR 1 PIZZA:

1/3 cup oil
2 cups flour
1 teaspoon baking powder
1 teaspoon salt
2/3 cup buttermilk

Cook sausage. Remove from pan and drain. In iron skillet heat enough oil to saute onion, green pepper and garlic. Cook until tender. Add ground beef and brown. Drain off most of liquid. Add tomatoes, tomato paste, spices and mushrooms. Simmer uncovered for 1 hour.
Crust: Add oil to flour, baking powder and salt. Blend until mixture resembles corn meal. Add buttermilk and blend. Roll out to fit a 12" round pan. Cook in 450° oven until done. Watch until crust turns golden brown. Cover baked crust with sauce and top with grated American cheese and sliced mozzarella cheese. Bake at 450° until cheeses melt. When serving, put bowls with anchovies, sausage, shrimp, black olives, chopped onion, etc. on table and let each guest make his own.

Helen Turner (Mrs. Franklin H., Jr.)

ORANGE-CELERY RICE

Serves: 10
Baking Time: 35 minutes

1-1/2 cups raw rice
6 Tablespoons butter
3/4 cup diced celery
1/2 teaspoon celery seed
Grated rind of 1 orange
Juice of 3 oranges
1 teaspoon salt
Optional: 4 spiced kumquats,
    julienne

Measure rice into a 1-1/2 quart casserole. Saute celery in butter. Stir in celery seed, rind, salt and orange juice and water combined to make 2-1/4 cups. About 35 minutes before serving, bring ingredients to a boil and pour over rice. Cover and bake 30 minutes in 350° oven. Stir in kumquats, fluff with fork and bake an additional 5 minutes.

Celine Hanan Lurey (Mrs. Michael)

GREEN RICE

Can do ahead
Serves: 6
Preparation: 15-20 minutes
Baking Time: 20 minutes

1 cup boiling water
1 (10-oz.) pkg. chopped broccoli
1 cup chopped celery
1/2 cup chopped onion
1/4 lb. margarine
1 (10-oz.) can cream of
   mushroom soup
1 (8-oz.) jar Cheez Whiz
2 cups cooked white rice

Pour boiling water over broccoli and cook 5 minutes. Drain. Saute onion and celery in margarine until just tender. Mix all ingredients together. Place in buttered casserole. Cover and bake 20 minutes in 375° oven. Serve with pork, chicken or ham.

Mary Bruce Rhodes Woody (Mrs. Stephen W.)

RICE PILAF

Can do ahead
Serves: 8
Preparation: 30 minutes
Baking Time: 45 minutes

3/4 cup butter
1 onion, chopped
1/2 lb. mushrooms, chopped
1 cup regular long-grained
   rice, uncooked
1 can beef consomme
1 can beef bouillon

Saute onions and mushrooms in butter. Combine this with rice and soups and boil 5 minutes. Transfer to medium-size casserole and bake for 45 minutes in 325° oven, covered.

Gay Woolard Coleman (Mrs. Stewart B.)

RICE SALAD

Must do ahead
Serves: 6-8

1 cup uncooked rice
6 Tablespoons salad oil
3 Tablespoons white wine or
   salad vinegar
1 teaspoon salt
Dash tarragon and pepper
1/2 cup green pepper, chopped
1/4 cup parsley
1/4 cup chopped onion
1 cup drained peas (canned)
1 small cucumber

Cook rice until tender. Combine oil, vinegar, salt, pepper and tarragon. Pour over hot rice. Cool. Fold in green pepper, parsley, onion and peas. Cover and refrigerate for at least four hours. At serving time, pare cucumber, cut into pieces and toss with rice mixture. Garnish with tomato slices and olives.

Bea Smolka Russell (Mrs. Jeffrey K.)

WILD RICE CASSEROLE

Serves: 8
Baking Time: 45-60 minutes

4 teaspoons butter or
    margarine
1/2 cup wild rice which has
    been soaked for at least 4
    hours and drained
1/2 cup white rice
1 can consomme soup
1-3/4 cup water
1 teaspoon salt
Pepper to taste
1/2 cup pimento, chopped
1/4 cup fresh or dried parsley,
    chopped
1/4 to 1/2 cup diced celery

Melt butter in skillet and add both kinds of rice. Saute gently 5 minutes or until browned. Heat consomme, water to boiling point. Add rest of ingredients. Pour into casserole with tight cover. Add rice. Bake in 350° oven for 45-60 minutes. Do not stir until ready to serve.

Suzanne Champine Byron (Mrs. Robert S.)

CREOLE EGG CASSEROLE

Can do ahead
Can freeze
Serves: 6
Baking Time: 15 minutes

8 eggs, hard-boiled
1 medium onion
1 small bell pepper
5 celery stalks
1 stick butter
1 can tomato soup
1 can mushroom soup
1 can sliced mushrooms
1 teaspoon chili powder
Dash of salt
Dash of Tabasco
Dash of Worcestershire sauce
Cracker crumbs
Grated sharp Cheddar cheese

Chop celery, onion, bell pepper and saute in stick of butter. Add tomato soup, simmer 20 minutes. Add mushrooms, mushroom soup, chili powder, salt, pepper, Tabasco, Worcestershire sauce. Simmer 5 minutes. Slice eggs and place in casserole. Cover with sauce, cracker crumbs, and grated cheese. Bake in hot oven at 450° for 15 minutes. Excellent with ham and hot fruit.

Sharon Snipes Harbin (Mrs. Thomas)

Hint:
When milk has slightly soured, add a pinch of soda and it can be used as fresh milk.

FARMERS OMELET

Serves: 2

4 slices bacon, cut in 1/2"
   pieces, cooked
2 Tablespoons butter
1 cup diced cooked potatoes
1/3 cup chopped onion
Salt and pepper, to taste
2 eggs per omelet
1 Tablespoon parsley

Melt butter; add potatoes. Saute until golden. Add bacon and onions, salt and pepper and parsley. Cook 3 to 5 minutes or until onion is soft. Put filling in an omelet. This is enough filling for two omelets.

Robyn Frankel Leslie (Mrs. William H.)

SICILY SANDWICH

Can be made ahead and frozen
Serves: 6
Preparation: 30 minutes
Baking Time: 45 minutes

12 slices of bread,
   crust removed
Margarine
6 Cheddar cheese slices
6 slices ham
2 cups milk
4 eggs
1 teaspoon salt
1 teaspoon paprika
SAUCE:

2 Tablespoons butter
2 Tablespoons flour
1-1/2 cups milk
1 can chopped asparagus
1 can sliced mushrooms

Spread butter or margarine on 6 slices of bread …put in casserole. Top each slice with 1 slice of ham and cheese. Put second piece of bread on top to form a sandwich. Mix milk, eggs, salt, and paprika; pour over sandwiches and refrigerate overnight. Bake for 45 minutes in 350° oven. Blend butter and flour in saucepan over medium heat. Add milk, mix until smooth and slightly thickened. Stir in drained asparagus and mushrooms. Serve over individual sandwiches.

Frances Smith Emrick (Mrs. Verl R., Jr.)

CHINESE MOLDS

Baking Time: 45 minutes

2 well-beaten eggs
1-1/4 cups milk
1 cup cooked rice
1 cup grated American cheese
1/2 teaspoon salt
1/8 teaspoon pepper

Mix well and turn into greased casserole or ring mold (sprayed with PAM or lined with waxed paper). Bake at 350° about 45 minutes or until knife inserted in center comes out clean. Good under creamed shrimp, crab or chicken.

Marian MacEachran Boggs (Mrs. Walter J.)

189

NOODLE KUGEL

Serves: 6
Baking Time: 65 minutes

1/2 lb. fine or medium noodles,
  cooked al dente
5 eggs, separated
1-1/4 cups sugar
1/2 pint sour cream
1 cup milk
8 oz. cottage cheese
8 oz. cream cheese
1 teaspoon vanilla
1 stick margarine, melted

Separate eggs. Beat egg yolks with sugar until thick, about 5 minutes. Add cream cheese, milk, sour cream, half of margarine and cottage cheese. Beat until mixed. Beat egg whites. Add first mixture to noodles. Add vanilla to mixture. Fold in whites. Grease pan with other half of margarine. Bake in 450° oven for 5 minutes, then 350° oven for 1 hour. Put cinnamon on top if desired. Cut when cool.

Jean Lipinsky Moore (Mrs. Michael)

BAKED ASPARAGUS CHEESE SANDWICHES

Can do ahead
Serves: 6
Baking Time: 35-40 minutes

6 thick slices of bread
6 slices of Swiss cheese
4 eggs
2 cups milk
1 teaspoon salt
1/8 teaspoon pepper
1/4 teaspoon nutmeg
1 Tablespoon finely
  chopped onion
18 cooked (canned) asparagus
  spears
1/2 cup shredded Cheddar
  cheese

Trim crusts from bread and arrange in bottom of 13x9x2" pan. Top each with a slice of Swiss cheese. Beat eggs slightly, add milk, seasonings and onion. Pour over sandwiches and bake in 325° oven for 25 minutes. Remove from oven, top each bread slice with 3 cooked asparagus spears, and sprinkle on shredded Cheddar cheese. Bake 10-15 minutes until custard sets and top is golden. Allow to stand 5 minutes before serving.

Carolyn Roberts Smith

FETTUCINI ST. AMBROSE

Serves: 4

1 onion
1 stalk celery
1 clove garlic
1/2 cup butter
1/2 cup white wine
Salt and pepper
1 cup heavy cream
1 Tablespoon tomato paste
12 oz. Ronzoni long fettucini
1 cup grated Parmesan cheese

Chop finely the onion, celery and garlic. Saute in butter over low heat until soft. Add wine (if using vermouth, cut amount to 1/3 cup) and cook over high heat until almost all liquid has evaporated. MAY BE PREPARED AHEAD TO THIS POINT. If prepared ahead, rewarm over low heat. Add the cream and tomato paste and stir until smooth. May be kept warm a short time. Cook pasta to the al dente stage in rapidly boiling, salted water. Drain thoroughly and combine with hot sauce. Serve immediately on hot plates, accompanied by a dish of freshly grated Parmesan cheese. Cheese may be combined with pasta and sauce in kitchen, if you prefer.

Celine Hanan Lurey (Mrs. Michael)

BROCCOLI FETTUCINE
A favorite meatless dish

Serves: 4
Preparation: 30 minutes

1 (8-oz.) pkg. medium noodles
  or spaghetti
1/4 cup oil
1 clove garlic, crushed
1 (10-oz.) pkg. frozen chopped
  broccoli, thawed
  and drained
1/2 cup canned condensed beef
  or chicken broth, undiluted
1/2 teaspoon basil
1/2 cup chopped parsley
1/4 cup grated Parmesan
  cheese
1 (8-oz.) carton cottage cheese
1/2 teaspoon salt
Dash of pepper

Cook noodles according to package directions. Drain. Saute garlic and broccoli in hot oil, stirring for 5 minutes. Add broth, basil, parsley, Parmesan cheese, cottage cheese, salt and pepper. Stir over low heat until blended. Toss broccoli mixture with noodles. Turn into heated serving dish.

Linda McFarland (Mrs. Edgar)

VEGETARIAN QUICHE

Serves: 6
Baking Time: 40 minutes

1 Tablespoon chopped chives
(or 1 small onion chopped)
1 unbaked, frozen deep-dish
pastry shell
1 cup sliced mushrooms
1 cup chopped green pepper
3/4 cup grated Swiss cheese
1/2 cup grated sharp
Cheddar cheese
3 eggs
1/2 cup milk
1/4 teaspoon nutmeg
1/2 teaspoon salt
Dash of pepper

Saute onions and green peppers. Add mushrooms for the last 1-2 minutes. Bake frozen pie shell 5-10 minutes at 450°. Fill shell with onions, green pepper, and mushrooms. Cover with cheese. Mix eggs, milk, nutmeg, salt and pepper, and pour mixture into pie shell. Bake for 10 minutes in 450° oven and then 30 minutes in 350° oven or until surface seems firm. Cool 5 minutes before serving.

Deborah Lynn Robinson

SPINACH QUICHE

Serves: 16
Baking Time: 30 minutes

2 9" pie shells partially baked
3 boxes frozen chopped spinach
3 Tablespoons chopped onion
6 Tablespoons butter
1 teaspoon salt (or more
to taste)
1/2 teaspoon freshly ground
black pepper (or more
to taste)
Nutmeg (at least 2
Tablespoons)
3 cups heavy cream
1/8 teaspoon pepper
1 cup grated Gruyere or
Swiss cheese
6 eggs

Cook spinach until barely tender and drain *well.* Saute onion in 4 tablespoons butter, until tender. Add spinach and stir over moderate heat for several minutes. Stir in salt, pepper, and nutmeg. Combine eggs, cream, pepper in large bowl; blend well. Add spinach and cheese. Add additional salt, pepper and nutmeg, if necessary. Pour mixture into pie shells. Dot with remaining butter. Bake in upper third of oven at 375° for 30 minutes.

Joyce Lichtenfels Cole

CREPES BOMBAY

Serves: 6

CREPES:

1/2 cup milk
1/2 cup beer
3 eggs
1 cup flour
3 Tablespoons butter, melted

FILLING:

2 Tablespoons vegetable oil
2 yellow onions, chopped
1 green pepper, cleaned and
  chopped
Salt and pepper
1-1/2 Tablespoons
  curry powder
2 Tablespoons flour
1 can chicken broth
1 can water
1/2 cup white, seedless raisins
1 lb. cleaned, whole raw shrimp

Put all the ingredients for crepes into a blender and blend well. Let the batter rest for at least 30 minutes. Take a crepe pan or small skillet and put a little butter in it. When very hot, wipe the pan with a paper towel so all excess fat is gone. Pour some of the batter in, making sure there is just enough to cover the bottom. Leave the crepe until it gets lightly brown on the edges, then turn over and leave for a couple of seconds more. Place the crepes on a piece of waxed paper. Continue until you have made 12 crepes. Filling: Heat the vegetable oil in a heavy sauce pan. Add the onions and brown them lightly, then add the pepper. Continue to saute for 2 minutes; then add the salt and pepper, curry powder and flour. Combine all ingredients well and add the chicken broth, water and raisins. Bring to a boil and simmer over low heat for about 30 minutes. Add the shrimp; keep the heat low and simmer for another 5 minutes. Fill each crepe with the shrimp mixture and roll them up. Pour the rest of the sauce over the crepes and sprinkle with some chopped parsley.

Joyce Lichtenfels Cole

AUNT NENNIE'S PINEAPPLE AND CHEESE CASSEROLE

Serves: 6
Baking time: 30 minutes

1 can pineapple chunks,
  unsweetened, drained
1 stick margarine
3/4 cup sugar
3 Tablespoons flour
1 cup grated sharp Cheddar
  cheese
3/4 sleeve Ritz crackers,
  crushed (about 25)

Melt margarine; add Ritz crackers. Place pineapple in casserole dish. Mix sugar, flour and cheese. Pour over pineapple. Cover top with crackers. Bake in 350° oven until slightly brown, for 30 minutes. Serve warm.

Reid Stratton Chapman (Mrs. James E.)

MACARONI MOUSSE

Serves: 4
Baking Time: 50 minutes

1 cup macaroni, broken in
   2" pieces
1-1/2 cups scalded milk
1 cup soft bread crumbs
1/4 cup melted butter
1 pimento, chopped
1 Tablespoon parsley, chopped
1 Tablespoon onion, chopped
1-1/2 cups cheese, grated
3/8 teaspoon salt
1/8 teaspoon pepper
Dash of paprika
3 eggs

MUSHROOM SAUCE:

1/4 cup butter
1 pint chicken broth
2 egg yolks
1/4 cup flour
1/4 cup cream or milk
1 teaspoon lemon juice
1 teaspoon parsley, chopped
1/2 lb. mushrooms
Salt and pepper, to taste

Cook the macaroni in boiling, salted water. Blanch in cold water and drain. Pour the scalded milk over the bread crumbs, add the butter, pimento, parsley, onion, grated cheese and seasonings. Add the well-beaten eggs. Put the macaroni in a thickly-buttered loaf pan and pour the milk and cheese mixture over it. Bake about 50 minutes in slow oven, or until the loaf is firm and will hold its shape when turned out onto a platter. Serve with mushroom sauce.

For sauce: Brown mushrooms in butter. Make smooth paste of broth and flour. Add to mushrooms. Mix beaten egg yolks with cream and mix with the remaining. Cook gently until the egg yolks are cooked.

Helen King Turner (Mrs. Franklin H., Jr.)

BARLEY CASSEROLE

Can do ahead
Serves: 8-10
Preparation: 20 minutes
Baking time: 60 minutes

1 cup (smallest) barley
1/2 cup butter
3 cups chicken stock (can use 1
   can chicken broth and water
   to make 3 cups)
1 large can chopped
   mushrooms, drained
1 can water chestnuts, drained
   and sliced
1/2 cup sliced almonds
1 teaspoon salt
3 Tablespoons dried parsley

Saute barley in butter until light brown. Add chicken stock and all other ingredients. Put in three-quart casserole. Cover and bake 1 hour in 350° oven, stirring occasionally. If too moist, remove cover and bake a little longer.
Serve with beef or chicken.

Betsy Rawleigh Simons (Mrs. William J.)

194

Vegetables

VEGETABLE TIPS

To retain nutrients, cook vegetables just until done—do not overcook. Also the less water used for cooking, the better; steaming recommended. Save broth from steamed or cooked vegetables for soups, gravy or to drink. *Or* feed this mineral-rich liquid to your houseplants—they will flourish!

Cook vegetables in chicken stock, beef stock or consomme for flavor variation.

To prevent crying while peeling onions, hold two matches, striking end out, in your teeth while peeling. Or try holding a stainless spoon in your mouth. It works!

Fresh parsley stays fresh longest stored in a screw-top jar in the refrigerator.

Use twice the amount of fresh herbs when substituting for dried herbs.

Store mushrooms in a brown paper bag in the refrigerator.

A little lemon juice added to sauteeing mushrooms helps prevent discoloration.

One-half teaspoon cream of tartar added while cooking vegetables makes their color brilliant.

Peel tomatoes easily by placing them in boiling water for a few seconds.

To remove vegetable stains, rub hands with lemon or raw potatoes.

As a general rule, vegetables grown underground should be covered for cooking; those grown above, should be cooked uncovered.

ARTICHOKES DEDE

Serves: 6
Preparation: 30 minutes
Baking Time: 1-1/2 hours

2 10-oz. pkgs. frozen artichoke
   hearts
1-1/2 cup chicken bouillon
1/4 cup white wine vinegar
1/2 cup vermouth
1 bay leaf
1/8 teaspoon thyme
4 sprigs parsley, chopped
Juice of 1 lemon
2 Tablespoons olive oil
Garlic salt and black pepper
   to taste

Combine all ingredients. Bake in 300° oven for 1-1/2 hours to evaporate most of the liquid. Remove bay leaf and serve.

Jean Moffat Frady (Mrs. A. Hampton, Jr.)

ASPARAGUS CASSEROLE

Can do ahead
Serves: 4
Preparation: 25 minutes
Baking Time: 20 minutes

1-1/2 Tablespoons butter
1-1/2 Tablespoons flour
1-1/2 cup hot milk
1/2 cup sharp grated cheese
1 can green asparagus spears
2 or 3 sliced, hard-cooked eggs
1/4 cup blanched slivered
*   toasted almonds*
Salt to taste

Make white sauce with first three ingredients. Add grated cheese; mix well. In a one-quart casserole arrange as follows in two layers: asparagus, sliced eggs, almonds. Pour sauce over all. Heat in 325° oven until bubbly (20 minutes.)

Mary Burhoe Gillam (Mrs. T. S.)

BARBEQUED BEANS

Can do ahead
Can freeze
Serves: 8-10
Preparation: 20 minutes
Baking Time: 1-1/2-2 hours

4 Tablespoons bacon drippings
3 medium onions, chopped
1 clove garlic, minced
1 can kidney beans (16 oz.),
*   drained*
1 can lima beans (15 oz.),
*   drained*
1 can pork and beans (16 oz.),
*   undrained*
1/2 cup brown sugar
1/2 cup catsup
1/4 cup vinegar
1 teaspoon salt
1/2 teaspoon black pepper

Saute onions and garlic in bacon drippings until soft. Combine beans. Add onions and remaining ingredients, mixing well. Pour into casserole and bake at 350° for 1-1/2 to 2 hours.

Sarah Greene Hensley (Mrs. Donald)

BLACK BEANS AND RICE

Must do ahead

1 lb. dried black beans
2-1/4 (approximately) cups
  water
2 Tablespoons butter or
  margarine
2 medium onions, chopped
2 cloves garlic, crushed
2 bay leaves
1/2 cup chopped green pepper
1 teaspoon ground cumin
3-1/2 cups beef broth
1 Tablespoon cider vinegar
1 teaspoon salt
1/8 teaspoon hot pepper sauce
3 cups hot, cooked yellow rice

Wash beans, discarding bad ones. Drain and place in large saucepan. Soak overnight in 2 and 1/4 cups water. (For quick-soak method, combine beans and 6 cups water; heat to boiling and boil 2 minutes. Cover and let stand 1 hour.) Drain beans, reserving soaking liquid. Melt butter in large saucepan and add next 5 ingredients, sautéing until onions are tender (3-5 minutes). Stir in beans and cook 3 minutes more. Pour in beef broth and 1 cup reserved soaking liquid. Simmer, partially covered, over low heat until beans are tender (about 1-2 hours). Stir occasionally. During last 30 minutes of cooking, stir in vinegar, salt, and hot pepper sauce. Cook yellow rice according to directions. Serve beans over rice.

Becky Rhodarmer York (Mrs. A Robert)

TWO BEAN FRITTERS

Yield: 24 fritters

1 cup fresh green beans
1 cup fresh wax beans
1 cup flour
3 teaspoons baking powder
3/4 teaspoon salt
1 egg, beaten
1 cup milk

Cook green beans and wax beans, covered, in a small amount of boiling salted water, until tender (about 20 minutes). Drain thoroughly. Stir together flour, baking powder and salt. Combine egg, milk and beans. Add to dry ingredients. Mix just until moist. Drop batter by the tablespoonful into deep hot fat. Fry until golden brown (3-4 minutes).

Margaret Lee Haggard

SWISS GREEN BEAN CASSEROLE

Can be done 2 days ahead
Can freeze
Serves: 6
Preparation: 15 minutes
Baking Time: 30 minutes

1 Tablespoon margarine
1 teaspoon salt
1 teaspoon sugar
2 teaspoons flour
1/4 teaspoon pepper
2 Tablespoons grated onion
1 cup sour cream
4 oz. (1-1/4 cups grated)
    Swiss cheese
2 (10 oz.) pkgs. frozen French
    green beans
Buttered bread crumbs

Cook beans until almost done; drain. Melt margarine; stir in flour, salt, pepper, sugar and onions. Add sour cream; stir until thick. Fold in beans and cheese. Put into a 1-3/4 quart casserole dish. Top with buttered crumbs (1 cup herbed stuffing mix and three tablespoons melted margarine is a good topping.) Bake in 350° oven for 30 minutes.

Kitty Oldham Young (Mrs. Marion J.)

TULU'S SHREDDED BEETS WITH SOUR CREAM

Can do ahead
Use processor
Serves: 6
Preparation: 15 minutes
Baking time: 50 minutes

4 large fresh beets
Boiling water to cover
1 teaspoon onion juice
2 Tablespoons lemon juice
1/2 teaspoon salt
1 teaspoon sugar
1/2 cup sour cream

Wash beets and cut off tops, leaving 3 inches attached. (This prevents beets from bleeding so badly.) Place unpeeled in a saucepan with water to cover. Boil, covered 30-50 minutes (depending on size of beets). Drain, cool and slip off skins and stem end. Shred beets and combine with onion juice, lemon juice, salt and sugar. Toss lightly. Serve warm or cold, topped with sour cream.

Lelia Kincaid Cort (Mrs. John)

QUICK BROCCOLI OR CAULIFLOWER PIE

Can partially do ahead
Can reheat for leftovers
Can freeze after baking and reheat for serving later
Serves: 6
Preparation: 20 minutes
Baking Time: 35-40 minutes

1 (10 oz.) pkg. frozen chopped broccoli (or 2 cups fresh broccoli, chopped)
or
1 (10 oz.) pkg. frozen cauliflower (or 2 cups fresh cauliflower cut into florettes)
1/2 cup chopped green pepper
1/2 cup chopped onion
Optional: 1/2 cup or 1 (4 oz.) can sliced mushrooms
1 cup grated extra sharp Cheddar cheese or more, if preferred
3/4 cup Bisquick
1-1/2 cups milk
3 eggs
1 teaspoon salt
Optional: 1/4 teaspoon pepper

Lightly grease (or spray with PAM) a 10x1-1/2" pie plate. Preheat oven to 400.°
If using fresh broccoli or cauliflower, cook in boiling water about 5 minutes. If using frozen broccoli or cauliflower, do not cook; but thaw and drain.
Mix together broccoli (or cauliflower), onions, green pepper, mushrooms, salt and cheese. Place in pie plate. Beat together milk, Bisquick and eggs until smooth (may use blender or hand mixer). Pour over vegetable mixture in pie plate. Bake in 400° oven for 35 to 40 minutes until top of pie is brown, and knife inserted into center comes out clean.

Mary Beth Baldwin

GOURMET CABBAGE

Can do ahead
Can freeze
Serves: 8
Preparation: 25 minutes
Baking Time: 45 minutes

2 cans cream of mushroom soup
Saltine crackers
2 lb. cabbage, sliced and par-boiled in salted water
1 stick butter, sliced
Cayenne to taste

Layer cabbage, saltines, butter and soup. Repeat and sprinkle with cayenne pepper. Top with cracker crumbs. Bake in 350° oven for 45 minutes. Top with canned onion rings last 15 minutes of baking.

Mattie Thompkins

Hint:
A little vinegar added to the cooking water of cabbage will keep the odor down...

200

CRUNCHY BROCCOLI RICE CASSEROLE

Must do ahead
Can freeze
Serves: 6
Preparation: 30 minutes
Baking Time: 30 minutes

2 cups cooked rice
1 pkg. frozen broccoli chopped
or
1 pkg. frozen chopped spinach
1 large onion, chopped
1/2 can cream of chicken soup
(undiluted)
1/2 lb. Cheddar cheese, cut up
1 cup water chestnuts, sliced
1/2 cup milk
1 teaspoon salt
1/2 teaspoon pepper

Cook rice and broccoli. Sauté onion in butter. Combine rice, broccoli and onion with cheese (save some for the top), undiluted soup and chestnuts. Add milk and mix. Top with remaining cheese. Bake in greased one and a half quart casserole for 30 minutes in 350° oven. Serves 6. To serve 12, double all but the chestnuts and cheese.

Dorothy Jane Schafly Brown (Mrs. Elbert S.)

ANNIE'S CARROTS VINDOLÉE

Can do ahead
Serves: 4-5
Preparation: 15 minutes
Baking Time: 20-30 minutes

3 Tablespoons butter
4-6 pared, thinly sliced carrots
1 medium onion, thinly sliced
Inner heart of celery, including
leaves, chopped
3 Tablespoons sugar
1/2 teaspoon dillweed
1/3 cup dry white wine

Melt butter and add remaining ingredients. Heat over medium heat, stirring gently, until sugar dissolves. Cover and reduce heat to low. Simmer 20-30 minutes until carrots are crisp tender.

Lelia Kincaid Cort (Mrs. John)

BRANDIED CARROTS

Baking Time: 30 minutes

2 lbs. carrots, scraped and
sliced thinly
1/2 cup butter, melted
3/4 teaspoon sugar
1/2 teaspoon salt
1/4 cup Grand Marnier

Parboil carrots 10 minutes or until slightly tender. Place in large casserole in a thin layer. Combine butter, sugar, salt and liqueur. Pour over carrots. Cover and bake for 30 minutes in a 325° oven.

Molly Riggins Sandridge (Mrs. David A.)

CARROT RING MOLD

Can partially do ahead
Serves: 6
Baking Time: 45 minutes

1-1/2 sticks butter, softened
1/2 cup brown sugar
2 eggs, separated
1-1/2 cups finely grated raw
   carrots
1 teaspoon cold water
1 teaspoon fresh lemon juice
1 cup plain flour
1/2 teaspoon baking soda
1 teaspoon baking powder
1/2 teaspoon salt
Bread crumbs

If planning to serve soon after preparation, pre-heat oven to 450.° In mixer cream butter and brown sugar. Add egg yolks and beat until thick. Add carrots, water, lemon juice, flour, soda, baking powder and salt. Mix thoroughly.
*At this point, refrigerate mixture if planning to serve at a later date.
On day of serving, bring egg whites and mixture to room temperature and proceed as follows: Beat egg whites until stiff peaks form and fold into carrot mixture. Generously oil 1-1/2 quart ring mold and dust with bread crumbs. Turn mixture into mold. Bake for 45 minutes in 450° oven, or until firm.
Turn out onto serving dish. Fill center with stuffed mushrooms, peas, or other green vegetable.

Barrie Muilenburg Sneed (Mrs. Albert L.)

ZESTY CARROTS
Especially good with beef

Can do ahead
Serves: 4-6
Preparation: 15 minutes
Baking Time: 20-30 minutes

12 carrots
1 cup mayonnaise
1 Tablespoon horseradish
1 small onion, grated
1/2 cup buttered bread crumbs
Ritz cracker crumbs

Wash carrots and cut into strips. Parboil until crisp tender. Mix mayonnaise, horseradish, onion, and bread crumbs. Add cooled, drained carrots and mix. Place in 1 quart casserole and top with cracker crumbs. Bake at 350° for 20-30 minutes.

Sara Oliver Bissette (Mrs. W. Louis)

CURRY CAULIFLOWER
Good served with beef or chicken

Can do ahead
Can freeze
Serves: 6
Preparation: 1 hour
Baking Time: 30 minutes

1 medium to large head
   cauliflower
1 teaspoon curry powder
1 cup grated sharp Cheddar
   cheese (save 1/4 cup)
1 can cream of chicken soup
1/3 cup mayonnaise
Buttered bread (or cracker)
   crumbs

Break cauliflower from main stem into small pieces. Cook in boiling water 5 minutes with salt and pepper. Drain. Combine with curry, cheese, soup and mayonnaise and put in baking dish. Top casserole with 1/4 cup cheese and buttered crumbs. Bake at 350° for 30 minutes.

Becky Rhodarmer York (Mrs. A. Robert)

CORN FRITTERS

Do not do ahead
Serves: 6
Preparation: 15-20 minutes

Salad oil
2 eggs
1 16 oz. can whole corn, drained
1 cup flour
3/4 teaspoon salt
1 teaspoon baking powder
1/4 cup milk
Syrup or confectioners sugar

Heat one-half inch of oil in a skillet. In a bowl with a fork, stir one tablespoon of salad oil and next six ingredients. Drop by tablespoonful into hot oil. Fry 3-5 minutes. Serve with hot syrup or dusted with confectioners sugar.

Gail Southwood Golding (Mrs. James N.)

CREAMED CORN

Serves: 6

8 ears corn
1 cup milk, or half and half
1 teaspoon salt
Optional: 2 teaspoons sugar
1/8 teaspoon pepper
2 Tablespoons butter

Cut corn off cob, about two-thirds the depth of the kernel. Scrape cob to remove the remaining corn, but not any of the cob. (You'll have about 4 cups). Combine corn with milk, salt, sugar and pepper. Place in greased 1-1/2 quart casserole. Dot with butter. Bake in 350° oven until corn is tender (40-50 minutes). Serve in individual bowls or sauce dishes.

Ginny Allday Webb (Mrs. Charles A.)

EGGPLANT AND TOMATO CASSEROLE

Baking Time: 25 minutes

1/4 cup salad oil
1 medium onion, chopped
Optional: 3/4 lb. mushrooms,
    sliced
1/2 medium green pepper,
    chopped
1 medium eggplant, peeled and
    cut into 1 inch cubes
1 can (1 lb.) tomatoes
1 teaspoon salt
1 Tablespoon parsley
Pinch of basil and oregano
1 cup each, grated Parmesan
    and shredded mozarella
    cheeses
2 eggs, beaten

Saute onion in oil in large frying pan; add mushrooms and green pepper and saute until limp. Stir in eggplant, tomatoes, salt, parsley, basil and oregano. Cover and simmer until eggplant is tender, stirring often. Uncover and reduce liquid if necessary. Combine cheeses with eggs. Spoon half of eggplant mixture in 2-1/2 quart casserole and top with half of cheese mixture. Repeat.
Bake uncovered at 350° for 25 minutes.

Wendy Weiland Burns (Mrs. Harry)

POLISH BAKED MUSHROOMS

Cannot be done ahead
Serves: 6
Preparation: 20 minutes
Baking Time: 12-15 minutes

1 lb. fresh mushrooms or two
    cans (6-8 oz. each) sliced
    mushrooms
3 Tablespoons butter
2 Tablespoons finely chopped
    onion
1/4 teaspoon salt
1/16 teaspoon ground white
    pepper
1 Tablespoon flour
1/4 cup grated Parmesan
    cheese
2 egg yolks, lightly beaten
3 Tablespoons fine soft bread
    crumbs
1 pint cream
Dill

Rinse, pat dry and slice fresh mushrooms (makes about 5 cups), or drain canned mushrooms. In a large skillet heat butter. Add mushrooms, onion, salt and white pepper. Cover and simmer 8 minutes. Remove cover. Stir in flour and cheese; cook 3 minutes. Turn into a buttered 8 inch cake pan or baking dish or individual ramekins. Sprinkle with dill. Mix cream with egg yolks. Pour over mushrooms. Sprinkle with bread crumbs. Bake in a preheated 425° oven for 12-15 minutes or until golden brown.

Elizabeth B. Thurlow

ONION TART KUCHEN
This one was worth crying over

Yield: 24 squares

CRUST:

1 pkg. dry yeast
1-1/2 teaspoons honey
1 cup lukewarm water
1 teaspoon salt
2 teaspoons oil
2 cups whole wheat flour
1 cup whole wheat pastry flour

FILLING:

3 Tablespoons butter
4 cups finely chopped onions
3/4 teaspoon salt
1 teaspoon caraway seeds
1 Tablespoon whole wheat
    pastry flour
3/4 cup cottage cheese
2 Tablespoons yogurt
2 Tablespoons milk
2 eggs, lightly beaten
1/4 cup sunflower seeds

To prepare crust: Dissolve yeast and honey in water. Let stand a few minutes. Add salt and oil, then the flours gradually; mix with spoon, then by hand. Knead dough on floured board for 5 minutes; additional flour may be necessary to prevent dough from sticking. Place dough in an oiled bowl, cover and let rise in a warm place about an hour. Punch down dough and let it rise a few minutes. Roll out on a lightly floured board to a thickness of 1/4 to 3/8 inch to fit an oiled baking sheet or jelly roll pan. Set in warm place to rise about 20 minutes. Meanwhile, preheat oven to 400° and prepare filling. To prepare filling: Heat butter in heavy skillet and add onion, salt and caraway seeds; stir, cover, and steam a few minutes or until onions are yellow, not brown, being careful they don't scorch. Sprinkle flour over onions, and stir until absorbed. Let mixture cool slightly. In a blender, whirl cottage cheese, yogurt and milk until satiny. Add to onions in skillet along with lightly beaten eggs. Cook slowly over very low heat, stirring constantly for a minute or two until thick and well blended. Add sunflower seeds. Spread filling over dough and allow to rise another 15 minutes. Bake in preheated oven for 30 minutes or until dough is crisp and brown around the edges and filling has set. Cut into squares and serve hot or cold. Refrigerate any not served immediately.

Mary Herndon Berg

FRENCH PEAS
A snazzy way to dress up plain old frozen peas

3 Tablespoons butter
1/4 cup iceburg lettuce, finely
    shredded
1 box frozen peas
1/4 cup finely minced green
    onion
1 large sprig parsley
2 teaspoons sugar
1/2 teaspoon salt
Dash white pepper

Melt butter in saucepan. Place lettuce on top of butter. Add remaining ingredients. Bring to a boil and turn down immediately. Simmer 4-5 minutes, stirring occasionally. Remove parsley and serve.

Barrie Muilenburg Sneed (Mrs. Albert L.)

205

STEWED OKRA AND TOMATOES

Can do ahead
Can freeze
Serves: 8-10
Cooking Time: 1-1/2 hours

3 lbs. fresh or frozen okra, sliced
  in rounds
1/3 cup bacon drippings
2 cups finely chopped onions
1 clove garlic, pressed
1/2 cup finely chopped celery
1 cup finely chopped green
  pepper
1 bay leaf
2 lbs. ripe tomatoes, peeled and
  diced
1 large can (16 oz.) corn
1 teaspoon salt
1/8 teaspoon thyme
3-4 dashes Tabasco
Pepper to taste
1/2 lb. bacon, crisply fried and
  crumbled

Fry okra in bacon drippings, stirring often, until there is no sign of ropiness, about 30 minutes. Add onions, garlic, celery, green pepper, bay leaf and cook until onions are transparent, about 15 minutes. Add tomatoes and cook 10 minutes more. Add corn, salt, thyme, Tabasco and pepper. Simmer, covered, for 30 more minutes. Remove bay leaf and serve garnished with bacon.
Add shrimp for a yummy gumbo.

Rebecca Johnson Kempson (Mrs. Barry)

EASY SCALLOPED POTATOES

Can do ahead
Can freeze
Serves: 16
Preparation: 15 minutes
Baking Time: 45 minutes

1 2 lb. pkg. frozen hash browns
  (thaw completely)
3/4 cup butter or margarine,
  melted
1/2 cup chopped onion
1 Tablespoon salt
1/4 teaspoon pepper
1 can cream of chicken soup
2 cups sour cream
2 cups grated Cheddar cheese
Corn flakes, crushed

Mix all of the ingredients except one-quarter cup of butter and the corn flakes. Put in an oblong casserole dish and top with crushed corn flakes mixed with the 1/4 cup of butter. Bake in 350° oven for 45 minutes.

Jamie Porter Armstrong (Mrs. Jeff)

POTATO PANCAKES

Serves: 2 (Easily multiplied)

1 egg, beaten
1 cup grated raw potatoes
(about 6 oz.)
1/2 Tablespoon fine bread
crumbs (whole wheat or
french)
1-1/2 Tablespoons grated carrot
Dash of baking powder
Dash of seasoned salt
Dash of pepper and cayenne
1 teaspoon butter
1 teaspoon corn oil

Combine beaten egg, raw potatoes, bread crumbs, carrot, baking powder, seasoned salt, pepper and cayenne. Heat in heavy skillet until bubbly, the 1 teaspoon of butter and one teaspoon corn oil. Stirring well, spoon half of potato mixture into hot butter and oil, making 3 4-1/2" pancakes. Brown, turn to brown the other side, adding butter or oil as needed. Repeat with the rest of the potato mixture.
Serve with fresh applesauce.

Sandy Farnam Sellers (Mrs. Danny)

SAUERKRAUT

Serve with German sausages, roast pork, game or smoked meats

Can be done ahead
Serves: 8-10
Preparation: 15 minutes
Baking Time: 2 hours

2 jars sauerkraut, rinsed well
1 pork knuckle or 1/2 lb. bacon
1 tart apple, unpeeled and
sectioned
1 small can crushed pineapple
Small handful juniper berries
10 peppercorns
2 bay leaves
2 big pinches caraway seeds
1 small onion, finely chopped
2 cloves
2 cups white wine
1 cup chicken stock

Mix all ingredients and cook in heavy Dutch oven or romertopf for 2 hours at 325°.
Can be reheated.

Lane Weaver Byrd (Mrs. Robert W. H.)

SPINACH PIE
As a side dish or first course

Can do ahead
Can freeze
Serves: 12
Preparation: 15-20 minutes
Baking Time: 45 minutes

2 10-oz. pkgs. chopped spinach
—thawed
1/2 cup chopped onions
2 Tablespoons olive oil
1/2 cup chopped parsley
1/2 lb. feta cheese, crumbled
Salt and pepper
6 eggs, separated
1/2 lb. melted butter
16 Filo pastry sheets

Drain and squeeze out excess water from spinach. Brown onions in olive oil. In large bowl, mix spinach, parsley, onion, cheese, salt, pepper and beaten egg yolks. Beat egg whites stiff and fold into spinach mixture. Grease a 13-1/2x9-1/2x2″ baking pan with melted butter and line bottom and sides with 8 pastry sheets, placing one on top of the other and brushing each pastry sheet generously with melted butter. Pour cheese mixture over the bottom stack of pastry sheets and spread evenly. Cover with the remaining sheets, brushing each sheet with melted butter. Brush top layer generously with butter. Bake at 375° for 45 minutes. When golden brown, remove from oven. Cool and cut in squares. May be frozen before baking. Let thaw in refrigerator and bake as instructed.

Celine Hanan Lurey (Mrs. Michael)

SQUASH CASSEROLE I

Can do ahead
Can freeze
Serves: 6-8
Preparation: 30 minutes
Baking Time: 30 minutes

2 lb. yellow squash, sliced
1 medium onion, chopped
1 cup cracker crumbs (Waverly
wafers)
1/2 teaspoon salt
Dash black pepper
1 cup grated cheese
3 Tablespoons butter
1/2 cup milk
1 egg

Cook squash and onion until tender. Remove from heat; drain. Add salt, pepper, butter, cheese, cracker crumbs, milk, egg. Stir until well blended. Pour into one-quart casserole. Sprinkle with grated cheese. Can put strips of bacon on top if desired. Bake for 30 minutes in 350° oven.

Alice Ward Griffin (Mrs. William R., III)

SQUASH CASSEROLE II

Can freeze
Baking Time: 30 minutes

2 lbs. squash
2 eggs
1 onion, grated
2 cups thick white sauce
1/2 lb. sharp Cheddar cheese
(1/2 cup grated Swiss
cheese can be substituted
for Cheddar cheese)

Cook squash and onion until tender. Drain and mash into fine pulp. Add beaten eggs, grated cheese and white sauce. Place in casserole dish. Top with bread crumbs. Freeze, or bake in 375° oven until bubbly hot (approximately 30 minutes). If frozen, bake for 45 minutes in 375° oven.

Barbara Morgan Nesbitt (Mrs. Charles E.)

BOBBIE PAYNE'S SPINACH SPECIAL

Delicious — may be used as a dressing, vegetable or bread.

Can do ahead
Serves: 6-8
Preparation: 10 minutes
Baking Time: 40-45 minutes

1 stick margarine
1 pkg. frozen chopped spinach
(cooked and drained well)
(Swiss chard works well too)
1 box Jiffy corn muffin mix
6 oz. cottage cheese
1/2 teaspoon salt
4 eggs
1 small onion, chopped

Melt margarine in two quart casserole. Pour margarine back into batter of other ingredients. Mix until ingredients are moist. Bake in same two-quart casserole in which you melted margarine, which contains excess margarine.
Bake 40-45 minutes in 350° oven until center is set.

Elizabeth Hudson McAnally (Mrs. Lon Wyatt)

SWEET POTATOES WITH APRICOTS

Can do ahead
Can freeze
Serves: 6-8
Preparation: 30 minutes
Baking Time: 45 minutes

6 oz. pkg. dried apricots
40 oz. can yams, drained
1 cup dark brown sugar
1/4 cup peach, apricot or
orange liqueur
Grated rind and juice
of 1 orange
4 Tablespoons butter, melted
1 cup pecans

Slice yams and mix with apricots, sugar, liqueur, butter, rind and juice. Place in a one and half quart well-greased casserole. Top with pecans (which have been tossed with a little melted butter, if desired).
Bake for 40-45 minutes in 350° oven.

Celine Hanan Lurey (Mrs. Michael)

SWEET POTATOES IN ORANGE SAUCE
Time consuming—but well worth it

Can do ahead
Serves: 8-10
Preparation: 2 hours
Baking Time: 20 minutes

3 lbs. sweet potatoes
1-1/2 cups water
1 orange
1 cup sugar
2-3 drops yellow coloring
6 Tablespoons butter, melted
2 Tablespoons flour
1/2 cup brown sugar
1 teaspoon cinnamon
1 teaspoon nutmeg
2 Tablespoons lemon juice
1 teaspoon salt
1 teaspoon vanilla

Cook potatoes in water; peel, slice and place in a 2 quart casserole. Cube orange, remove seeds, and grind orange (including peel); add cooking water, sugar and coloring. Cook until mixture resembles syrup (about 30 minutes.) Mix flour and melted butter, Add to syrup with the remaining ingredients. Blend well and pour over sweet potatoes in 2 quart casserole. Bake at 350° for 20 minutes or until bubbly.

Jan Stauffer Schulhof (Mrs. Lary A.)

TOMATOES WITH ARTICHOKE

Can do ahead, but don't cook
Serves: 4
Preparation: 15 minutes
Baking Time: 25 minutes

4 large, ripe, firm tomatoes
1 large or 2 small jars marinated
   artichoke hearts
1 stick butter
1 cup bread crumbs
Salt and pepper, to taste
1 cup vermouth
Parmesan cheese

Wash, dry and cut the tops off tomatoes. Scoop out the pulp and sprinkle with salt and pepper. Turn upside down on toweling and allow tomatoes to drain while preparing filling.
Drain liquid from artichokes and reserve. Chop hearts and add to melted butter in skillet. Add bread crumbs and mix. Add reserved liquid if mixture seems dry. Fill tomatoes with mixture and top with Parmesan cheese. Place in pan containing vermouth and bake at 325° for 25 minutes. Before serving, spoon pan liquids over tomatoes.

Rebecca Johnson Kempson (Mrs. Barry)

CHERRY TOMATOES IN CREAM

May not be done ahead
May not be frozen
Serves: 4
Preparation: 5 minutes
Cooking Time: 3 minutes

1 pint cherry tomatoes
2 Tablespoons butter
1/4 teaspoon salt
2 Tablespoons brown sugar
1/4 cup heavy cream
Chopped fresh parsley for
garnish

Saute rinsed tomatoes in butter with salt and brown sugar for 2 to 3 minutes, stirring constantly. Remove tomatoes to serving dish. Add cream to pan juices, stir and pour over tomatoes. Garnish with chopped parsley and serve immediately.

Barrie Muilenburg Sneed (Mrs. Albert L.)

TOMATO PIE

Baking Time: 20-25 minutes

5 medium tomatoes, peeled,
sliced and drained
9" pie crust, pre-baked
1/2 cup mayonnaise
1/2 cup Parmesan cheese
1 clove garlic, crushed
1/4 teaspoon pepper
1/4 cup Ritz cracker crumbs
(8 crackers)
2 teaspoons butter

Preheat oven to 425.° Arrange tomatoes in the pie shell. Mix mayonnaise, Parmesan cheese, garlic and pepper; spread over the tomatoes. Sprinkle cracker crumbs on top and dot with butter. Bake for 20-25 minutes.
Also delicious without the pie crust, as a casserole. A good dish to serve with bland meat.

Kathleen Fairburn Armstrong (Mrs. Robert)

BAKED SHREDDED ZUCCHINI

Serves: 2 (Easily multiplied)
Preparation: 5 minutes
Baking Time: 20 minutes

2 cups coarsely grated zucchini
1/4 cup grated Parmesan
cheese
1 egg, beaten
1/4 teaspoon pepper
1/4 teaspoon basil

Combine all ingredients and transfer to buttered 1 quart baking dish. Bake at 350° for 20 minutes.

Sandy Farnam Sellers (Mrs. Danny)

MRS. MARTIN'S ZUCCHINI STUFFING CASSEROLE

Can do ahead
Serves: 6-8
Preparation: 30 minutes
Baking Time: 30 minutes

1/4 cup butter
2 carrots, grated
1 large onion, chopped
2-1/2 cups stuffing mix
1 10-3/4 oz. can cream of
*   mushroom or chicken soup*
1/2 cup sour cream
4 medium zucchinis, sliced
*   into 1/2" thick pieces*
2 Tablespoon butter, melted

Preheat oven to 350.° In melted butter, saute carrots and onions until tender. Stir in 2 cups stuffing mix, soup and sour cream. Remove from heat. Cook zucchini in boiling salted water a few minutes, just until tender. Add to vegetable mixture. Pour into buttered casserole dish. Mix remaining 1/2 cup of stuffing mix with two tablespoons melted butter and sprinkle on top. Bake for 30 minutes in 350° oven.

Elizabeth Glenn Biggers (Mrs. Carl)

THREE VEGETABLE CASSEROLE

Serves: 6-8
Preparation: 10 minutes
Baking Time: 1 hour 15 minutes

4 medium potatoes (1-1/4 lb.)
*   pared and thinly sliced*
2 medium onions, peeled, thinly
*   sliced and separated into*
*   rings*
4 small yellow straightneck
*   squash (1-1/4 lbs.) washed,*
*   unpared and thinly sliced*
Salt and pepper, to taste
1 stick butter
1 cup grated Parmesan cheese
1 cup commercial sour cream

Butter a shallow baking dish that holds 2-1/2 quarts which can go into the oven and under the broiler. In it layer 1/2 the potatoes, sprinkling with salt and pepper; dot with a generous pat of butter. In the same way, layer 1/2 the onion and 1/2 the squash, sprinkling with salt and pepper; dot with butter. Repeat layers, ending with squash and butter. Cover tightly with foil and bake in preheated 350° oven until potatoes are very tender when pierced with fork—about 1 hour 15 minutes.

Stir together the Parmesan cheese and sour cream (the mixture will be thick). Spread over top of vegetables. Broil, watching carefully, about 6-8 inches from high heat, until topping is browned in spots (3-5 minutes). Serve at once, adding some of the butter from bottom of dish to each serving.

Lynn Holmes Trotter (Mrs. Benjamin)

VEGETABLE CASSEROLE I

Serves: 10

4 Tablespoons cooking oil
1 green pepper
2 or 3 spring onions
2 celery stalks, thinly sliced
2 peeled carrots, thinly sliced
4 zucchini (2 if large), thinly
    sliced
4 small yellow squash, thinly
    sliced
4 or 5 fresh tomatoes, peeled,
    cut in quarters
1/2 lb. sliced fresh
    mushrooms
1 teaspoon sugar
1/2 teaspoon oregano
1/2 teaspoon basil
Salt and pepper to taste
1/2 lb. grated Cheddar cheese
Toasted slivered almonds

Saute onions and green pepper in oil. Add celery, carrots, zucchini, squash and cook all until just tender. Add mushrooms and seasonings and part of cheese. Put in casserole dish. Sprinkle with remaining cheese and toasted almonds.
Keep warm in 200° oven until ready to serve.

Ione Wright Morgan (Mrs. Charles W.)

VEGETABLE CASSEROLE II

Can do ahead
Serves:8
Preparation: 30 minutes
Baking Time: 1 hour

6 Tablespoons butter, melted
1 Tablespoon tapioca
1 can stewed tomatoes
1 pkg. frozen string beans
1-1/2 cups raw julienne carrots
1-1/2 cup chopped celery
1-1/2 cups raw onions—julienne
3/4 cup bell pepper, chopped
1 can water chestnuts, sliced
1 Tablespoon sugar
2-1/2 teaspoons salt
1/2 teaspoon pepper

Melt butter and combine with tapioca. In a three-quart casserole, layer the vegetables with sugar, salt and pepper. Pour stewed tomatoes and butter over vegetables. Bake for one hour in 350° oven.

Elizabeth B. Thurlow

CREAM SOUP SOUFFLE

Baking Time: 45 minutes

*Use any kind of cream soup
(Asparagus is good)
4 eggs, separated
1/2 teaspoon Worcestershire
sauce*

Beat yolks of 4 eggs well and combine with soup. Whip egg whites stiff and fold in soup mixture. Season with Worcestershire sauce. Place in greased casserole. Sprinkle paprika on top. Bake for 45 minutes in 300° oven.

Margaret Fearrington Baumann

FRUIT BAKE
Easy to fix

*Can do ahead
Serves: 10
Baking Time: 20 minutes*

*1/2 lb. prunes—stewed
1 lb. carrots—stewed
1 #2 can chunk pineapple
1/4 stick butter
2-1/2 Tablespoons flour
1/2 cup sugar
Juice from pineapple*

Melt butter. Put flour, sugar and pineapple juice in—bring to boil and pour over fruit. Bake for 20 minutes in 350° oven.

Susan Hunter Baumann (Mrs. Carl)

FROSTED GRAPE COMPOTE

*Can do ahead early in day
Serves: 8*

*2 lbs. white seedless grapes
1/4 cup brandy
1/2 cup sour cream
1/2 cup heavy cream
2 Tablespoons confectioners
sugar
Brown sugar*

Wash grapes; place in shallow bowl. Sprinkle with brandy. Toss lightly. Whip cream; combine with sour cream and confectioners sugar. Pour cream mixture over grapes and toss. Place in freezer for about 10 minutes. Serve with brown sugar sprinkled over top. You can do this early in the day.

Lelia Kincaid Cort (Mrs. John)

GRAM'S PINEAPPLE CASSEROLE

Delicious with turkey, ham or pork. A good substitute for sweet potatoes.
Also can be served as a pineapple bread pudding for dessert.

Can do ahead
Serves: 6-8
Preparation: 10 minutes
Baking Time: 40-45 minutes

3 eggs
2 Tablespoons flour
1/2 cup sugar
Pinch salt
1 #2-1/2 can crushed pineapple
1/2—1 stick butter
4 slices fresh bread (remove
   crusts and cut into cubes)

Beat eggs; add sugar, salt and flour. Beat mixture until fluffy. Pour pineapple into mixture and blend. Place in greased 2 quart casserole. You may stop here and refrigerate. When ready to bake, place cubed bread on top in geometric pattern. Slice butter and place on top of bread. Bake at 400° for 40-45 minutes.

Bettie Griffin Watts (Mrs. Nelson B.)

APPLE AND TOMATO CASSEROLE

Can do ahead until time to bake
Serves: 6
Preparation: 10 minutes
Baking Time: 20-30 minutes

1 (16 oz.) can stewed tomatoes
1 (16 oz.) can apples
2 Tablespoons brown sugar
1 teaspoon cinnamon
Buttered bread crumbs

Mix brown sugar and cinnamon together and add to apples and tomatoes. Put into one-quart casserole (greased or sprayed with PAM). Cover with buttered crumbs. Heat in 350° oven until hot and bubbly (20 minutes or more if casserole has been refrigerated before baking.) Leftovers heat well.

Betty Bryan Coleman (Mrs. Richard L.)

HOT FRUIT SALAD

Serves: 8-10
Baking Time: 60 minutes

1 No. 2 can pineapple slices
1 No. 1 can pear halves
1 No. 1 can peach halves
1 No. 1 can apricot halves
3/4 cup brown sugar
2 teaspoons of curry powder
Lemon juice
1/3 cup butter

Melt butter and add brown sugar. Place fruit in layers beginning with pineapple. Squirt with lemon juice. Pour butter mixture over fruit. Bake 1 hour in 325° oven. Serve hot. Good with ham.

Jamie Porter Armstrong (Mrs. Jeff)

FRIED CHINESE CABBAGE
From Chinese cooking class taken in Okinawa

Serves: 6

CABBAGE MIXTURE:

4 Tablespoons oil
4 cups cabbage, Chinese or round, chopped and separated into pieces 1" x 3-1/2" (about 1 pound)
1 clove garlic, crushed
Optional: 2 or 3 pieces hot pepper sliced
2 Tablespoons soy sauce
Salt to taste

SEASONINGS:

2 Tablespoons water
1-1/2 Tablespoons vinegar
1 teaspoon Accent
Optional: 1 teaspoon sugar
3 green onions slivered

Heat 4 tablespoons oil in frying pan. Brown red pepper, garlic, salt and soy sauce. Add cabbage; cover. Stir and fry 1-2 minutes.
Sprinkle seasonings ingredients over cabbage in pan. Cook 1 minute; then add onion. Serve warm.
Serve this with Chinese egg drop soup, rice, tea, almond cookies with chilled mandarin oranges.

Diana Roscoe Bilbrey (Mrs. George M., Jr.)

Salads

SPINACH AND ARTICHOKE SALAD
The dressing makes this salad—a food processor makes preparation easy

May do ahead
Serves: 8-10
Preparation: 35-45 minutes

1-1/2 lbs. spinach, washed,
   dried—take stems off—
   tear into bite-sized pieces
3 hard-boiled eggs, sliced
1/2 lb. bacon crisply fried
   and crumbled
1 can artichoke hearts—
   drained and chopped
   (use food processor)
8 oz. of fresh mushrooms sliced
   in food processor (use thin
   slicing blade)

DRESSING:

2/3 cup of sugar
1 teaspoon dry mustard
1 teaspoon salt
1 cup salad oil
1 medium onion
1 Tablespoon plus 1/2 teaspoon
   celery seed
1/2 cup plus 1 Tablespoon
   vinegar

Mix spinach, eggs, bacon, artichoke hearts and mushrooms in a large bowl.
Dressing: Combine first 5 ingredients in bowl of food processor. Use metal blade; process 1-1/2 minutes, stopping once or twice to scrape side of bowl. Add celery seed and vinegar. Process 45 seconds. Chill.

Kathleen Kennedy Noyes

SPINACH SALAD

Serves: 10-12
Preparation: 30 minutes

1 bag spinach, washed
   and drained
1 can water chestnuts, drained
   and chopped
1 can bean sprouts, drained
3 hard-boiled eggs, sliced
1/2 lb. bacon, fried and
   crumbled
1 large onion, cut in thin slices
   (mild, red onion)

Toss spinach, chestnuts and sprouts. Add bacon, eggs and onion. Blend dressing ingredients and pour over salad just before serving.

DRESSING:

1 cup salad oil
3/4 cup sugar
1/2 cup dark vinegar
2 teaspoons salt
1/2 cup ketchup   Susan Murray Daniel (Mrs. John N., Jr.)

24 HOUR VEGETABLE SALAD

Must do ahead
Serves: 12
Preparation: 30 minutes

6 cups chopped lettuce
Salt, pepper, sugar
6 hard-boiled eggs, sliced
1 10-oz. pkg. peas, thawed
16 oz. bacon, cooked
    and crumbled
8 oz. Swiss cheese, shredded
1 cup mayonnaise
1/4 cup sliced green onions
    with tops
Paprika

Place 3 cups lettuce in bottom of large bowl. Sprinkle with salt, pepper and sugar. Layer eggs atop lettuce. Sprinkle with salt. Layer in order: peas, remaining lettuce, bacon, cheese. Spread mayonnaise over top, sealing to edge of bowl. Cover and chill 24 hours. Garnish with onions and paprika. Toss before serving.

Sandra Pappas Byrd (Mrs. Jones P.)

BOARD ORIENTATION GREEK SALAD

1 can pitted ripe olives
1 bunch diced green onions
1 green pepper, cut into rings
Torn, washed and dried good
    quality lettuce, several
    bunches
3 wedged tomatoes
1 cup feta cheese or Swiss
    cheese chunks*
3 cups of hot boiled potatoes,
    diced and combined with
    garlic powder, dash of red
    wine vinegar and
    mayonnaise and salt
Salt to taste
Parsley to taste

Divide the ingredients among your committee. Have each member bring one or two items. Combine at the last minute.
*You may add or substitute 1 can of shrimp, smoked oysters or chopped ham.
Toss with Italian dressing.

SNOW PEA SALAD

Serves: 8

1 head iceberg lettuce, shredded
1 lb. snow peas, steamed
   30 seconds
Red lettuce

SESAME SEED
DRESSING:

1/2 cup chopped parsley
1/4 cup sesame seeds, toasted
2/3 cup salad oil
2 Tablespoons lemon juice
2 Tablespoons vinegar
2 Tablespoons sugar
1 clove garlic, crushed
1-1/2 teaspoons salt

Place peas and shredded lettuce on top of red lettuce leaves. To prepare sesame seed dressing, blend all ingredients except sesame seeds. Next add seeds. Toss salad. Dressing keeps well.

Ruth Bowles Carson (Mrs. Philip G.)

ITALIAN MARINATED VEGETABLE SALAD

Must do ahead
Serves: 8-10

1 cup button mushrooms,
   drained
1 green pepper, cut in strips
1 carrot, sliced and steamed
   gently
2 cups uncooked cauliflower,
   broken in pieces
6 green onions, sliced
1 cup stuffed olives
1 can heart of palms, sliced
1 can artichoke hearts, drained,
   cut in quarters
1 pkg. frozen baby Brussels
   sprouts, gently steamed
Cherry tomatoes
Minced parsley

MARINADE:

1-1/2 cups wine vinegar
1 teaspoon sugar
1-1/2 teaspoons salt
1/2 teaspoon pepper
2 teaspoons oregano
1/2 cup salad oil
1/2 cup olive oil

Combine all vegetables except tomatoes and parsley in a large bowl. Heat vinegar, combine with oils. Add sugar, salt, pepper and oregano. Pour over vegetables. Mix well, cover and refrigerate for 24 hours before serving.
To serve: Drain, arrange on lettuce adding cherry tomatoes and parsley.

Lee Tickle Mynatt (Mrs. William)

BROCCOLI-CAULIFLOWER SALAD
Easy to do—nice and crunchy

Must do ahead
Preparation: 30 minutes

1 head cauliflower, chopped
   very fine
1 head broccoli, chopped
   very fine
1 large onion, chopped very fine
1 can water chestnuts, sliced
1 cup slivered almonds
1 pkg. frozen green peas—
   cooked until tender, drain
1 bottle Casear's creamy
   salad dressing

Place ingredients in large glass bowl and marinate overnight in the refrigerator.

Nancy Kouns Worley (Mrs. Charles R.)

SUE'S CAULIFLOWER SLAW

Must do ahead
Serves: 6
Preparation: 15-20 minutes

1 large head of cauliflower (raw)
6 green onions, chopped
1 Tablespoon chopped parsley
1 cup sour cream
1 cup chopped celery leaves
1-1/4 teaspoons dill weed
1/2 cup Italian salad dressing

Finely slice cauliflower. Combine with rest of the ingredients and refrigerate at least four hours or overnight.

Martha Blackshear Salisbury (Mrs. Kent)

SLAW

Can do ahead

1 head green cabbage, chopped
   or grated
1 green pepper, chopped
2 medium onions, chopped
3 pieces celery, chopped
3/4 cup oil
3/4 cup sugar
1 cup white vinegar
1 Tablespoon salt

Put vinegar, salt, sugar and oil in saucepan and boil for five minutes. Let cool. Then mix with other ingredients. This keeps well in the refrigerator.

Lynn Holmes Trotter (Mrs. Benjamin)

COLE SLAW

Can do ahead
Serves: 6-8

TOSS:

1 head white cabbage, shredded
1 small carrot, shredded
1 Tablespoon celery seed
1/2 cup crushed pineapple,
    drained but not dry
1 cup salad dressing
    (recipe follows)

SALAD DRESSING:

2 whole eggs
1/2 cup vinegar
1/2 cup water
1 Tablespoon butter
1 Tablespoon sugar
1/2 teaspoon dry mustard
Heaping Tablespoon of flour
1 teaspoon salt
3 good dashes Tabasco
1/2 to 1 cup salad oil

Mix sugar, mustard, flour, salt, with butter, vinegar and water and Tabasco. Place in double boiler and cook until smooth. Add well beaten eggs. Stir constantly until thickened. Remove from heat and cool. Beat in oil until dressing has absorbed as much as it will hold. Can be placed in jar for future use.

Margaret Fearrington Baumann

ASHEVILLE SALAD
A special tomato aspic.

Must do ahead
Serves: 8-10

2 cans tomato soup
2 pkgs. cream cheese, 3 oz.
1 cup celery, onion and green
    pepper, cut fine and mixed
1 cup mayonnaise
1/2 cup pecan meats
1 pkg. gelatin dissolved in
    1/3 cup cold water

Put cheese and soup together on heat to dissolve cheese. Add gelatin and mix until gelatin is dissolved well. Cool. Add nuts and vegetables, and last of all add mayonnaise. Pour into a mold to congeal. Serve on lettuce with a portion of mayonnaise.

Margaret Fearrington Baumann
Lynn Mernin Salley (Mrs. Alfred N.)

EASY TOMATO ASPIC

*Looks good on a salad plate served with chicken salad,
cottage cheese and fruit. Great for luncheon.*

Must do ahead
Serves: 10-12
Preparation: 20 minutes
Chilling: 24 hours

1 pkg. lemon gelatin
2 cups V-8 juice, heated
2 Tablespoons vinegar or
    lemon juice
1/2 cucumber, grated
1/2 onion, grated
1/4 chopped green pepper
2 stalks celery, chopped
Sliced green olives
Dash of Tabasco sauce

Dissolve gelatin in hot V-8 juice, add remaining
ingredients and cool. Pour into molds, and chill
for 24 hours.

Bettie Griffin Watts (Mrs. Nelson B.)

BEET SALAD

Men love this salad!

Must do ahead
Serves: 16-18

3 pkgs. lemon gelatin
6 cans strained (baby
    food) beets
1 small jar horseradish (hot)
Salt to taste (quite a lot)
6 cups liquid, including beets
    and horseradish, add water
    to make necessary amount
    of liquid.

Heat beets and water. Dissolve gelatin in same.
Add salt and horseradish. Pour into mold or
8-1/2x13" casserole. Chill until set. Serve with
dressing.
Dressing: Soak 2 large cucumbers, seeded and
sliced, in salt water. Drain and chop fine; add to
2 cups sour cream.

DRESSING:

2 large cucumbers
2 cups sour cream

COLD BEET SALAD AUX FINES HERBS

Must do ahead
Serves: 6-8

1 cup Creme Fraiche
2 Tablespoons olive oil
1-1/2 Tablespoons red wine
  vinegar
1 teaspoon dried tarragon
2 Tablespoons finely minced
  fresh herbs (parsley, chives,
  and chervil)
4 cups freshly cooked,
  cubed beets
Freshly ground white pepper
2 Tablespoons finely minced
  fresh parsley

In a serving bowl, combine the creme fraiche, olive oil, vinegar and herbs. Stir the mixture until well blended, then add the beets and fold them into the dressing. Season with pepper and a pinch of salt and chill for 2 to 4 hours before serving. Forty-five minutes before serving, bring the salad back to room temperature taste and correct the seasoning, then sprinkle with parsley and serve as part of an hors d'oeuvre table or as a garnish to roast chicken, poached fish, or cold roast beef.

CREME FRAICHE:

Yield: 2 cups

2 cups very fresh heavy cream
6 teaspoons buttermilk

Combine the cream and buttermilk in a jar and whisk the mixture until well blended. Cover the jar and let it stand in a warm place for 24 hours, checking the cream once or twice and whisking again. It is done when it has the consistency of sour cream. Refrigerate. This keeps well for 1 to 2 weeks. Can also be sugared and served with berries or poached fruit.
Note: Creme Fraiche will not curdle in a hot sauce.

Sandy Farnam Sellers (Mrs. Danny)

CRANBERRY FROZEN SALAD

Must do ahead
Serves: 8-10

2 3-oz. pkgs. cream cheese
2 teaspoons mayonnaise
2 teaspoons sugar
1 lb. can whole cranberry sauce
1 7-oz. can crushed pineapple,
  drained
1/2 cup chopped nuts
1 cup whipped cream

Soften cheese. Blend in mayonnaise and sugar. Add fruits and nuts. Fold in whipped cream. Pour in loaf pan. Freeze firm. Cut in squares.

Ann Buchanan Robinson (Mrs. Robert J.)

CHERRY SALAD
Coke in this recipe gives it a different flavor

Must do ahead
Serves: 12
Preparation: 20 minutes

2 pkgs. cherry gelatin
1 pkg. frozen dark sweet
    cherries or canned, pitted
1 20-oz. can crushed pineapple
1 12-oz. Coke, chilled
1 lemon or 2 Tablespoons of
    lemon juice
3/4 cup nuts, chopped

Thaw cherries, drain and reserve. Add water to cherry juice to make 1 cup. Heat and pour over gelatin. Cool. Add coke and lemon juice. Refrigerate till almost set. Add cherries cut in pieces, nuts, and drained pineapple. Chill until firm.

Jeannie Renick Davis (Mrs. John N., Jr.)

CUCUMBER/PINEAPPLE MOLD

Must do ahead
Serves: 8
Preparation: 15 minutes

2 envelopes unflavored gelatin
1/2 cup cold water
2/3 cup sugar
1/2 cup water
1 teaspoon salt
1 lb. can crushed pineapple,
    undrained
1 cup grated cucumber
1/3 cup lemon juice
1 cup sour cream
Grated rind of 1/2 lemon

Soften gelatin in the *cold* water. Bring other 1/2 cup of water, sugar and salt to a boil. Remove from heat and stir in gelatin until dissolved. Cool. Add remainder of ingredients. Pour into 1-quart ring mold that has been sprayed with Pam. Chill. Unmold on endive, watercress or Bibb lettuce.

Carolyn Roda Smith (Mrs. Canie B.)

MANDARIN GELATIN MOLD

Must do ahead

2 can Mandarin oranges,
    drained
2 small pkgs. (3 oz.)
    orange gelatin
2 cups boiling water
1 pint orange sherbert
2 cups Cool Whip

Dissolve gelatin in water and add sherbert until dissolved. Add Cool Whip and put in refrigerator until partially set. Add the oranges and pour into 2 quart mold. Chill. You may garnish mold with extra can of oranges.

Joyce Lichtenfels Cole

LEMON-HORSERADISH GELATIN MOLD
Serve this with a colorful meal.

Must do ahead
Serves: 8
Preparation: 60 minutes
Chilling: 24 hours

2 pkgs. lemon gelatin
1-1/2 cups hot water
1-1/2 cups cold water
1 cup whipping cream, whipped
1 cup mayonnaise
1/2 cup horseradish
Sliced olives (about 15)

Prepare gelatin with hot and cold water. Let it set slightly. Whip cream and fold into gelatin. Add mayonnaise, horseradish and sliced olives. Allow to set in either mold or oblong pan to chill for 24 hours.

Sue Hein McClinton (Mrs. Raymond)

SPICED PEACH SALAD
Spicy-tart and very good with poultry!

Must do ahead
Yield: 1 large mold or 10 small ones
Preparation: 20 minutes

1 29-oz. jar spiced peaches
1/2 cup water
1 cup chopped pecans
1 small jar maraschino cherries,
    drained and chopped
2 small pkgs. lemon gelatin
4 large juicy oranges, peeled
    and chopped

Drain spiced peaches and heat the juice. Pour hot juice over the gelatin to dissolve and add 1/2 cup of water. Chop spiced peaches into small pieces. Add peaches, oranges and their juices, chopped pecans and cherries to gelatin. Pour into mold and congeal.

Helen King Turner (Mrs. Franklin H., Jr.)

FRUIT SALAD

Must do ahead (marinate)
Preparation: 1-2 hours

2 pkgs. frozen blueberries
2 pkgs. frozen or fresh
    strawberries
1 cantaloupe, cut up
3 or 4 peaches, cut in pieces
2 cans chunk pineapple,
    drained

Let fruit marinate about two hours before serving.

Continued...

MARINADE:

2 cups orange juice
1 cup sugar
1/2 teaspoon almond extract
1/2 teaspoon vanilla
1/4 cup cream sherry   *Deborah Daniel Killian (Mrs. Leon)*

FROZEN FRUIT CUPS
Try these as an after school snack

Must do ahead and freeze
Serves: 18
Preparation: 20 minutes

1 16-oz. carton plain yogurt
   (I use home-made)
2 Tablespoons lemon juice
3/4 cup sugar
1/8 teaspoon salt
1/4 cup pecans, chopped
1/2 cup miniature
   marshmallows, chopped
8-1/4-oz. can crushed
   pineapple, undrained
1/4 cup maraschino cherries,
   chopped
3 bananas, peeled and chopped

Combine all ingredients and pour into muffin tins lined with paper muffin cups. Freeze in tins until firm. Remove from tins and store in plastic bags in freezer. Great for "after-school snacks" or as fruit salad on lettuce.

Bonnie Tyler Brannon (Mrs. Russell)

MOLDED PINEAPPLE AND CHEESE SALAD

Must do ahead
Yield: 12-18 portions

1 pkg. lemon gelatin
1 pkg. lime gelatin
2 cups boiling water
1 cup evaporated milk
2 Tablespoons lemon juice
1 lb. creamed cottage cheese
2 cups crushed pineapple,
   drained
1 cup chopped celery
1 cup chopped walnuts

Combine lime and lemon gelatin and dissolve in boiling water. *Cool.* Stir in evaporated milk and lemon juice. Chill until slightly thickened. Add remainder of ingredients. Pour into 2-quart ring mold. Chill until firm (overnight).

DRESSING:

1 cup mayonnaise
2 teaspoons red horseradish   *Jean C. Moran (Mrs. Raymond F.)*

MACARONI AND CHEESE SALAD

This could almost be used as a main dish. Very filling; you don't need much else to go with it.

Can do ahead
Serves: 6
Preparation: 60 minutes

6 oz. seashell macaroni
   (1-1/2 cups)
1 cup sliced celery
1 cup shredded carrots
1/4 cup chopped onion
1 can condensed Cheddar
   cheese soup
1/4 cup cooking oil
2 Tablespoons vinegar
1 teaspoon sugar
1 teaspoon prepared mustard
1 teaspoon Worchestershire
   sauce
1/2 teaspoon salt
Dash of pepper

Cook macaroni according to package directions. Drain. Combine macaroni, celery, carrots and onion. In small mixer bowl, combine condensed cheese soup, oil, vinegar, sugar and mustard, Worchestershire sauce, salt and pepper and mix until well blended. Spoon atop macaroni mixture and mix well. Chill several hours.

Becky Rhodarmer York (Mrs. Robert A.)

SEAFOOD VERMICELLI SALAD

Serves: 8-12

12-oz. pkg. Vermicelli
   spaghetti, cooked "al dente,"
   drained and rinsed
5 hard-boiled eggs, chopped
5 stalks celery, chopped
4-6 Tablespoons sweet pickle
   relish to taste, or 6 sweet
   pickles, chopped
1 small onion, diced
Salt
1-1/2 to 2 cups mayonnaise
2 cans shrimp or crab, drained
   (4-1/2 oz. size)

Mix all ingredients together. Refrigerate. Salad is also good with diced cooked chicken or turkey. Can also be made without any meat and used as a side dish, instead of potato salad.

Clara Crumpler Bitter (Mrs. Stephen)

RICE SALAD

Must do ahead
Serves: 8-10

1 cup long grain rice, uncooked
1/2 cup salad oil
1/4 cup cider vinegar
2 Tablespoons soy sauce
1/2 teaspoon salt
1 cup thinly sliced celery
1 (8-1/2-oz.) can water
    chestnuts, drained
    and sliced
1 cup sliced fresh mushrooms
1 (11-oz.) can mandarin
    oranges, drained
Lettuce
1 cup green pepper, chopped
3/4 cup raisins
1/2 cup walnuts, chopped

Cook rice, according to package directions. Let cool to room temperature. Combine salad oil, vinegar, soy sauce, salt, celery, green pepper; stir in rice. Fold in water chestnuts, mushrooms and oranges just until blended. Stir in nuts and raisins. Chill thoroughly and serve in a lettuce-lined bowl.

Deborah Lyn Robinson

FRENCH POTATO SALAD

Serves 6-8

2 lbs. new or boiling potatoes
Freshly ground black pepper
2 Tablespoons dry white
    vermouth
2 Tablespoons beef bouillon
2 Tablespoons wine vinegar
6 Tablespoons olive oil
2 Tablespoons minced shallots
1 teaspoon Dijon mustard
Chopped fresh parsley

Boil potatoes in their jackets until tender. Peel and slice while still hot. Place them in a shallow serving dish. Season with salt and pepper and pour vermouth and bouillon over all. Toss gently and let set for a few minutes. Make a French dressing by combining all remaining ingredients except parsley in a screw-top container. Shake well. Pour dressing over potatoes. Toss gently and sprinkle with parsley.

Sandy Farnam Sellers (Mrs. Danny)

GROUND STEAK SALAD

Serves: 5-6
Preparation: 30 minutes

1 lb. ground round
1 teaspoon chili powder
1 teaspoon crazy salt
Small head of lettuce
1 cucumber
1 tomato
1 red onion, sliced
1 green pepper
Optional: 1 ripe avocado
1/2 lb. shredded Cheddar
    cheese
1 small jar Thousand Island
    dressing
Optional: crushed corn chips

Cook 1 lb. ground round with 1 teaspoon chili powder and 1 teaspoon crazy salt. Cool and drain. Toss with remaining ingredients.

Patricia Stancil Smith (Mrs. Philip J.)

BLENDER CAESAR DRESSING

1 teaspoon salt
1/2 teaspoon pepper
1 clove garlic, crushed
1 teaspoon Worcestershire
    sauce
1/4 cup salad oil
1 egg
Another 1/2 cup salad oil
1/4 cup lemon juice
1/4 cup grated
    Parmesan cheese

Put first 5 ingredients into blender. Coddle egg one minute. Put into blender and turn motor on. Immediately remove the cover and add 1/2 cup more salad oil. Turn off; add lemon juice and cheese. Turn blender on again—then off quickly and it is done.
Serve with Romaine and croutons.

Molly Riggins Sandridge (Mrs. David A.)

TARRAGON SALAD DRESSING

Serves: 4 (can double or triple)

6 Tablespoons salad oil
2 Tablespoons tarragon
    vinegar
1/2 teaspoon salt
Dash white pepper
1/2 teaspoon Accent

Combine ingredients and blend.
Added touch: chop small amounts of fresh mint into salad greens.

Ruth Bowles Carson (Mrs. Philip G.)

230

"BUCKS RESTAURANT" BLUE CHEESE DRESSING

Can do ahead
Yield: 2 cups
Preparation: 5 minutes

1/4 cup blue cheese
1 cup mayonnaise
3/4 cup buttermilk
1 Tablespoon Worcestershire
    sauce
1 teaspoon garlic salt

Crumble blue cheese into mayonnaise; mix well. Add buttermilk, Worcestershire sauce and garlic salt.

Gay Woolard Coleman (Mrs. Stewart B.)

CHUTNEY DRESSING
This is especially good on spinach salad

Must do ahead
Serves: 8

3/4 cup safflower oil
1/4 cup white wine vinegar
1 Tablespoon chopped chutney
1 teaspoon curry powder
1/2 teaspoon dry mustard
Salt and freshly ground pepper

Combine all ingredients in bowl or jar with tight-fitting lid and whisk or shake until well blended. Refrigerate several hours or overnight.

Emily Caddell Gordon (Mrs. Alan F.)

FRUIT MAYONNAISE
Good over congealed salads and fruit salads

Must do ahead
Yield: 2 cups
Preparation: 20 minutes

1 Tablespoon butter
2 Tablespoons flour
1-1/2 cups fruit juices
    (pineapple or grapefruit,
    unsweetened)
Juice of 1 lemon
Juice of 1 orange
2 eggs, separated
1/2 cup whipping cream
Sugar

Melt butter, add flour and blend. Add fruit juices and sweeten to taste. Cook over medium heat, stirring until thickened. Remove from heat and slowly pour over beaten egg yolks, stirring vigorously. Let mixture cool. Carefully fold in stiffly beaten egg whites and whipped cream. Chill and serve over salad.

Mary Jane Dillingham Westall (Mrs. Jack W., Jr.)

231

HONEY DRESSING

Can do ahead
Yield: 2 cups

2/3 cup sugar
1 teaspoon dry mustard
1 teaspoon paprika
1/4 teaspoon salt
1 teaspoon celery seed
1/3 cup strained honey
5 Tablespoons vinegar
1 Tablespoon lemon juice
1 teaspoon onion, grated
1 cup salad oil

Mix dry ingredients; add honey, vinegar, lemon juice and grated onion. Pour oil into mixture very slowly, beating constantly with rotary beater.

Shirley Ann Freeman McCullough (Mrs. Charles T.)

ELIZA'S SALAD DRESSING

1/2 cup sugar
1/4 cup vinegar
1/2 cup oil
1/4 cup ketchup
1/2 teaspoon salt
1 Tablespoon minced onion
Dash pepper

Mix all ingredients well. Store in refrigerator. Keeps for weeks.

Stuart Pegram Bradfield (Mrs. S. Smith)

FRENCH DRESSING

1/3 cup tarragon vinegar
1 Tablespoon paprika
1 teaspoon salt
Dash of cayenne
1 small clove garlic, pressed
1/4 cup sugar
1 egg
1 cup salad oil

In blender or food processor, mix all ingredients except oil. With motor on, slowly dribble oil in until thick. Chill. Keeps in refrigerator about 5 days.

Emily Caddell Gordon (Mrs. Alan F.)

ITALIAN DRESSING

Must do ahead
Yield: 2 cups

1-1/3 cups vegetable oil
1/2 cup tarragon vinegar
5 cloves garlic, minced
1 teaspoon salt
1 teaspoon pepper
3 Tablespoons chopped fresh
    parsley
1 teaspoon whole basil leaves
1 teaspoon oregano
1 Tablespoon anchovy paste
1/3 cup pimento-stuffed olives
1 Tablespoon capers
1/4 cup grated Parmesan cheese
1 Tablespoon lemon juice
2 teaspoons sugar

Combine all ingredients in container of an electric blender. Blend well. Refrigerate at least one hour before serving.

Molly Riggins Sandridge (Mrs. David A.)

POPPY SEED DRESSING

Can do ahead
Serves: 14-16
Preparation: 10 minutes

3/4 cup sugar
1 teaspoon salt
1 teaspoon paprika
1/4 cup orange juice, or more
2-1/2 Tablespoons lemon juice,
    or more
1 cup salad oil
1 teaspoon grated onion
1 Tablespoon poppy seeds

SUGGESTED FRUIT
SALAD COMBINATIONS:

1 cantaloupe
1 lb. seedless, green grapes,
    halved
2 bananas, sliced
2 apples, diced
1 11-oz. can pineapple tidbits,
    drained
1 11-oz. can mandarin orange
    sections, drained

Combine ingredients in bottle or jar and serve over fruit salad. A fruit salad with this dressing goes well with curried eggs for brunch. Any favorite fruit combination may be used depending upon which fruits are in season. Strawberries tend to lend an elegant air when needed.
Fruit Salad: With a melon scoop shape cantaloupe into balls. Gently combine fruits and use the sauce above for a dressing.

Gail Roscoe (Mrs. Ronald R.)

POTATO SALAD DRESSING

Can do ahead
Yield: 3/4 cup
Preparation: 15 minutes

1/2 cup sugar
1 Tablespoon flour
1 egg
Dash of salt
1/4 cup vinegar
1 Tablespoon water
1 Tablespoon mayonnaise
1 Tablespoon prepared mustard

Beat sugar, flour, egg and salt together until creamy. Add vinegar and water. Cook over low heat, stirring often, until thick. When done, blend in mayonnaise and mustard. This amount is sufficient for about 5 to 6 cups cubed, cooked potatoes (plus pickles, celery, onions, etc.).

Nell Cundiff Staples (Mrs. Lawrence H.)

MUSTARD-ONION DRESSING

Can do ahead
Yield: 3/4 cup
Preparation: 5-10 minutes

2 teaspoons onion, grated
1/2 teaspoon salt
1/2 teaspoon pepper
2 teaspoons prepared mustard
2 Tablespoons wine vinegar
8 Tablespoons oil
1/4 teaspoon lemon juice

Mix the onion, salt, pepper, prepared mustard and wine vinegar. Then add gradually 8 tablespoons oil and finally add 1/4 teaspoon lemon juice. Great with spinach/orange salad, as well as any green salad.

Bitsy Murphee Powell (Mrs. James)

Desserts

DESSERT HINTS

For a curdled custard, slowly blend a beaten egg into the hot liquid.

When separating an egg, if a bit of yolk gets into the white, remove with a piece of egg shell.

Dust a little flour or cornstarch on cake before icing to prevent icing running off.

Egg whites will yield more volume if beaten at room temperature.

Igniting the brandy or Cognac takes away the raw taste and sends calories up in smoke. Also a cheap brandy is all right for flaming dishes.

Egg whites may be kept in the refrigerator for several weeks if placed in a closed jar.

Be certain a meringue topping on a pie touches the edge of the crust so that it won't shrink from the sides.

When sending cookies to children, pack in popcorn to prevent breaking.

Cream is easiest to whip when chilled. Also chill bowl and beaters.

When melting chocolate, first grease pot in which it is to be melted.

When using glass ovenware, lower the temperature by 25°.

To scald milk without scorching, rinse pan in hot water before using.

For a nice meringue on pie, add 1 tablespoon sugar to every egg white, add a little cream of tartar and bake at a slow heat, about 250° for about 15 minutes.

When baking a cake, add 2 tablespoons of boiling water to the butter and sugar mixture. This makes a fine textured cake.

To keep cookies fresh and crisp in the jar, place crumpled tissue paper in the bottom.

In creaming butter and sugar for a cake, a little hot milk added will aid in the creaming process.

BANANA CAKE

Can do ahead
Can freeze
Yield: 1 loaf
Preparation: 10 minutes
Baking Time: 45-60 minutes

1/2 cup butter
1 cup sugar
2 eggs
3 bananas
1-1/2 cups flour
1 teaspoon soda
1 teaspoon vanilla
1/2 cup nuts, chopped

Cream butter and sugar; add breaten eggs. Sift flour with soda and with other ingredients. Put in greased loaf pan and bake for 45-60 minutes or until done in 350° oven.

Celine Hanan Lurey (Mrs. Michael)

ALMOND CAKE

Can do ahead
Can freeze
Yield: 24-30 squares
Preparation: 15 minutes
Baking Time: 30 minutes

1 can almond paste
1 lb. butter
1-1/2 cups sugar
2 eggs
2 teaspoons almond extract
4 cups sifted flour
1/2 cup sliced almonds

Preheat oven to 350°. Mix butter and sugar until fluffy. Separate eggs—set whites aside—beat yolks into butter mixture. Beat in almond paste and extract until smooth. Add flour and mix until just combined. Press into an ungreased pan—you can use a 9x12 pan or for a thinner cake can bake in a 10x15 jelly roll pan. Beat egg whites until fluffy and brush over the top. Cover with sliced almonds and bake at 350° for 30 minutes.

Celine Hanan Lurey (Mrs. Michael)

FRESH APPLE CAKE

Baking Time: 45 minutes

2 eggs
2 cups sugar
1/2 cup oil
1 teaspoon vanilla
2 cups regular flour, sifted
1/2 teaspoon salt
1 teaspoon baking soda
2 teaspoons cinnamon
1/4 teaspoon nutmeg
4 cups peeled, diced apples
1 cup chopped pecans

ICING:

3 oz. pkg. cream cheese
3 Tablespoons margarine,
    softened
1/2 teaspoon vanilla
1-1/2 cups 4x confectioners'
    sugar

Grease and flour 9x13" pan or bundt pan. Beat eggs well, and gradually add sugar, oil, vanilla. Sift next 5 ingredients and add to eggs. Stir in apples and pecans—mixture will be stiff. Bake for 45 minutes in 350° oven if using a 9x13" pan or 1 hour if a bundt pan. Let cool 15 minutes on rack then spread with cream cheese icing. Remove from bundt pan to ice.
Blend all ingredients for frosting until smooth and then ice cooled cake.

Emmie Field (Mrs. Arthur)

Hint:
Frosting won't stick to waxed paper if you butter the paper lightly before wrapping.

APPLESAUCE FRUIT CAKE
Expensive but very special!

Freezes well
Can do ahead
Serves: 16
Preparation: 20 minutes
Baking time: 1 hour, 15 minutes

1-1/2 cups brown sugar
1 quart applesauce
1/2 lb. margarine, melted
1 cup raisins
1 cup figs, chopped
1 cup dates, chopped
1 cup nuts, chopped
1 teaspoon cinnamon
3/4 teaspoon cloves
3/4 teasoon allspice
1/2 teaspoon nutmeg
3 cups plain flour
3 teaspoons soda
1/2 teaspoon salt

Mix nuts, fruits, sugar and spices together in a large mixing bowl. Stir melted butter into mixture then flour and soda; mix well. Pour into a well-greased and floured tube pan and bake in a 350° oven for one hour and 15 minutes, or until done.

A Christmas favorite in our house. The recipe came from my grandmother.

Nancy Young Hunnicutt (Mrs. Thomas B.)

JO CRUMPLER'S CHEESECAKE
A delicious cheesecake!

Must do ahead
Can freeze
Serves: 8
Baking Time: 30 minutes

1 pound cream cheese
3 eggs, separated
1 pint sour cream
1/2 cup sugar
1 teaspoon vanilla
1 Tablespoon sugar
Graham cracker crust in
    10" spring pan

Bring cream cheese to room temperature, stir to cream it slightly. Beat egg yolks, add cream cheese and 1/2 of the sour cream and the 1/2 cup sugar. Mix until blended. Fold in the stiffly beaten (not dry) egg whites. Pour into graham cracker crust. Bake 30 minutes at 350°. Meanwhile prepare topping: mix remaining sour cream with 1 teaspoon vanilla and 1 tablespoon sugar. When cake is done turn off oven. Spread topping on cake, return to oven to cool for two hours. Chill before serving. Keeps well in refrigerator for 1 week; may be frozen.

Clara Crumpler Bitter (Mrs. Stephen)

CHESS CAKE

Can do ahead
Can freeze
Yield: 15 to 18 squares
Baking Time: 40 minutes

1 box yellow cake mix
1 stick butter
1 egg

TOPPING:

2 eggs
1 box powdered sugar
1 teaspoon lemon extract
1 8-oz. pkg. cream cheese,
    softened
Vanilla to taste

Blend together first three ingredients and put in a well-greased 9x13″ pan. (This will be dough like.) Mix together remaining ingredients and pour over top (this will be soupy). Bake at 350° for 40-45 minutes or until it tests done.

Lynn Holmes Trotter (Mrs. Ben W., Jr.)
Sandi Tucker Holt (Mrs. Stan E.)

ELIZA'S REFRIGERATOR CAKE

Must do ahead
Serves: 8-10
Preparation: 30 minutes
Baking Time: 30 minutes

1 yellow cake mix
1/2 cup oil
4 eggs
1 can mandarin oranges

FROSTING:

1 regular box vanilla
    pudding mix
1 large can crushed pineapple
1 large bowl Cool Whip

Mix cake mix, oil, 4 eggs and mandarin oranges and pour into two 9″ cake pans. Bake at 350° for 30 minutes or until done.
For frosting make pudding according to directions; add pineapple and Cool Whip to pudding. Ice cake.

Stuart Pegram Bradfield (Mrs. S. Smith)

Hint:
A pinch of baking soda put in the water while cooking green vegetables helps hold their color.

ITALIAN CREAM CAKE

Can do ahead
Serves: 10
Preparation: 30 minutes
Baking Time: 25 minutes

1 stick butter
1/2 cup Crisco
2 cups sugar
5 eggs, divided
2 cups flour, sifted with
*   1 teaspoon soda*
1 cup buttermilk
1 teaspoon vanilla
1 small can coconut
1 cup chopped nuts

FROSTING:

1 8-oz. pkg. cream cheese,
*   softened*
1/2 stick butter, softened
1 box powdered sugar, sifted
1 teaspoon vanilla

Cream well butter, Crisco and sugar. Add 5 egg yolks, one at a time. Beat well. Add flour and buttermilk. Beat well. Add remaining 3 ingredients. Beat egg whites and fold into mixture. Makes 3 or 4 layers. Bake at 350° for 25 minutes. Cool and frost.
Combine frosting ingredients and frost cake when cool. Refrigerate.

Peggy Freeman Byrd (Mrs. Grady G., Jr.)
Susan Murray Daniel (Mrs. John N., Jr.)

HUMMINGBIRD CAKE

Can do ahead
Yield: 1 cake
Preparation: 15 minutes
Baking Time: 75 minutes

3 cups flour, sifted
2 cups sugar
1 teaspoon salt
1 teaspoon baking soda
1 heaping teaspoon cinnamon
1 cup Crisco oil
3 beaten eggs
2 cups firm bananas, chopped
1 or 2 cups pecans, chopped
1-1/2 teaspoons vanilla

Combine ingredients and stir with fork. Bake in tube pan at 325° for one hour and 15 minutes.

Jean Rankin Roberts (Mrs. Landon)

LANE CAKE
Expensive, but worth it

Can do ahead
Serves: 16-20
Preparation: 45 minutes
Baking Time: About 20 minutes

1 cup butter
2 cups sugar
Pinch of salt
1 cup milk
8 egg whites (beaten)
3-1/4 cups flour
2 teaspoons baking powder
1 teaspoon vanilla

FILLING:

8 egg yolks
1 cup sugar
1/2 cup butter
1 jigger of whiskey
1 teaspoon vanilla
1 cup raisins
1/2 of a grated coconut
    (about 8 oz.)
2 cups chopped pecans

7-MINUTE ICING:

2 egg whites, room temperature
1-1/2 cups sugar
5 Tablespoons cold water
1/4 teaspoon cream of tartar
1 to 2 teaspoons vanilla

Cream butter and 2 cups of sugar until light and fluffy. Add milk and dry ingredients alternately. Then add vanilla and fold in beaten egg whites. Pour into 3 greased and floured layer cake pans. Bake in a 350° oven just until done. Do not overbake or cake will be dry.

For filling, beat yolks and add sugar and butter. Cook in a double boiler until thick; remove and stir in other ingredients, beginning with raisins. When cake is cool, spread between and on top of layers. Frost with 7-minute icing and put remaining coconut on top and sides of cake. This makes a tall, beautiful and delicious cake. It has been made at Christmas in our family for three generations.

For icing: Place all ingredients except vanilla in top of double boiler, which is over boiling water. Beat constantly for 7 minutes. Remove from heat and add vanilla. Continue beating until icing is right consistency to spread—about 1 minute.

Nancy Young Hunnicut (Mrs. Thomas B.)

Hint:
To make nut meats come out whole, soak nuts in salt water overnight before cracking.

PINEAPPLE CARROT CAKE

A good cake to take on a picnic or for casual suppers.
Better if allowed to sit one day to blend flavors.

Must do ahead
Baking Time: 25-30 minutes

1-1/2 cups plain flour
1 cup sugar
1 teaspoon baking power
1 teaspoon baking soda
1 teaspoon cinnamon
1/2 teaspoon salt
2/3 cup cooking oil
2 eggs
1 cup finely shredded
    raw carrot
1/2 cup crushed pineapple
    (with syrup)
1 teaspoon vanilla

Stir together dry ingredients in large bowl. Add oil, eggs, carrot, pineapple and vanilla. Mix until moistened. Beat with electric mixer 2 minutes at medium speed. Pour batter into greased and lightly floured 9x13″ pan. Bake at 350° for about 25 to 30 minutes. Cool.
Frosting: Beat cream cheese and butter together. Add vanilla and dash of salt. Gradually add sugar. Blend well. Stir in pecans. Frost.

FROSTING:

2 3-oz. pkgs. cream cheese,
    softened
1 stick butter, softened
2 teaspoons vanilla
Dash salt
5 cups sifted 10x sugar
1 cup chopped pecans

Lynn Roda Smith (Mrs. Canie)

DUMP CAKE
EASY, EASY, EASY! GOOD, GOOD, GOOD!

Can do ahead
Serves: 8-10
Preparation: 30 minutes
Baking Time: 60 minutes

1 22-oz. can cherry pie filling
1 15-1/4-oz. can crushed
pineapple, undrained
1 18-1/2-oz. pkg. yellow
    cake mix
1 cup melted butter
    or margarine
1 3-1/2-oz. can flaked coconut
1 cup pecans (pieces)

Layer in order listed in a 9x13 pyrex pan. Bake at 325° for 1 hour.

Becky Rhoadarmer York (Mrs. A. Robert)

PECAN ICE BOX CAKE

Expensive but easy. Good substitute for traditional fruit cake.

Must do ahead
Serves: At least 24
Preparation: 15-20 minutes

1 lb. box vanilla wafers
1 lb. box dark seedless raisins
1 quart pecans (pieces and
halves mixed) (4 cups)
1 can condensed milk

Crush vanilla wafers with rolling pin. Then in a bowl mix thoroughly crushed wafers, raisins and nuts. Add condensed milk. Rinse can out with 3 or 4 tablespoons of water and add to mixture. Ingredients should be moist. Pack firmly in tube pan lightly greased. Place in refrigerator overnight before using.

Nancy Mays Thrash (Mrs. Virgil)

PLUM GOOD CAKE

The best of spice cakes

Can do ahead
Freezes well
Yield: 1 cake
Preparation: 15 minutes
Baking Time: 1 hour

1 cup salad oil
3 eggs
2 cups sugar
1 teaspoon cinnamon
1 teaspoon ground cloves
1 teaspoon nutmeg
2 cups self-rising flour
2 jars (4-3/4 oz.) baby food
apricots with tapioca
Optional: 1 cup chopped nuts

GLAZE:

2 cups confectioners' sugar
1/4 teaspoon allspice
1/4 teaspoon cinnamon
1/3 cup butter
1-1/2 teaspoons vanilla
2 to 4 Tablespoons hot water

Beat together oil and eggs, add sugar and spices, add flour and baby food. Pour into a greased and floured bundt pan. Bake in preheated 350° oven for one hour.
Glaze: Melt butter. Blend in sugar, vanilla and spices. Add hot water, one tablespoon at a time until proper consistency. Drizzle over cool cake.

Kathleen Kennedy Noyes

STRAWBERRY CAKE

Must do ahead
Serves: 8
Preparation: 30 minutes
Baking Time: 30 minutes
Yield: 1 cake

1 box white cake mix
1 box (3 oz.) strawberry jello
4 eggs
1/2 cup Wesson oil
1/2 cup water
1/2 cup strawberry juice and
    mashed strawberries (use
    10 oz. pkg. frozen
    strawberries, saving
    leftover juice and berries
    for icing)

ICING:

1 box powdered sugar
1/2 lb. margarine, softened
Add enough mashed
    strawberries and juice
    to make icing spread

Grease and flour a tube or loaf pan. Combine cake mix, jello, eggs, oil, water and strawberries and beat well. Pour into pan and bake at 350° for 25 to 30 minutes.

For icing: Beat all ingredients well and spread on well cooled cake.

Helen King Turner (Mrs. Franklin H., Jr.)

AUNT BETTY'S PLUM CAKE

Must do ahead
Serves: 6
Preparation: 20 minutes
Baking Time: 60 minutes

1 stick of butter, plus
    generous piece
4 Tablespoons sugar
1 egg
1 cup flour
2 lbs. Italian purple plums
    (these plus are plentiful in
    late summer and early fall)
3 Tablespoons granulated
    sugar
1 teaspoon vanilla

Cream butter until soft. Add sugar and cream together. Add egg. Add flour and stir until the dough forms a tender ball. Flour hands and press dough into greased 9″ pie pan. With heel of hand, shape into shell form. Prick dough with fork. Quarter plums. Begin at outside edge and continue placing quartered plums side by side until plums meet at center. Bake at 350° for 1 hour. Remove from oven and immediately sprinkle with 3 tablespoons of granulated sugar mixed with 1 teaspoon vanilla. Cool and serve topped with whipped cream.

Martha Blackshear Salisbury (Mrs. Kent)

WATERGATE CAKE

Can do ahead
Serves: 8
Preparation: 20 minutes
Baking Time: 25-30 minutes

1 pkg. white cake mix
1 pkg. pistachio
   instant pudding
1 cup club soda
1 cup oil
3 eggs
1/2 cup chopped nuts

Mix all ingredients. Place in a greased 9x13″ baking pan or dish. Bake at 350° for 25 to 30 minutes. Let cool.
Icing: Combine Cool Whip and pistachio pudding (dry) and spread on cake. Sprinkle with additional chopped pecans, if desired.

ICING:

1 9-oz. bowl Cool Whip
1 pkg. pistachio pudding

Mrs. Howard K. Poe

5 FLAVOR POUND CAKE

Can freeze
Serves: 12-15
Preparation: 45 minutes
Baking Time: 1 hour, 30 minutes

CAKE:

2 sticks butter
1/2 cup vegetable shortening
3 cups sugar
5 eggs, well beaten
3 cups all-purpose flour
1/2 teaspoon baking powder
1 cup milk
1 teaspoon coconut extract
1 teaspoon rum extract
1 teaspoon lemon extract
1 teaspoon vanilla extract
1 teaspoon butter extract

Cream butter, shortening and sugar until lightly fluffy. Add eggs which have been beaten until lemon colored. Combine flour and baking powder and add to creamed mixture alternately with milk. Stir in flavorings. Spoon into a greased and papered 10″ tube pan and bake at 325° for 1 hour and 30 minutes. For glaze, combine ingredients in heavy saucepan. Bring to a boil and stir until sugar is melted; pour over cake just out of oven. Let sit in pan until cake is cool.

GLAZE:

1 cup sugar
1/2 cup water
1 teaspoon coconut extract
1 teaspoon rum extract
1 teaspoon butter extract
1 teaspoon lemon extract
1 teaspoon vanilla extract
1 teaspoon almond extract

Sarah Greene Hensley (Mrs. Donald)

245

FULLER'S FINEST POUND CAKE

Can freeze
Can do ahead
Yield: 1 12-cup cake or 2 6-cup cakes
Preparation: 20 minutes
Baking Time: 1-1/2 to 2 hours

3 cups sugar
2 sticks margarine
1 stick butter
1 8-oz. pkg. cream cheese
8 eggs
1 teaspoon vanilla
1 teaspoon rum flavoring
3 cups flour

Cream butter, margarine and cream cheese. Add sugar and cream until light in color. Add flavorings and eggs one at a time, beating well after each one. Add flour slowly and blend well. Grease and flour one 12 cup tube pan or 2 six cup tube pans. Bake in 12 cup tube pan at 250° for 1-1/2 to 2 hours. (Bake only 1-1/2 hours if using 2 six cup tube pans.)

Jo Clark Shuford (Mrs. Fuller A.)

BOURBON POUND CAKE

Can do ahead
Can freeze
Serves: 16-20
Preparation: 30 minutes
Baking Time: 1-1/2 hours

1 pound butter
3 cups white sugar
8 eggs
3 cups cake flour, sifted
1/4 teaspoon salt
2 Tablespoons bourbon
3 teaspoons vanilla
1/2 cup pecans

Cream butter and sugar. Add yolks of eggs one at a time. Beat after each one. Add cake flour, salt. Add egg whites, beaten stiff. Add bourbon and vanilla. Grease and flour tube pan. Line the bottom with wax paper. Chop 1/2 cup pecans and place on wax paper. Pour batter over nuts. Bake at 325° for 1-1/2 hours. Let stand in pan 5 minutes before turning out.

Mrs. Pearl Wright

Hint:
A bay leaf in your flour and other staples will keep the bugs away.

BLACKBERRY CREAM PIE
A deliciously different blackberry pie

Can do ahead
Serves: 6-8
Preparation: 15-20 minutes
Baking Time: 40-45 minutes

1 cup sugar
1 cup sour cream
3 Tablespoons flour
1/4 teaspoon salt
4 cups blackberries, rinsed or
    16 oz. bag, if frozen, berries
1 9" unbaked pie crust
1/4 cup fine dry bread crumbs
2 Tablespoons sugar
1 Tablespoon butter, melted

In a bowl combine sugar, flour and salt and stir. Add sour cream and stir until blended. Pour blackberries in crust and spread evenly. Pour sour cream mixture over berries. Combine melted butter, crumbs and sugar. Sprinkle over top. Bake at 375° for 40-45 minutes. Serve warm or cool.

Gail Northen Rogers (Mrs. George H., Jr.)

BUTTERMILK PIE

Can freeze
Serves: 8
Preparation: 15 minutes
Baking Time: 50 minutes

1/2 cup butter, or margarine
2 scant cups sugar
3 eggs
1/4 cup all-purpose flour
1 cup buttermilk
Dash of ground nutmeg or
    1 teaspoon vanilla (I use
    the vanilla)
1 unbaked deep dish pie shell

Combine butter or margarine and sugar, creaming well. Add eggs and flour...beat until fluffy (about 2 minutes). Fold in buttermilk and flavoring. Pour into pastry shell. Bake at 325° for 50 minutes. Cool thoroughly before cutting.

Mary Claire Krause Israel (Mrs. Thomas M., II)

PEANUT BUTTER PIE

Can do ahead
Can freeze
Yield: 4 pies or about 48 tarts
Preparation: 20 minutes

4 regular or chocolate graham
    cracker crusts
12 oz. smooth peanut butter
8 oz. cream cheese, softened
1 lb. confectioners' sugar
1-1/2 cups milk
2 9-oz. pkgs. Cool Whip

Mix together peanut butter, cream cheese, sugar and milk. Blend in Cool Whip. Pour into pie shells and freeze.

Lynn Holmes Trotter (Mrs. Ben W., Jr.)

CHIFFON SQUASH PIE
I prefer this to pumpkin pie—very light and delicious

Can do ahead—the same day
Serves: 4-6
Preparation: 20 minutes

9" baked pie shell, cooled
3 eggs, separated
1 Tablespoon gelatin
1/2 cup heavy cream
1/2 teaspoon salt
1/2 teaspoon ginger
1-1/2 cups cooked butternut
    squash, mashed
2 Tablespoons white sugar
1 cup brown sugar
2 teaspoons cinnamon
1/4 teaspoon allspice

Soften gelatin in cold water. Combine squash, brown sugar, egg yolks, spices and salt in double boiler or heavy pan and cook until thickened— stirring constantly. Add gelatin to hot mixture until it dissolves. Chill until thick. Mix sugar into stiffly beaten egg whites and add to first mixture. Pour into pie shell. Refrigerate. Top with whipped cream before serving.

Karen Altizer Fields (Mrs. Jay, Jr.)

FRUIT SALAD PIE
Our family's traditional Christmas pie.

Must do ahead
Yield: 2 pies
Preparation: 20 minutes (some the day ahead)

1 large can crushed pineapple
2 cups sugar
1 jar maraschino cherries
1/4 cup water
1 egg, beaten
1 Tablespoon flour
Dash salt
6 bananas, sliced
1 cup nuts
2 9-inch pie shells, baked
Whipped cream

Mix can of crushed pineapple and sugar. This *must* set overnight. Drain off juice the following day. Heat pineapple juice and cherry juice. Add egg and enough flour to thicken to the one-quarter cup of water. This mixture and a dash of salt should be added to the hot juices. Cook to boiling. Cool. Mix in bananas, nuts, pineapple and cherries. This filling may be made several days ahead. It's best to add filling to pie shells just before serving. Top with whipped cream.

Susan Lee Drenning (Mrs. Dennis)

Hint:
Brown sugar will soften if placed in the frige for a few days.

MERINGUE PIE

Can do ahead
Serves: 6-8
Baking Time: 15-20 minutes

1 cup Ritz cracker crumbs
    (about 20 crackers)
3 egg whites
1 teaspoon vanilla
1 cup sugar
1 teaspoon baking powder
1/2 cup nuts
1/2 cup chocolate bits

Crush crackers. Beat egg whites, adding sugar and vanilla gradually. Fold in other ingredients. Pour in well greased 9" pie pan. Bake at 350° for 15 to 20 minutes.

Lynn Holmes Trotter (Mrs. Ben W., Jr.)

MY FAVORITE PECAN PIE

Can do ahead
Yield: 1 pie
Preparation: 15 minutes
Baking Time: 45 minutes

1 cup white corn syrup
1 cup light brown sugar
1/3 teaspoon salt
1/3 cup melted butter
1 teaspoon vanilla
3 whole eggs
1 heaping cup shelled and
    broken pecans

Mix corn syrup, sugar, salt, butter and vanilla. Combine with lightly beaten eggs. Pour into 9" pie shell and sprinkle with pecans. Bake in 350° oven for 45 minutes.

James E. Chapman

PUMPKIN PIE

Can do ahead
Yield: 1 9" pie
Preparation: 15 minutes
Baking Time: 45 minutes

1-1/2 cups pumpkin, cooked
    and mashed
1/2 cup brown sugar
1/2 cup white sugar
1/2 teaspoon salt
1 teaspoon cinnamon
1 teaspoon ginger
1/8 teaspoon allspice
2 eggs, slightly beaten
1 cup evaporated milk
1 pie shell, unbaked

Mix pumpkin, sugars and spices together. Add eggs and milk and mix thoroughly. Pour into your favorite *unbaked* pie shell. Bake at 425° for 40 to 45 minutes. When pie is done a knife inserted in the center will come out clean. Serve with whipped cream.

Anne Hirzel Rector (Mrs. Frederick)

PINA COLADA PIE

Must do ahead
Serves: 6-8
Preparation: 30 minutes

CRUST:

1-1/4 cup graham cracker
*   crumbs*
3 Tablespoons granulated
*   sugar*
1/3 cup melted butter

FILLING:

1-1/4 cup Pina Colada Mix
*   (by Holland House)*
1-1/2 Tablespoons flour
3 eggs, well beaten
2 Tablespoons butter, or
*   margarine*
2 Tablespoons light rum
1 8-1/4-oz. can crushed
*   pineapple, drained*
1/4 teaspoon coconut flavoring
1/4 teaspoon rum flavoring
1 cup Cool Whip
3/4 cup angel flake coconut

Crust: Mix graham cracker crumbs, sugar and butter together and press into 9″ pie plate. Chill. **Filling:** In top of double boiler, mix together pina colada mix, flour, eggs, butter and rum. Cook in double boiler over high heat until thick, about 5-10 minutes. Cool by immersing pan in bowl of ice water. Add crushed pineapple, both flavorings, and mix well. Fold in Cool Whip and most of coconut. Pour into chilled pie shell. Sprinkle remaining coconut over top. Chill.

Jeannie Renick Davis (Mrs. John N., Jr.)

RUM CREAM PIE
Superb!

Must do ahead
Can freeze
Serves: 6-8
Preparation: 20 minutes

1/2 Tablespoon Knox gelatin
1/4 cup water
1/2 cup sugar
1/8 teaspoon salt
3 egg yolks (from large eggs)
1/4 cup white rum
1 cup heavy cream, whipped
1 8″ graham cracker pie crust
Chocolate curl garnish

Sprinkle gelatin over water to soften. Add sugar, salt, egg yolks, and stir over medium heat until gelatin dissolves and eggs thicken. Do not boil. Remove from heat. Add rum and cool until mixture thickens. Fold in whipped cream and pour into pie shell. Chill several hours or overnight. Serve at room temperature and garnish with chocolate curls. This will keep up to 2 weeks in the refrigerator.

Elsie Allport Bennett (Mrs. Harold K.)

RASPBERRY MACAROON PIE

Must do ahead
Can freeze
Serves: 8
Preparation: 2 hours

3 dozen macaroons
3/4 cup sherry
3/4 cup toasted sliced almonds
1 10-oz. pkg. frozen raspberries,
    thawed
1 pint (good) vanilla ice cream

Soak macaroons in sherry for 1/2 to 3/4 hour. Crumble and press into well greased pie pan. Alternate raspberries, ice cream and almonds, ending with almonds. Freeze.

If peaches are in season, a few peach slices soaked in sherry with a little sugar is a nice garnish. Add these just before serving. Remove pie from freezer 15 to 20 minutes before serving.

Lynn Roda Smith (Mrs. Canie)

THE WORLD'S BEST COOKIES
And they really are!

Can do ahead
Yield: 8 dozen
Preparation: 15 minutes
Baking Time: 12 minutes "per batch"

1 cup butter
1 cup sugar
1 cup brown sugar; firmly
    packed
1 egg
1 cup salad oil
1-1/2 cups rolled oats, regular
1 cup crushed Grape-Nut
    flakes
1 cup shredded coconut
3/4 cup chopped walnuts
    or pecans
3-1/2 cups sifted all-purpose
    flour
1 teaspoon soda
1 teaspoon vanilla extract
1/2 teaspoon coconut extract
1/2 teaspoon salt

Preheat oven to 325°. Cream together butter and sugars until light and fluffy. Add egg, mixing well, then salad oil, mixing well. Add oats, Grape Nut flakes, coconut, and nuts, stirring well. Then add flour, soda, salt and flavoring. Mix well and form into balls the size of small walnuts and place on ungreased cookie sheet. Flatten with a fork dipped in water. Bake for 12 minutes. Allow to cool on cookie sheet for a few minutes before removing.

Nancy Young Hunnicutt (Mrs. Thomas B.)

BLONDE BROWNIES
These will never make it to the freezer!! Delicious and easy!

Can do ahead
Can freeze
Yield: 16-20 squares
Preparation: 20 minutes
Baking Time: 25-30 minutes

1 stick butter
1 cup flour
1 cup sugar
2 eggs
1 egg yolk
1/2 cup nuts
1 teaspoon vanilla

Soften butter. Blend in sugar and flour. Add eggs one at a time. Fold in nuts and vanilla. Bake in 8" greased cake pan at 350° for 25-30 minutes. Cut into squares when cooled . Store in separate tin.

Holly Hall Mason (Mrs. Christopher P.)

AUNT GOODY'S GOODIES

Must do ahead
Serves: 12
Preparation: 20 minutes
Refrigerator: 2 hours

2 sticks butter, melted
1 cup sugar
1 egg
1/2 cup milk
1 cup nuts
1 can coconut
1 cup crushed grahams
TOPPING:
3/4 cup butter
2 cups powdered sugar
1 Tablespoon milk
1 teaspoon vanilla

Grease 9x13" pan and line with whole graham crackers. Put two sticks butter, 1 cup sugar, egg and 1/2 cup milk in saucepan and let boil over medium heat about 1 minute. Add nuts, coconut, cup crushed grahams; pour over crust. Chill 2 hours. Blend topping ingredients in blender and spread over chilled mixture.

Bette Huntsman Marlowe (Mrs. L. Gilbert)

CHEESE SUGAR COOKIES

Can do ahead
Yield: 150 to 200 cookies
Preparation: 15 minutes

1 pound butter
1/2 cup sugar
5 cups flour
3/4 pounds grated sharp cheese
1 egg yolk

Melt butter, cream in sugar. Fold in flour. Add egg yolk and knead in cheese. Form into small balls. Slightly flatten with finger. Bake at 350° 8 to 12 minutes (watch). Roll in granulated sugar. Store in separate tin.

CAROB-CHIP WHOLE WHEAT COOKIES
A healthy cookie!

Can do ahead
Yield: 60
Preparation: 20 minutes
Baking Time: 8-12 minutes "per batch"

2-1/2 cups whole wheat flour
1/3 cup instant non-fat dry
*   milk powder*
1 teaspoon baking soda
1/2 teaspoon salt
1 cup unsalted butter, softened
1 teaspoon vanilla
1-1/2 cups firmly packed dark
*   brown sugar*
3 eggs
Optional: 1-1/2 cups coarsely
*   broken walnuts or pecans*
1-1/2 cups carob chips
*   (available at health*
*   food stores)*

Stir flour, dry milk powder, baking soda and salt in a medium-size bowl until blended. Beat butter, vanilla, sugar and eggs in large bowl with electric mixer on high speed until well blended and lighter color. Turn mixer to low speed. Gradually beat in flour mixture just until blended. Stir in nuts and carob chips.

Preheat oven to 375°. Line cookie sheet with aluminum foil. Drop dough by rounded teaspoonfuls on to foil-lined sheets, spacing about 1-1/2 inches apart. They do not spread much. Bake 8 to 12 minutes depending upon your oven, until they feel semi-firm to the touch and are slightly darkened. Cool on wire racks.

Deborah Lynn Robinson

CREAM CHEESE COOKIES

Can do ahead
Yield: 3-4 dozen
Baking Time: 20 minutes

1 cup butter
6 oz. cream cheese, softened
1 cup sugar
1/4 teaspoon salt
1 teaspoon vanilla
1 egg
1 Tablespoon milk
2 cups flour
1/2 cup coconut
Nuts or cherries

Cream butter, cheese, sugar, salt and vanilla. Add eggs and milk, beat well. Add flour and stir in coconut. Drop from teaspoon on *ungreased* cookie sheet. Top with nut halves. Bake at 325° for 20 minutes. DO NOT LET BROWN!

Celine Hanan Lurey (Mrs. Michael)

CINNAMON RAISIN BARS

Can do ahead
Serves: 12-15
Preparation: 30 minutes
Baking Time: 35 minutes

1/2 cup margarine
1 cup brown sugar
1-1/2 cups flour
1/2 teaspoon soda
1/2 teaspoon salt
1-1/2 cups oatmeal
   (quick 1 minute)

RAISIN FILLING:

1/4 cup sugar
1 Tablespoon cornstarch
1 cup water
2 cups raisins

ICING:

2 cups 10x sugar
1/2 teaspoon cinnamon
2 Tablespoons milk

Put sugar and cornstarch in saucepan. Stir in water and add raisins. Cook over medium heat until thick and bubbly; cool.
While mixture is cooling, cream butter and sugar. Add dry ingredients, flour, soda, salt and oats. Add 1 to 2 tablespoons water. Mix until crumbly. Firmly pat half mixture in 13x9″ greased pan. Spread cooled raisin filling over mixture. Mix remaining crumbs with 1 to 2 tablespoons water. Spoon over raisin filling. Pat smooth. Bake at 350° for 35 minutes. Remove from oven and top with cinnamon icing. Mix the sugar, cinnamon and milk (can heat to spread) and spread over top of cooked mixture.

Ann Mendenhall Campbell (Mrs. R. Donald)

DREAM BARS

Can do ahead
Can freeze
Yield: 48 cookies
Preparation: 20 minutes
Baking Time: 45 minutes

1 cup vegetable shortening
3 cups brown sugar
2 cups sifted flour
1 teaspoon salt
2 teaspoons vanilla
4 eggs
4 Tablespoons flour
1 teaspoon baking powder
3 cups coconut
2 cups broken nuts
1 pkg. dried apricots, cooked
   and finely chopped

Cream shortening with one cup of sugar. Add 2 cups flour and salt. Mix well. Spread in greased 10-1/2x15-1/2″ pan or two 8x8″ pans. Bake at 350° for 15 mintues. Cool.
Mix remaining sugar, vanilla, and eggs and beat thoroughly. Add 4 tablespoons flour, baking powder, coconut, nuts and apricots. Pour this mixture on top of first baked mixture and bake at 350° for 25 minutes or until done.

Jan Stauffer Schulhof (Mrs. Lary A.)

CRUNCHY LADYFINGERS

Can do ahead
Yield: 3 dozen
Preparation: 30 minutes
Baking Time: 25 minutes

1 cup butter—no substitute
6 Tablespoons confectioners'
sugar
2 cups flour
1 cup nuts
2 teaspoons vanilla

Combine to form stiff dough. Roll out in hands —into finger shape. Bake at 350° for 25 minutes or less. You don't want them to color. Roll in powdered sugar.

Elaine Newman Schulman (Mrs. Dick)

MOTHER'S DATE NUT ROLL

Must do ahead
Serves: 8-10
Preparation: 30 minutes

1-1/2 cups graham cracker
crumbs
1 cup chopped dates
1 Tablespoon orange juice
1/8 teaspoon salt
36 miniature marshmallows
1/4 cup pecans, chopped
1/2 cup cream, whipped

Pour orange juice over dates; add salt. Fold dates, nuts and marshmallows into cream. Fold in cracker crumbs, reserving about 1 tablespoon. Sprinkle unused crumbs in a sheet of waxed paper brushed with butter. Turn date mixture onto paper and shape into long roll about 3″ wide. Roll in paper and put in refrigerator for at least 12 hours. Cut into 1/2 inch slices and serve with extra whipped cream. (Cream can be flavored with rum or brandy.)

Boots Uzzell Spencer (Mrs. William C.)

LEMON BISQUE
Quick and easy! Melts in your mouth.

Can do ahead
Can freeze
Serves: 6-8
Preparation: 10 minutes

1 tall can carnation milk,
chilled
1 cup sugar
1/4 cup lemon juice
Grated rind of 1 lemon
Graham cracker crumbs,
enough for at least one
pie crust

Whip the milk until stiff. Add sugar, lemon juice and grated lemon rind. Line square pyrex dish or icetray with graham cracker crumbs. Pour in mixture and top with more graham cracker crumbs. Freeze.
Can be made in food processor. Do not use blender for whipping milk.

Alice Ward Griffin (Mrs. William R., III)

FROSTED LEMON BARS

Can do ahead
Freezes well
Yield: 4 dozen
Preparation: 30 minutes
Baking Time: 45 minutes

CRUST:

1 cup butter
  (NOT margarine)
2 cups flour
1/2 cup powdered sugar

Make crust and press into 9x12 baking sheet. Bake at 350° for 20 minutes. Pour filling on to crust; bake 25 minutes more. Cool before frosting.

FILLING:

4 beaten eggs
4 Tablespoons lemon juice
2 teaspoons lemon rind
2 cups sugar
4 Tablespoons flour
1 teaspoon baking powder

FROSTING:

3 cups powdered sugar
3 Tablespoons softened butter
1 Tablespoon lemon juice
1 to 2 Tablespoons heavy cream
2 teaspoons vanilla

Holly Hall Mason (Mrs. Christopher)

JAM STREUSEL BAR
Good with breakfast or brunch

Can do ahead
Can freeze
Serves: 12
Preparation: 15 minutes
Baking Time: 25 minutes

1-1/2 cups flour
1 cup packed brown sugar
1 teaspoon salt
3/4 cup butter
2 cups oatmeal
1-1/2 cups jam (strawberry,
  blackberry, grape or
  your favorite)
1/2 cup chopped pecans

Combine flour, sugar, salt and oatmeal. Cut in butter. Grease 13x9″ pan. Press in 1/2 of flour mixture evenly. Spread jam over this and top with remaining flour, oatmeal mixture. Dot with 2 tablespoons butter and nuts. Bake at 375° for 25 minutes.

Jane Brown McNeil (Mrs. M. Kerney)

OATMEAL LACE COOKIES

Can do ahead
Yield: 5-6 dozen
Preparation: 20 minutes
Baking Time: 7 minutes per batch

1/2 lb. butter, melted
2-1/4 cups Old Fashioned
Quaker Oats
2-1/4 cups light brown sugar
3 Tablespoons flour
1/2 teaspoon salt
1 egg, slightly beaten
1 teaspoon vanilla

Grease lightly 2 cookie sheets. Stir oats, sugar, flour and salt together. Melt butter and add to mixture while hot. Mix well. Next, add slightly beaten egg and vanilla. Mix well again.

Drop by the teaspoonful, spaced apart, on cookie sheet (1 dozen to a sheet).

Bake at 375° for about 7 minutes. Prepare one "batch" while one cooks. the "trick" is to remove cookies with a spatula when *slightly* cooled, to waxed paper...just about a minute. Store in tin for crispness.

Adelene Barnett Watts (Mrs. Walter M., Jr.)

MIMI'S CHRISTMAS PECOONS

Note: This recipe was carefully cultured by my grandmother and is still the Christmas tradition for all the Dulins who have inherited the recipe.

Can do ahead
Can freeze
Yield: 36
Preparation: 15 minutes
Baking time: 30 minutes

1-1/2 sticks butter (or 1/2
butter and 1/2 margarine)
1/4 cup white sugar
1 cup pecans, finely chopped
2 teaspoons cold water
2 cups plain flour, sifted
2 teaspoons vanilla
Dash salt

Cream butter and sugar, add vanilla and nuts. Add water, then flour and salt and mix thoroughly. Roll small amount at a time by hand into a roll the size of your finger and about 2" long. Cook in a preheated 300° oven or until very lightly browned. When cool enough to handle, roll in powdered sugar to cover well. Before putting in a covered container, roll again in powdered sugar. The flavor improves with age.

Barrie Muilenburg Sneed (Mrs. Albert Lee)

ORANGE COCONUT COOKIES

Can do ahead
Yield: 16 squares
Baking Time: 25 minutes

2 cups Bakers Angel
    Flake coconut
1/2 cup soft oleo
2 cups sugar
2 eggs
2 Tablespoons fresh
    orange rind
2 Tablespoons milk
1 cup sifted flour
1 teaspoon baking powder
1 teaspoon salt

Cream margarine and sugar until light. Add eggs, orange rind and milk. Sift flour, baking powder and salt together. Stir into butter-egg mixture. Add coconut. Put into two 8″ square pans lined with waxed paper. Bake at 350° for 25 minutes. Allow to cool and cut into 16 squares.

Elizabeth B. Thurlow

SPRITZ COOKIES

Can do ahead
Can freeze
Preheat oven to 375°
Baking Time: 8-10 minutes

2-1/4 cups flour
1/4 teaspoon salt
1 cup butter
1-1/4 cup unsifted
    confectioners' sugar
2 egg yolks
1/2 teaspoon almond extract
1 teaspoon vanilla extract

Mix flour and salt. Put butter in mixer and add sugar. Beat in eggs. Add flour mixture. Put in cookie press and press onto greased cookie sheet. Sprinkle with colored sugar.

Harriet Maybank Hutson (Mrs. Henry C.)

NUTTY BUTTERSCOTCH TREATS

Must do ahead
Serves: 12
Baking Time: 30-35 minutes

1 cup plain flour
1 stick margarine, softened
1 cup nuts, chopped
1 8-oz. pkg. cream cheese,
    softened
1 cup powdered sugar
1 large bowl Cool Whip
2 boxes instant butterscotch
    pudding
3 cups milk

Mix together flour, margarine and nuts with a little water, if necessary. Spread evenly in greased 9x12 pan and bake at 350° for 30-35 minutes or until golden brown. Mix together cream cheese, powdered sugar and 1/2 Cool Whip and chill. Spread over cooled crust. Mix together butterscotch pudding and milk and spread over cream cheese mixture and top with remaining Cool Whip and chill.

Anne Simmons Stewart (Mrs. John E.)

ALMOND PUDDING LOAF

Serves: 6-8
Baking Time: 50 minutes

1/2 cup toasted and finely
    chopped Blue Diamond
    whole natural almonds
1 cup candied chopped fruit
2-1/2 cups Bisquick
1/4 cup sugar
1 pkg. (3-3/4-oz.) vanilla
    instant pudding and
    pie filling
2/3 cup milk
1/4 cup vegetable oil

GLAZE:

1 cup powdered sugar
1 teaspoon rum extract
1 to 2 Tablespoons milk

Heat oven to 350°. Generously grease loaf pan, 9x5x3," sprinkle 1/3 cup almonds over bottom and sides, pressing if necessary. Beat remaining ingredients except glaze in large mixer bowl on low speed, scraping bowl occasionally, for 3 minutes. Pour into pan. Bake until wooden pick inserted in center comes out clean—about 50 minutes. Immediately remove from pan. Cool completely on wire rack, then glaze. Beat powdered sugar, rum extract and milk until smooth, and glaze loaf.

Caney Brown Shuford (Mrs. John F.)

SPELL-BINDERS

Can do ahead
Can freeze
Yield: 4 dozen
Baking Time: 12-15 minutes

1-1/2 cups flour
1-1/2 teaspoons baking powder
1 teaspoon soda
1 cup firmly packed
    brown sugar
1 cup soft butter
1 egg
1 cup quick-cooking rolled oats
1 cup flaked coconut
1 cup pecans, chopped
1/2 cup finely crushed
    corn flakes

ICING:

2 Tablespoons butter
1 cup confectioners' sugar
1 Tablespoon hot water
1 teaspoon vanilla extract

Combine flour, baking powder and soda. Gradually add sugar to butter in mixing bowl, creaming until light and fluffy. Add egg; beat well. Gradually add dry ingredients, blending after each. Stir in oats, coconut, pecans and corn flakes. Drop by rounded teaspoonfuls onto ungreased cookie sheets. Flatten slightly with bottom of glass dipped in additional cornflakes. Bake at 350° for 12-15 minutes. Drizzle with icing.

Icing: Melt butter in 2-cup container. Add confectioners' sugar, hot water and vanilla extract. Beat until consistency of a glaze. If necessary, may thin with a few drops of hot water.

Suzanne Latham Carter (Mrs. David)

PECAN ROLL

Must be done ahead
Serves: 10-12
Preparation: 30 minutes
Baking Time: 15-20 minutes

7 eggs, separated
3/4 cup sugar
1-1/2 cup pecans,
    coarsely ground
1 teaspoon baking powder
Powdered sugar
1/2 pint whipping cream
1 teaspoon almond extract
1 Tablespoon sugar

Brush 15-1/2x10-1/2x1" jelly roll pan with oil. Line with waxed paper and oil the paper well. Separate 7 eggs. With electric beater, beat egg yolks with 3/4 cup sugar until mixture pales and is thick enough to fall into ribbons. Stir in nuts and baking powder. Beat egg whites until stiff and fold into pecan mixture. Spread batter in pan, making sure pecans are evenly distributed over all of pan. Bake at 350° for 15 to 20 minutes or until golden brown. Cool cake in pan. Place a damp dish cloth over top of pastry and chill in refrigerator. (This may be done several hours in advance.)

Cut two pieces of waxed paper and overlap. Dust cold cake with powdered sugar. Turn cake out onto waxed paper. Carefully strip waxed paper from bottom and sides of cake. (It is often more difficult to remove from edges.) Beat 1/2 pint whipping cream and almond extract and 1 tablespoon sugar. Spread evenly over cake. Roll up cake using waxed paper as an aid and slide onto flat serving platter. Sprinkle with more powdered sugar.

Note: Do not fill with whipped cream too far ahead of serving.

Linda Worthington Bell (Mrs. Richard B., Jr.)

APRICOT MOUSSE

Must do ahead
Can freeze
Serves: 6-8

1 cup apricot nectar (juice) or
    pureed apricots
20 marshmallows (large ones)
1 cup cream, whipped
2 Tablespoons orange juice
1 teaspoon lemon juice
1 egg white

Heat in double boiler: the 1 cup apricot nectar (juice) or pureed canned apricots, 20 marshmallows. When marshmallows are melted, remove from heat and cool. Add beaten white of 1 egg, 1 cup cream, whipped, 2 tablespoons orange juice, 1 teaspoon lemon juice. Pour into pyrex pan 6x10 and let set in refrigerator for a soft dessert. Can also be frozen. Good with ginger snaps.

Marian MacEachran Boggs (Mrs. Walter J.)

BUTTER PECAN TORTE
Excellent and versatile

Must do ahead
Serves: 12

LAYER #1:

1-1/2 cups plain flour
1-1/2 sticks margarine
1 cup chopped pecans

LAYER #2:

1 8-oz. pkg. cream cheese
1 9-oz. bowl Cool Whip
1-1/2 cups powdered sugar

LAYER #3:

2 pkg. butter pecan instant
*   pudding (or chocolate)*
3 cups milk

LAYER #4:

1 9-oz. bowl Cool Whip

Mix and press Layer #1 ingredients into 9x13 pan, and bake at 350° until slightly brown; then cool. Mix and spread Layer #2 over Layer #1. Mix and spread Layer #3 over Layer #2. Place Layer #4 over Layer #3 and chill at least 5 hours before serving.

Carol Anne Freeman (Mrs. Michael M.)

ELEGANT MACAROON DESSERT

Can do ahead
Serves: 10-12
Preparation: 60 minutes

24 large almond macaroons
1/2 cup rum
1/2 cup bourbon
1 cup chopped almonds
4 eggs, separated
2/3 cup sugar
2 env. gelatin, soaked in
*   1/4 cup water*
1/2 pint whipping cream

Break up macaroons and soak in whiskey and crunch. Add chopped almonds. Beat egg yolks with 1/3 cup sugar and mix with gelatin mixture. Stir this over hot water until it makes a custard. Cool. Beat egg whites and add 1/3 cup sugar to them. Whip cream. Fold whipped cream and egg whites together. Take 1/3 of egg white-whipped cream mixture and stir into other mixture and then fold in the rest. Pour into your best serving dish and chill. Can serve with dots of whipped cream on top.

Anne Mitchell Betty (Mrs. Tyson)

261

HAZELNUT TORTE

Must do ahead
Serves: 12
Baking Time: 25 minutes

7 eggs, separated
1/4 teaspoon salt
3/4 cup granulated sugar
2 teaspoons grated lemon rind
1 teaspoon vanilla
2 cups ground hazelnuts
1/3 cup breadcrumbs
1 teaspoon baking powder
1 cup heavy cream
1/4 cup confectioners' sugar
Mocha butter cream
   (recipe follows)
2 Tablespoons unsweetened
   cocoa powder

MOCHA BUTTER CREAM:

1/2 cup (1 stick) butter
1 egg yolk
2-3/4 cups confectioners' sugar
3 Tablespoons unsweetened
   cocoa powder
3 teaspoons instant
   coffee powder
1/3 cup cold water

Line 3 8x1-1/2" round layer pans with waxed paper. Beat egg whites with salt in a large bowl with an electric mixer at high speed until foamy. Beat in 1/2 cup sugar, 1 tablespoon at a time, until meringue forms soft peaks. With same beaters, beat egg yolks with remaining sugar until very thick and fluffy. Beat in lemon rind and vanilla. Fold yolk mixture into meringue. Combine nuts, breadcrumbs and baking powder; gently fold into egg mixture. Pour into prepared pans, dividing evenly, and smooth tops. Bake in moderate (375°) oven for 25 minutes or until center springs back when touched lightly. Turn upside down on wire racks. Cool completely. Loosen cakes from edges with knife; turn out of pans and peel off waxed paper. Beat cream and sugar until stiff. Stack torte layers on serving plate with whipped cream between each layer. Refrigerate while making mocha butter cream. Spread butter cream on side and top of torte, reserving about 1 cup. Add 2 tablespoons unsweetened cocoa powder to reserved butter cream and pipe through decorating tube onto top and around base of cake. Decorate with whole hazelnuts. Refrigerate 3 hours before serving. For mocha butter cream: Beat butter in mixing bowl until soft; beat in egg yolk, 1 cup of sugar and cocoa. Dissolve coffee in water. Beat in alternately with remaining sugar until smooth.

Emily Caddell Gordon (Mrs. Alan F.)

CREME De MENTHE MOUSSE

Must do ahead
Must freeze
Serves: 12
Preparation: 15 minutes

1/2 gallon vanilla ice cream
1 medium bottle green cherries,
   chopped and drained
20 coconut macaroons, crushed
3/4 cup green Creme de Menthe
1/2 cup toasted almonds

Soften ice cream. Mix well with remaining ingredients. Pour into clear glass or silver container. Freeze. Garnish with mint leaves.

Beverly Maury Bagley (Mrs. Carter S.)

FORGOTTEN DESSERT

Must do ahead
Cooks overnight
Serves: 8-10

5 egg whites
1/4 teaspoon salt
1 teaspoon vanilla
1/2 teaspoon cream of tartar
1-1/2 cups sugar
1 cup heavy cream, whipped
1 teaspoon sugar
Vanilla ice cream
Fresh or frozen berries

Preheat oven to 450°. Beat 5 egg whites with salt, vanilla and cream of tartar, until forms stiff peaks. Add 1-1/2 cups of sugar one teaspoon at a time and continue beating about 15 minutes. Put in greased 9x13" pan. Put dessert in electric oven and turn oven off. Leave overnight.

Next morning, whip cream with 1 teaspoon sugar. Spread over dessert and refrigerate several hours. Top with vanilla ice cream and then fresh or frozen berries. (Frozen raspberries or strawberries with juice work particularly well.)

Carol Abbott McCollum (Mrs. Hugh)

FROZEN LEMON SOUFFLE

Must freeze
Serves: 20 plus
Preparation: 30 minutes

7 oz. box vanilla wafers,
    crushed
1-1/2 cups sugar
9 Tablespoons lemon juice
6 eggs, separated
3 cups whipped cream
Dash salt

Dissolve sugar in lemon juice, add slightly beaten egg yolks. Add cream and salt. Fold in beaten whites. Pour into two 7" springform pans with 2/3 of wafer crumbs on the bottom, the rest on top. Freeze. Move to the refrigerator 2 to 3 hours before serving. Can serve topped with whipped cream.

Anne Mitchell Betty (Mrs. Tyson)

RUSSIAN CREAM
Excellent!!

Must do ahead
Cannot freeze
Serves: 6
Preparation: 15 minutes

3/4 cup sugar
1 env. unflavored gelatin
1 cup heavy cream
1-1/2 cups sour cream
1 teaspoon vanilla

Blend together sugar and gelatin in small pan. Add water and mix well. Let stand about 5 minutes; then bring to a full, rolling boil, stirring. Remove the sugar mixture from heat and pour in the cream. In a small bowl, mix sour cream and vanilla. Gradually beat in the hot sugar mixture. Pour into a 3 cup mold or individual dishes. Serve with marinated fruit (i.e. nectarines with amaretto.)

Jan Stauffer Schulhof (Mrs. Lary A.)

MACAROON PUDDING
A light and delicious dessert!

Must do ahead
Serves: 6-8
Preparation: 20 minutes

1 quart milk
2 envelopes Knox gelatin
4 eggs
1 cup sugar
8 to 10 macaroons
1 teaspoon vanilla

Dissolve gelatin, add milk. Beat egg yolks with sugar. Add to milk and heat over low heat. When *well* curdled add stiffly beaten egg whites and vanilla. Crumble macaroons over the bottom of a 9x12 bowl. Pour mixture over macaroons and chill.

Mrs. James H. Glenn

CHERRIES JUBILEE
A quick "show stopper"

Serves: 6
Preparation: 10 minutes

3/4 cup currant jelly
1 can pitted bing cherries,
   drained
2 Tablespoons Curacao or
   Grand Marnier
6 Tablespoons dark or
   light rum
6 dishes vanilla ice cream

Melt currant jelly in a chafing dish or frying pan. Stir in cherries and heat. Pour in Curacao and rum and wait no logner than 30 seconds. Light, stirring until the flames die out. Ladle over vanilla ice cream, which has been previously dished out and kept cold in the freezer.

Ellen Resnikoff Carr (Mrs. Robert)

ENGLISH TRIFLE
Traditional English holiday dessert, elegant but light and lovely when served at table from a glass or crystal bowl.

Must make ahead
Serves: 6-8
Preparation: 20 minutes

2 pkgs. lady fingers
Raspberry jam
1 pkg. vanilla pudding
   (not instant)
2-1/2 cups milk
1 large can pears
Sherry or brandy
1/2 pint sweetened
   whipped cream

Spread jam between lady fingers. Line bottom and sides of glass bowl with 1/2 to 3/4 lady fingers. Put a layer of pears and mash with tines of fork (may want to mash pears slightly before layering over lady fingers.) Sprinkle pears generously with sherry or brandy. Make the pudding, using 2-1/2 cups of milk. Pudding will be fairly thin. Pour 1/2 pudding over pears. Repeat layers of filled lady fingers, pears, sherry and ending with remaining 1/2 pudding. Let stand overnight in refrigerator. Before serving, spread sweetened whipped cream over top; garnish with cherries and nuts.

Patricia Stancil Smith (Mrs. Philip J.)

POPPY SEED TORTE

Can do ahead
Preparation: 45 minutes
Baking Time: 20 minutes

1/2 lb. graham crackers,
*   rolled fine*
1/4 cup sugar
1/2 cup butter, melted
3 cups milk
1 cup sugar
1/4 cup poppy seeds
1 teaspoon vanilla
3 Tablespoons cornstarch
1 Tablespoon butter
4 egg yolks
4 egg whites
4 Tablespoons sugar
1 teaspoon vanilla
1/2 cup chopped nuts

Mix first three ingredients and pat into 9x13 pan.
Mix well milk, sugar, poppy seeds, cornstarch, butter and egg yolks. Cook in double boiler until thick, add vanilla. Pour into crust.
Beat egg whites until stiff; add sugar and vanilla. Spread on top of custard. Sprinkle with nuts. Bake at 350° for 15-20 minutes or until browned. Refrigerate.

Linda McFarland (Mrs. Edgar)

BRIE CHEESE

Can do ahead
Serves: 12
Preparation: 20 minutes
Baking time: 30 minutes

1 9" pie crust
4 eggs, separated
1-1/2 cups light cream
1 lb. Brie cheese, broken
*   in pieces*
1/8 teaspoon salt

Preheat oven to 375°. Line a 9" quiche or pie pan with pastry. Bake for 10 minutes. Cool and set aside. Beat egg yolks and cream thoroughly, blend in cheese and salt. Beat egg whites until stiff. Stir in 3 tablespoons of the egg whites and blend to lighten the mixture. Fold in remaining egg whites. Pour into the crust and bake at 350° for 30 minutes or until the custard is set. Allow to cool slightly before cutting. Delicious served with ripe pears and crisp apples.

Barry Muilenburg Sneed (Mrs. Albert Lee)

SUET PUDDING (Steamed Pudding)
Very old family recipe

Must do ahead
Can freeze
Serves: 8-10
Preparation: a day or two!
Baking Time: 3 hours

1 cup chopped nuts
1 cup brown sugar
1 cup sour milk (Milk with 1
*   Tablespoon vinegar added)*
1 cup currants or mixed fruit
1 cup raisins
1 cup ground suet
2 eggs
1 teaspoon cinnamon
1 teaspoon nutmeg
Flour enough for a stiff batter
*   (about 1-1/2 cups)*

SAUCE:

1 cup sugar
1/2 cup rum or brandy
1/2 cup butter
1 Tablespoon flour
1 cup boiling water
1 teaspoon vanilla

Day or two before: Flour fuit and raisins. Mix with remaining ingredients and then add flour to make stiff batter. Turn into a buttered 2-quart pudding mold with a tight-fitting cover or use 2 buttered 1-lb. coffee cans tightly covered with aluminum foil. Fill no more than two-thirds full. Refrigerate with cover in place.

About 3 hours before serving time: Place pudding on trivet (rack or canning jar lids) in deep kettle. Into kettle, pour boiling water to come halfway up sides of pudding mold; cover and steam for 3 hours. Adjust the heat to keep the water gently boiling throughout the steaming; add more water as it steams away.

To unmold: Set mold in cold water for a few seconds. Uncover and turn out. Serve hot; spoon some sauce over top and pass the rest.

Sauce Mix flour and sugar; cream with butter; add boiling water. Boil a few minutes and then add vanilla when cool. Add rum or brandy.

Note: this pudding may be made several days in advance, cooled, then wrapped in foil and kept in the refrigerator. To reheat bake at 325° for about 1 hour or until hot. Or steam in same mold or in a collander about an hour until hot. Can also be frozen for several months. Thaw in refrigerator overnight, then heat using either method described above.

Nancy Kouns Worley (Mrs. Charles R.)

FRIED ICE CREAM (Chinese)
Serve with a Chinese meal

Must do ahead
Serves: 12
Preparation: 15 minutes

1 frozen sponge cake
1/2 gallon ice cream,
   any flavor
5 egg whites
1/2 teaspoon cream of tartar
3 Tablespoons flour
3 Tablespoons cornstarch
3 Tablespoons sugar

One day ahead, slice frozen sponge cake into very thin slices. Cut ice cream into 1-1/2" squares. Wrap sponge cake slices around ice cream, cover and press down edges. Wrap securely with plastic wrap and refreeze.

Fold last 4 ingredients into stiff egg whites. Dip frozen ice cream squares in batter, one at a time. Drop individually in oil heated in wok to 420°. Ice cream will pop right up. Flip over quickly and immediately remove. Entire cooking time is about 10 seconds. (Meringue will brown instantly!) Continue frying until all are fried. Pour flaming brandy over each and serve.

Nancy Reid Graham (Mrs. Frank P.)

LEMON CHARLOTTE ROUSSE

Can do ahead
Serves: 12

1 env. unflavored gelatin
1/2 cup fresh lemon juice
4 eggs, separated
1-1/2 cups sugar
1/8 teaspoon salt
3 Tablespoons butter
1-1/2 teaspoons grated
   lemon peel
1 teaspoon vanilla
Lady Fingers
1 cup heavy cream, whipped

Soften gelatin in lemon juice—reserve. Beat egg yolks, 1 cup sugar and salt until thick. In top of double boiler, combine egg mixture, gelatin and butter. Cook until thickened, stirring constantly (about 10 minutes). Stir in peel and vanilla. Cool. Line spring mold with Lady Fingers. Beat egg whites until soft peaks form. Gradually add remaining sugar (1/2 cup) and beat until stiff. Fold egg whites and whipped cream into lemon mixture. Turn into spring form pan. Refrigerate until firm. Unmold on to serving plate. Garnish with whipped cream.

Frances Hall (mother of Holly Mason)

Chocolate

HELPFUL HINTS IN WORKING WITH CHOCOLATE

How to melt unsweetened baking chocolate:

Method 1: Place baking chocolate in top of double boiler; melt over simmering water.

Method 2: Place baking chocolate in custard cup; set in a pan of hot water.

Method 3: Place chocolate block(s) in original wrapper on piece of foil on cookie sheet. Place in warm oven. *Watch carefully.* Remove chocolate as soon as soft.

How to melt other forms of chocolate:

Melt milk chocolate or semisweet chocolate in top of double boiler over *warm* water. Melt dark, chocolate-flavored baking chips in top of a double boiler over hot, not boiling, water.

The chocolate will melt in a few minutes, depending on its thickness. Chopping or breaking the bar into small pieces and stirring while heating will speed the melting process.

Do not attempt to speed the melting process of either chocolate by boiling the water. High temperatures will only cause the chocolate to thicken.

As soon as the chocolate has melted, remove from heat and use. Further heating will only make the chocolate thicker.

If, after stirring, the chocolate is not thin enough for your purposes, it may be thinned with vegetable shortening (not butter or margarine). Do not use more than four teaspoons of shortening to six ounces of chocolate. Stir in shortening with the melted chocolate and rewarm slightly, if necessary.

Substitutions:

If a recipe calls for cocoa and all you have is solid chocolate blocks, or vice versa, you may substitute.

To substitute cocoa for baking chocolate (unsweetened): Use three tablespoons of cocoa plus one tablespoon of shortening for each ounce of unsweetened chocolate.

To substitute baking chocolate (unsweetened) for semisweet chocolate: For one cup (six-ounce package) of semisweet chocolate, substitute two ounces baking chocolate, seven tablespoons sugar and two tablespoons shortening.

To substitute premelted baking chocolate-type product for baking chocolate or cocoa: One ounce (one package) of premelted product is equivalent to one ounce of baking chocolate or three tablespoons cocoa plus one tablespoon shortening.

Note: Do not substutite semisweet or milk chocolate for unsweetened baking chocolate in recipes. Also, when recipes call for melting milk chocolate chips *with* semisweet chocolate chips, do not substitute baking chips for semisweet chips.

Accurately measure unsweetened cocoa by lightly packing coca into measuring cup and levelling with a spatula.

If additional fat is required when melting baking chips, use shortening, *not* butter or margarine.

Prevent skin from forming on top of cooked puddings and pie fillings by lightly pressing waxed paper or plastic wrap directly onto surface before cooling.

Beat hot chocolate beverages with a rotary beater or wire whisk until foaming to prevent formation of a skin and to enhance flavor.

For chocolate curls, draw blade of vegetable parer over smooth side of a slightly warm block of unsweetened baking chocolate or dark, sweet chocolate bar.

Chocolate deflates stiffly beaten egg white mixtures, so fold in carefully—just until blended, but not mixed.

An opened can of chocolate-flavored syrup should be stored in the refrigerator.

BITTERSWEET CHOCOLATE FROSTING
The perfect adornment for your favorite yellow cake

Can do ahead
Yield: Frost 2 8" layers
Preparation: 20 minutes

4 squares (4 oz.) unsweetened
    chocolate
1 cup granulated sugar
1-1/2 cups milk
3 Tablespoons cornstarch
2 Tablespoons cold water
2 Tablespoons butter or
    margarine
1 teaspoon vanilla

Melt chocolate in top of double boiler. Add sugar, milk and cornstarch which has been mixed with cold water. Place over direct heat and cook until thickened, stirring constantly. Remove from heat. Add butter and vanilla. Cool and spread on cake.

Leslie Anderson

$100 CAKE

*A New York chef charged $100 to give out this recipe...magnificent mocha...
accolades guaranteed!*

Can do ahead
Can freeze
Serves: 16
Preparation: 1 hour
Baking Time: 20 minutes

2-1/2 cups sugar
1 cup shortening
5 eggs
1 cup buttermilk
3 cups flour
5 Tablespoons strong coffee
4 teaspoons cocoa
1 teaspoon soda
Pinch of salt
2 teaspoons vanilla

$100 ICING:

3/4 cup butter
1 egg yolk
3 teaspoons cocoa
5 Tablespoons strong coffee
1-1/2 teaspoon vanilla
1-1/2 boxes powdered sugar

Cream shortening; add sugar. In separate bowl, sift dry ingredients. Separate eggs. Beat egg yolks and add to shortening/sugar mixture with alternate additions of buttermilk and dry ingredients. Stir in coffee and vanilla. Fold in stiffy-beaten egg whites. Grease and flour 4 round cake layer pans. Divide batter into the four pans. Bake in 350° oven for 20 minutes. Cool. Frost with $100 icing.

Prepare icing while cake is cooking. Sift sugar and cocoa. Cream with butter. Add egg yolk, coffee and vanilla. Beat until fluffy. Ice cooled cake.

Ione Wright Morgan (Mrs. C. W.)

AUNTIE NORMA'S CHOCOLATE CAKE

Absolutely delicious—old fashioned goodness in every bite!

Can do ahead
Can freeze
Serves: 12-16
Preparation: 15 minutes
Baking Time: 30 minutes

1-1/2 oz. chocolate
  (unsweetened)
1 cup water
1/2 cup Crisco
1 stick margarine
2 cups flour, all-purpose
2 scant cups sugar
2 eggs
1/2 cup buttermilk
1 teaspoon soda
1 teaspoon vanilla
Pinch of salt

In a saucepan, boil one minute: chocolate, water, Crisco, and margarine. Pour this over flour, sugar and stir. Then add eggs, buttermilk, soda, vanilla and salt. Bake in ungreased 10x13″ pan for 30 minutes in 350° oven. Five minutes before done melt in saucepan ingredients for frosting, except sugar and nuts, and boil one minute. Add sugar and nuts. Stir until dissolved. Take cake out of oven and pour frosting over it. Let it set and cool. Try two teaspoons of cinnamon for variation.

Continued...

FROSTING:

6 Tablespoons sweet milk
1-1/2 oz. chocolate
   (unsweetened)
1 stick margarine
1 teaspoon vanilla
1 box powdered sugar
1 cup chopped nuts

Elizabeth Carpenter Boys (Mrs. G. W., Jr.)
Sarah Ann Raynor Lamm (Mrs. Riddick, Jr.)
Elizabeth Glenn Biggers (Mrs. Carl)

MOCHA APPLE CAKE
Moist and luscious

Can do ahead
Freezes well
Serves: 12
Preparation: 15 minutes
Baking Time: 70 minutes

3 eggs
2 cups sugar
1-1/2 cups oil
2 Tablespoons cocoa
1-1/2 teaspoons salt
1 teaspoon baking soda
1 teaspoon vanilla
3 cups all-purpose flour
3 cups diced baking apples

FROSTING:

1 scant Tablespoon instant
   coffee powder
2 Tablespoons boiling water
3 Tablespoons butter, softened
1-1/2 Tablespoons cocoa
2 cups powdered sugar
1 teaspoon vanilla
1 cup chopped walnuts, toasted

Preheat oven to 350°. Grease a 9x13" pan or a 10" tube pan. Using medium speed on mixer, beat eggs in large bowl. Add sugar and oil and continue beating until well mixed. Blend in cocoa, salt, baking soda and vanilla. Add flour and continue beating until ingredients are combined. Fold in apples. Spread batter in prepared pan and bake 70 minutes or until cake pulls away from side of pan and inserted toothpick comes out clean. Cool on rack. If using tube pan, remove cake from pan.

For frosting: Dissolve coffee in boiling water in medium bowl. Stir in butter and cocoa. Mix until combined well. Add sugar and vanilla and stir until frosting is smooth and spreadable. (You may need to add a bit more boiling water.) Spread over cooled cake and sprinkle with nuts.

Millicent Bitter Elmore (Mrs. Miles)

LINCOLN LOG
Advance preparation required but well worth it!

Must do ahead
Servings: 6-8 generously
Preparation: 30 minutes
Baking Time: 25 minutes

1/2 cup sugar
1/4 cup flour
3 rounded Tablespoons of cocoa
1/4 teaspoon salt
5 eggs
1/2 teaspoon cream of tartar
1/2 cup sugar
1 teaspoon vanilla
Powdered sugar
1 pint whipping cream

SAUCE:

1/2 cup sugar
1-1/2 Tablespoons cornstarch
1 oz. unsweetened chocolate
1/2 cup water
Dash of salt
2 Tablespoons butter
1/2 teaspoon vanilla
Chopped nuts

Sift together twice: 1/2 cup sugar, flour, cocoa and salt. Beat 5 egg whites until stiff, but not dry with cream of tartar. Gradually add 1/2 cup sugar. Beat one minute. Beat 5 egg yolks well with vanilla. Fold dry ingredients into yolk mixture. Blend well. Fold into egg whites. Pour batter into jelly roll pan, lined with buttered waxed paper. Bake in 325° oven for 25 minutes. Sprinkle powdered sugar on a tea towel. Turn out chocolate roll onto towel. Immediately roll up from side to side, not end to end. Put aside to cool.

Whip one pint of whipping cream. Unroll cake and fill with cream. Roll cake up. Wrap with waxed paper and refrigerate.

Mix sugar, cornstarch, chocolate, water and salt well. Cook until thick. Remove from heat and add butter and vanilla. Spoon hot sauce over cake. Sprinkle with nuts. Cut into serving pieces.

Betty Lou McCarty Davis (Mrs. P. C.)

CHOCOLATE VELVET
A cool, smooth dessert to climax your next dinner party.

Must do ahead
Serves: 8

12 oz semi-sweet chocolate bits
1-1/2 cups milk
1-1/2 envelopes gelatin
1/2 cup water
1/2 cup sugar
Dash salt
1/2 cup light cream
2 Tablespoons brandy
2 cups whipping cream
3 Tablespoons sugar
Optional: Kahlua

Scald milk with chocolate in top of double boiler until chocolate melts. Soften gelatin in cold water. Beat chocolate and milk with rotary beater. Allow to cool slightly. Add softened gelatin, sugar and salt. Stir until dissolved. Add light cream, 1 tablespoon brandy and 1 cup whipping cream, whipped. Blend until smooth with a wooden spoon. Pour into 5 cup mold. Chill. When ready to serve, whip 1 cup whipping cream with 1 tablespoon brandy and 3 tablespoons sugar. Spoon onto unmolded desert. Pour Kahlua over top.

Jo-Ann McGowan Grimes (Mrs. C. W.)

A CHOCOHOLIC'S FANTASY
White chocolate and fudge combine in an elegant cake

Can do ahead
Can freeze
Yield: 16 slices
Preparation: 15 minutes
Baking Time: 40-45 minutes

1 cup butter
2 cups sugar
4 eggs
1/4 lb. white chocolate melted
    in 1/2 cup of boiling water
2-1/2 cups cake flour
1 teaspoon soda
1 cup buttermilk
1 teaspoon vanilla

Cream butter and sugar. Add eggs, one at a time, beating after each. Cool chocolate and add to egg mixture. Add flour, soda and butter to mixture, alternately. Add vanilla. Pour into 2 9" greased and floured cake pans. Bake in 350° oven for 40-45 minutes. Cool. Cut layers in half for four-layer cake.

ICING:

Boil 2 cups sugar
2 sticks butter
2/3 cup evaporated milk for
    1 minute
Add 1 cup semi-sweet chocolate
    chips
Remove from heat and beat
    until thickened (5 minutes).

Ruth Bowles Carson (Mrs. Philip G.)

CHOCOLATE BOURBON PIE
Wow your last-minute company with this!

Freezes well
Preparation: 15 minutes
Baking Time: 45 minutes

2 eggs
1 cup sugar
1/2 cup melted butter
4 Tablespoons Bourbon
1/4 cup cornstarch
1 cup pecans, chopped
1 cup semisweet chocolate bits
1 9" pie shell
1 cup whipped cream

Beat eggs, gradually adding sugar. Add butter and Bourbon. Blend in cornstarch. Stir in pecans and chocolate bits. Pour into shell. Bake for 45 minutes in 350° oven. Serve slightly warm with whipped cream.

Beverly Maury Bagley (Mrs. C. S.)

CHOCOLATE ANGEL PIE

This heavenly dessert will answer all your prayers...yumm!

Refrigerator Time: 2 hours
Serves: 8
Preparation: 10/15 minutes
Baking Time: 50-55 minutes

2 egg whites,
    at room temperature
1/8 teaspoon salt
1/8 teaspoon cream of tartar
1/2 cup sugar
1/2 teaspoon vanilla
1/2 cup finely chopped walnuts
    or pecans

PIE FILLING:

1 bar (4 oz.) Baker's German
    Sweet chocolate
3 Tablespoons water
1 teaspoon vanilla
1 cup whipping cream

Meringue shell: Beat egg whites with salt and cream of tartar until foamy. Add sugar, 2 Tablespoons at a time, beating well after each addition. Beat to very stiff peaks. Fold in vanilla and nuts. Spoon into lightly buttered 8″ pie pan, spreading it to look like a pastry shell. Build up sides about half an inch above the side of the pan. Bake in 300° oven for 50-55 minutes. Cool. Pie Filling: Stir chocolate in the water over low heat until blended, smoothing out any lumps. Cool until thickened. Add vanilla. Whip the cream, fold in cooled chocolate mixture. Pile into meringue shell. Chill 2 hours. Garnish with curls made of dark chocolate. Yumm.

Virginia Cooper Taylor (Mrs. W. F.)
Candy Stell Shivers (Mrs. J. A.)

CHOCOLATE CHESS PIE

Serve this warm or cold—delicious either way

Can do ahead
Serves: 8
Baking Time: 40 minutes

PIE CRUST:

Make pate brisee, substituting 1 teaspoon sugar for salt. (Or use a regular pie shell.) Roll it out to 10″ circle on lightly-floured board. Fit dough into 9″ pie pan and crimp edges. Prick shell with fork and chill for 1 hour. Line shell with waxed paper and fill with raw rice or pie weights and bake in hot oven at 400° for 10 minutes. Carefully remove paper and rice and bake the shell 10 more minutes, or until LIGHT brown. Let cool.

In saucepan, melt butter and unsweetened chocolate. Remove from heat and add brown sugar, granulated sugar combined with flour. Beat in eggs, evaporated milk and vanilla. Pour into cooled shell and bake in 325° oven for 25-40 minutes or until set.
Serve warm with whipped cream flavored with rum.

Continued...

PIE FILLING:

1 stick butter
1-1/2 oz. unsweetened
chocolate
1 cup brown sugar (packed)
1/2 cup granulated sugar
1 Tablespoon flour
2 eggs
2 Tablespoons evaporated milk
1 teaspoon vanilla   *Lynn Roda Smith (Mrs. C. B.)*

CHOCOLATE CHEESECAKE
Fabulously rich...unbelievably delicious...suspend your calorie count for this one

Must be made ahead
Can be frozen
Yield: 8
Preparation: 20 minutes
Cooking Time: 2 hours

3/4 cup graham
*   cracker crumbs*
5 Tablespoons melted butter
2 Tablespoons sugar
2 Tablespoons grated
*   semisweet chocolate*
3 eggs
1 cup sugar
3 (8-oz.) pkgs. cream cheese,
*   softened*
12 oz. semisweet chocolate,
*   grated*
1 cup sour cream
1-1/2 sticks butter (3/4 cup)
1 teaspoon vanilla
1 cup coarsely chopped pecans
Whipped cream

In bowl, combine graham cracker crumbs, butter, 2 tablespoons sugar and 2 tablespoons grated chocolate. Press mixture firmly into bottom of 8″ springform pan. In bowl of electric mixer, beat eggs with sugar until mixture ribbons when beater is lifted. In another bowl, beat cream cheese until very soft. Add cheese to egg mixture and beat well. In top of double boiler, combine 12 oz. chocolate, sour cream, butter and vanilla. Set pan over simmering water and heat until chocolate is melted. Stir into cheese mixture and fold in 1 cup coarsely chopped pecans.
Pour batter into pan and bake in 325° oven for 2 hours or until center is firm. Let cake cool on wire rack and remove from pan. Chill 12 hours. Serve with whipped cream.

Lane Weaver Byrd (Mrs. R.W.H.)

FRENCH CHOCOLATE ICE CREAM

This easy ice cream is smooth and will not form ice crystals no matter how long it stays in your freezer.

1/4 cup sugar
1/3 cup water
1 6-oz. pkg. semi-sweet
  chocolate chips
3 egg yolks
1-1/2 cup cream, whipped

In a saucepan, combine water and sugar. Bring to a boil rapidly 3 minutes. Into a blender container put chocolate chips. Add hot mixture of water and sugar. Cover and blend at high speed for 20 seconds or until sauce is smooth. Add egg yolks. Stir to combine. Cover and blend 10 seconds. Fold chocolate mixture into whipped cream. Spoon into 2 refrigerator trays and cover with waxed paper. Freeze 2-3 hours. Yield: 1 quart.

Diana Roscoe Bilbrey (Mrs. G. M., Jr.)

FUDGE SUNDAE CRUNCH

Children especially will love fixing and eating this!

Must do ahead
Serves: 8
Preparation: 2 hours (No baking)

1/4 cup corn syrup
2 Tablespoons firmly packed
  brown sugar
3 Tablespoons butter,
  or margarine
2-1/2 cups Rice Crispies
1/2 cup peanut butter
1/2 cup (or more) fudge sauce
  for ice cream
6 Tablespoons corn syrup
1 quart (or more) ice cream

Combine 1/4 cup corn syrup, brown sugar and margarine in medium-size saucepan (large enough to hold 2-1/2 cups Rice Crispies and mixing).
Cook over low heat, stirring occasionally until mixture begins to boil. Remove from heat. Add 2-1/2 cups Rice Crispies, stirring until well coated. Press into 9" greased pie plate or 9" greased square pan. (We found the square cut easier). Stir together peanut butter, fudge sauce and corn syrup. Spread 1/2 of peanut butter mixture over crust. Freeze until firm (about 45 minutes). Allow ice cream to soften slightly; spoon into frozen pie crust spreading evenly. Warm remaining peanut butter mixture and drizzle over top. Cover with foil and freeze until firm. Let stand at room temperature (about 10 minutes) before cutting.

Mrs. John F. Purnell
Hendersonville, North Carolina

ICED INDIAN PUFFS WITH WHIPPED CREAM
Fabulous Viennese Pastries!

Can do ahead
Yield: 2 dozen
Preparation: 30 minutes
Baking Time: 20 minutes

6 egg yolks
3/4 cup sugar
3 Tablespoons water
1 cup flour, sifted
6 egg whites
2 Tablespoons sugar
1-1/2 cups whipped cream
3 teaspoons sugar

CHOCOLATE ICING:

3 oz. semisweet chocolate
2 Tablespoons water
4 Tablespoons unsalted butter
4 Tablespoons confectioners
   sugar, sifted

Beat egg yolks and sugar until light and fluffy. Add water and flour. Beat egg whites until almost stiff. Add 2 Tablespoons sugar and continue beating until stiff. Combine with egg and flour mixture. Spoon into greased muffin tins or into special Indianer forms which have a rounded bottom. Bake in 275° oven for 15-20 minutes. Remove from pans while hot. Cut off slice at top. Scoop out insides. Put top back in place and ice with chocolate icing. When ready to serve, remove top again and fill inside of cakes with whipped cream, sweetened with 3 teaspoons sugar (or ice cream and whipped cream).

For icing: Into a saucepan put chocolate and water. Heat mixture until chocolate melts. Remove from heat. Add butter and sugar. Allow to cool before spreading.

Greta Halward (Mrs. Eugene)
Statesville

CHOCOLATE SNAKE
SSSSimple...SSSScrumptious...Fudge

4 oz. unsweetened chocolate
6 oz. cream cheese, softened
1 teaspoon vanilla
1/8 teaspoon salt
1 lb. confectioners' sugar,
   sifted

Melt chocolate in top of double boiler over moderate heat. Using an electric mixer, beat cream cheese until smooth. Add vanilla and salt. Gradually beat in sugar, then chocolate until smooth. Roll fudge into a sausage shape, about 1-1/2" in diameter. Wrap in plastic wrap and chill in refrigerator until firm. Keep in fridge until it disappears.

Jeanne Forsyth Powell (Mrs. B. P.)

279

MARTHA WASHINGTON JETS
An easy confection that looks professional!

Can do ahead
Can freeze
Yield: 28-30
Preparation: 35-45 minutes

1 stick softened butter
  (not margarine)
1 box (1 lb.) confectioners' sugar
1 teaspoon vanilla, or rum,
  or mint, etc.
1 Tablespoon evaporated milk
1/2-1 lb. whole pecan halves
5 oz. unsweetened chocolate
2-1/2 oz. cooking paraffin
Toothpicks (about 10)
Optional: red or green
  food coloring

Cream together softened butter and sugar. This can be done by hand or in food processor. Add vanilla and milk. Here food coloring may be added also. If coloring is left out, a little more evaporated milk may be added until the mixture can be easily rolled into small balls, using about 1 tablespoon of dough for each. Place balls on waxed paper and be careful not to let them dry out. A damp towel will prevent this.
Melt chocolate and paraffin together using twice as much chocolate as paraffin. Let cool slightly. Dip each ball into chocolate, using toothpicks. Return to waxed paper and immediately place pecan half on each one.

Gay Woolard Coleman (Mrs. S. B.)

CHOCOLATE TRUFFLES
Bet you can't eat just one!

Must be made ahead
Can be frozen
Should be kept chilled
Yield: 30 3/4" balls
Preparation: 15 minutes
Cooking Time: 10 minutes
Frige Time: 4 hours

1 Tablespoon instant Espresso
3 Tablespoons boiling water
8 oz. semisweet chocolate,
  cut into pieces
1 stick sweet butter
3 Tablespoons brandy,
  Grand Marnier or
  your favorite liqueur
Unsweetened cocoa

In top of double boiler over hot water, combine espresso, water and chocolate until chocolate is dissolved. Remove from heat. Beat in butter, one piece at a time, adding each piece just before the previous one is incorporated. Beat in brandy and chill at least 4 hours until firm. Form into 3/4" balls by shaving mixture with a melon ball scooper and roll in cocoa. These can also be cut into squares and powdered with cocoa. Store in cool place in airtight tin. Keeps indefinitely.

Lane Weaver Byrd (Mrs. R.W.H.)

CHOCOLATE MINT BROWNIES
Luscious green and dark chocolate—pleasing to the eye as well as the palate.

Can do ahead
Can freeze
Yield: 1-1/2 to 2 dozen
Preparation: 20-30 minutes
Baking Time: 30 minutes

1/2 stick margarine
1/2 stick butter
2 squares unsweetened
*   chocolate*
1 cup sugar
2 eggs
1/2 cup flour
1/4 teaspoon salt
1/2 teaspoon vanilla

MINT LAYER:

2 Tablespoons butter
1 cup powdered sugar
1 Tablespoon milk
3/4 teaspoon mint extract
Green food coloring

GLAZE:

1 square chocolate
1 Tablespoon butter

Melt and cool the margarine, butter and chocolate. Beat in the sugar and eggs with a spoon. Add flour, salt and vanilla. Bake in 350° oven for 30 minutes in greased 8″ square pan. When brownies are cool, spread with mint layer and glaze. For mint layer: melt butter and add remaining ingredients, spread and chill.
For glaze: Melt chocolate and butter and spread over mint layer.

Sarah Greene Hensley (Mrs. Donald)

THE WORLD'S RICHEST BROWNIES
Cut squares small

Can do ahead
Can freeze
Yield: 4 dozen
Preparation: 15 minutes
Baking Time: 30-35 minutes

1 cup butter
4 oz. unsweetened chocolate
2-1/2 cups sugar
4 eggs, well beaten
1 (6-oz.) pkg. semisweet
*   chocolate chips*
1 cup flour

Melt butter and chocolate in double boiler. Remove from heat and add sugar while mixture is still hot. Cool and add remaining ingredients. Place in greased 12x15″ pan. Bake in 325° oven for 30-35 minutes.

Beverly Maury Bagley (Mrs. C. S.)

BEST FUDGE CAKE EVER

Bridge Club...Picnic...Camp Care Package...
Wherever a brownie is truly appreciated.

Can do ahead
Can freeze
Yield: 2 dozen
Preparation: 15 minutes
Baking Time: 30-35 minutes

3-1/2 squares semisweet
   chocolate
2 sticks of butter
2 cups sugar
1-1/2 cups of flour
1/4 teaspoon salt
1/2 teaspoon baking powder
4 eggs
2 teaspoons vanilla
Optional: 2 cups nuts

Melt butter, sugar, chocolate together. Sift flour and baking powder into same pan. Add eggs, vanilla, salt and broken nuts. Blend well. Bake in 325° oven for 30-35 minutes. Let cool for 20 minutes, then cut.

Jeanne Forsyth Powell (Mrs. B. P.)

CUCKOO COOKIES

These are great favorites of children and men;
not recommended as a tea-party kind of cookie.

Can do ahead
Can freeze, but chocolate turns color
Yield: 48-60

1-3/4 cup sifted Swans Down
   Cake Flour
1/2 teaspoon soda
1/2 teaspoon salt
1/2 cup cocoa
1/2 cup shortening (Crisco)
1 cup sugar
1 egg
1 teaspoon vanilla
1/2 cup milk
1/2 cup pecans, chopped

Sift together flour, soda, salt and cocoa. Cream shortening and sugar. Beat in egg and vanilla. Add alternately flour and milk. Stir in chopped pecans. Drop by teaspoon on greased baking sheet. Bake in 375° oven for 8 minutes. Remove, top each cookie with half a marshmallow, pressing gently; bake 4 minutes more. When cookies are cool, spread (or dip) with cocoa glaze.
When making glaze, add more hot water, about 1/4 teaspoonful at a time, to get desired consistency.

COCOA GLAZE:

1/2 cup cocoa
1-1/2 cup powdered sugar
3 Tablespoons hot water
1/3 cup butter, melted

Virginia Cooper Taylor (Mrs. W. F.)

CHOCOLATE ICE BOX CAKE

This dazzling dessert should be done the day before...let your diners enjoy its beauty before they eat it!

Must do ahead
Serves: 8—maybe more—very rich
Preparation: 3 hours

8 egg yolks
3/4 cup sugar
2 cups milk
1/2 to 1 teaspoon vanilla extract
2 Tablespoons gelatin
4 Tablespoons cold water
1-1/2 oz. bitter chocolate,
    melted
2 Tablespoons melted butter
1/4 cup rum or Kirsch
2 cups heavy cream
Lady fingers (12)
Kirsch and water
Whipped cream
Optional: walnuts

Combine egg yolks and sugar in top of double boiler and work the mixture with a wooden spoon until smooth. Bring the milk to a boil and add vanilla extract; then add milk gradually to the yolk mixture, stirring rapidly with a wire whisk. Cook over boiling water until the mixture becomes smooth and thick. Do not allow mixture to boil, or it will curdle. Soften the gelatin in cold water and add it to the hot custard, stirring until it dissolves. Cool the custard but do not let it set. Divide the custard into 2 portions and add melted chocolate, melted butter and rum or Kirsch to one portion. Whip cream until stiff and fold half of it into each of the 2 mixtures. Line the sides of a medium spring-form cake pan with lady fingers dipped in equal quantities of Kirsch and water. Fill the mold with alternating layers of chocolate and vanilla cream, allowing each layer to set in refrigerator for about 30 minutes before adding the next. Set the cake (still in its pan) in refrigerator to chill for at *least 12 hours* or overnight.

When ready to serve, remove sides of pan from the cake, leaving the cake in the bottom of the pan. Top with whipped cream and walnuts.

Helen King Turner (Mrs. F. H., Jr.)

FUDGE PIE

Absolutely delicious and easy as pie!

Serves: 6-8
Preparation: 10-15 minutes
Baking Time: 30 minutes

2 eggs
1/2 cup butter, softened
1 cup sugar
2 oz. bitter chocolate, melted
1/2 cup all-purpose flour
1 teaspoon vanilla
1/2 teaspoon salt

Combine butter, sugar, eggs and chocolate, mixing thoroughly. Add a bit at a time, the flour, blending well. Finally blend in the vanilla and salt. Pour into a greased 8" pie plate and bake for 30 minutes in 325° oven. Serve warm with vanilla ice cream or whipped cream.

Barrie Muilenburg Sneed (Mrs. A. L.)
Mildred Matthews Robinson (Mrs. C. L.)

CHOCOLATE POUND CAKE
Moist and delicious—a favorite for mountain picnics

Can do ahead
Can freeze
Preparation: 20 minutes
Baking Time: 90 minutes

1-1/2 cups butter, or margarine
3 cups sugar
5 eggs
3 cups flour, sifted
1/2 teaspoon baking powder
1/2 teaspoon salt
5 Tablespoons cocoa
1 cup milk
1 Tablespoon vanilla
Optional: 1 cup nuts

GLAZE:

3 oz. (1/2 cup) semi-sweet
   chocolate chips
1 Tablespoon margarine
1/4 cup water
1 cup sifted confectioners' sugar
Dash salt
1/2 teaspoon vanilla

Cream butter and sugar; add eggs, one at a time. Sift flour, baking powder, salt and cocoa. Add dry ingredients alternately with milk. Add vanilla and nuts.

Put in greased 10″ tube pan. Bake for 1-1/2 hours in 325° oven.

For glaze: Melt chocolate, margarine in water and add remaining ingredients.

Elizabeth Murphree Powell (Mrs. J. B.)
Melanie Huntsman Hudgins (Mrs. R. M., Jr.)
Patricia Stancil Smith (Mrs. P. J.)

COCOA SURPRISE COOKIES
Children (and grown-ups!) love the surprise of the first bite!

Can do ahead
Yield: 4 dozen
Baking Time: 10-12 minutes

1 cup butter, softened
2/3 cup sugar
1 teaspoon vanilla
1-2/3 cups flour
1/4 cup cocoa
1 cup finely chopped pecans
Small bag Hershey Kisses

Cream butter, sugar and vanilla. Gradually add flour and cocoa. Add nuts and mix. Chill.

Unwrap kisses and then shape dough (about 1 tablespoon) around each Kiss so it is completely covered and roll into a ball.

Place on ungreased cookie sheet and bake in 375° oven for 10-12 minutes. Cool slightly and then put on wire racks to cool completely.

Gay Woolard Coleman (Mrs. S. B.)

MOCHA PIE
Rich and savory

Must do ahead
Can freeze
Serves: 8
Preparation: 30 minutes

20 whole oreo cookies, crushed
1/4 cup butter, melted
1 qt. coffee ice cream, softened
3 oz. unsweetened chocolate,
   melted
1/4 cup butter
2/3 cup sugar
2/3 cup evaporated milk
1 teaspoon vanilla
1 cup heavy cream, whipped
Optional: chopped pecans or
   chocolate shavings

Combine cookies and melted butter; press into 9" pie plate. Spread ice cream over crust and freeze.
Bring chocolate, butter and sugar to boil. Gradually add evaporated milk and cook until thickened. Cool and add vanilla. Spread over ice cream and return to freezer. When set, top with whipped cream. Garnish with nuts or chocolate shavings.

Carol Abbott McCollum (Mrs. Hugh)

CHOCOLATE MOUSSE

Use food processor
Chill or can freeze
Serves: 6

1/4 cup sugar
1/3 cup water
1-1/2 cups heavy cream
1 6-oz. pkg. semisweet
   chocolate pieces
3 Tablespoons dark rum
3 egg yolks
1/2 cup toasted almonds

Combine sugar and water in saucepan and boil for 3 minutes. With metal blade of processor, add cream to beaker and process until a very thick cream forms—about 1 minute. Transfer cream to a large bowl. Without washing beaker, process chocolate pieces for 15-20 seconds. Continue processing and pour in hot syrup, rum and yolks. Add almonds and process until coarsely chopped. Scrape chocolate almond mixture over whipped cream and fold together. Freeze or chill. Spoon into champagne glasses and garnish with chocolate curl to serve.

Beth Walker Hill (Mrs. Haywood N.)

QUICK FRENCH CREAMS
A super holiday gift for your favorite teacher

Can do ahead
Yield: 35-40 pieces
Preparation: 10-15 minutes

8 oz. semi-sweet cooking
  chocolate
1 cup sifted powdered sugar
1 Tablespoon milk
1 egg, well beaten
1/3 cup chocolate sprinkles

In top of double boiler over hot, but not boiling, water, melt chocolate, stirring until smooth. Remove from over water and quickly stir in powdered sugar, milk and egg. Refrigerate until firm enough to shape. Form into 1″ balls. Roll in chocolate sprinkles.

Maureen Kelly Coleman (Mrs. R. L., Jr.)

BUCKEYE CANDY
Let your children help dip these

Yield: 6-7 dozen
Preparation: 90 minutes

1-1/2 1-lb. boxes confectioners'
  sugar
1 lb. jar chunky-style peanut
  butter
1-1/2 Tablespoons vanilla
2 sticks (8 oz.) butter,
  room temperature
1 12-oz. pkg. semi-sweet
  chocolate chips
1/4 bar Paraffin (4 oz.)

Combine sugar, peanut butter and butter. Knead until sugar is blended thoroughly. Mixture will be doughlike in consistency. Form into small balls the size of a buckeye. Melt chocolate chips and paraffin in a double boiler. Dip balls into chocolate with a toothpick, leave top uncovered to look like a buckeye.

Sally Spencer Sword (Mrs. W. C.)

DARK CHOCOLATE SAUCE
A lustrous semi-sweet sauce

Can do ahead
Preparation: 10 minutes
Cooking Time: 5 minutes

1 cup water
1-1/4 cup sugar
1 cup cocoa

Heat water and sugar until it boils hard over the whole surface. Then take off heat and pour in cocoa. Stir with a whip until sauce becomes free of lumps.

Yvonne Eriksson Day (Mrs. J.K.M.)

QUICK 'N EASY POT DU CREME
This is very rich and a little goes a long way

Must do ahead at least 4 hours
(preferably overnight)
Serves: 4
Preparation: 5 minutes
Refrigerator time: 4 hours

1 (6-oz.) pkg. semi-sweet
   chocolate chips
2 Tablespoons sugar
Dash salt
1 Tablespoon brandy
1 egg
3/4 cup milk

Place in bowl of food processor or blender container the chocolate chips, sugar, salt, brandy and egg. In a saucepan, bring 3/4 cup milk just to boiling point. Pour milk into container gradually and blend for 1 minute until mixture is thoroughly whipped. Pour into small pot du creme cups or other small containers and chill. Serve with whipped cream, if desired.

Barrie Muilenburg Sneed (Mrs. A. L.)

BUTTER PECAN TURTLE COOKIES
Watch these disappear at your next meeting!

Can do ahead
Can freeze
Yield: 35-40
Preparation: 20 minutes
Baking time: 18-20 minutes

CRUST:

2 cups flour
1 cup packed brown sugar
1/2 cup softened butter
1 cup whole pecan halves

CARAMEL LAYER:

2/3 cup butter
1/2 cup packed brown sugar

TOP:

1 cup milk chocolate chips

Preheat oven to 350°. In large bowl, combine crust ingredients. Mix at medium speed 2 to 3 minutes, or use pastry blender to cut butter in. Pat into 9x13" pan. Sprinkle pecans on top.
Prepare caramel layer in one quart pan. Combine brown sugar and butter. Cook over medium heat, stirring constantly until entire surface begins to boil. Boil 30-60 seconds, stirring constantly. Pour over crust.
Bake near center of oven for 18-20 minutes until caramel layer is bubbly and crust is light golden brown. Remove from oven and sprinkle with chocolate chips. Allow to melt for several minutes, then swirl with a knife.
Cool completely before cutting.

Nancy Sauer Crosby (Mrs. E. B.)

CHOCOLATE EASTER EGG NESTS
Children love this; something fun to do at Easter besides dying eggs.

Must do ahead
Can freeze
Yield: 12
Preparation: 15 minutes plus at least 1 hour frige time

NEST:

1 pkg. (12 oz.) milk chocolate
  morsels
2 Tablespoons shortening
12 cupcake baking cups

Melt chocolate chips and shortening. Pour into baking cups, covering bottom and sides to desired thickness. Refrigerate at least 1 hour. Remove baking cups carefully. Fill with green mint ice cream; top with coconut and jelly beans.

FILLING:

Green mint ice cream

Jeanne Forsyth Powell (Mrs. B. P.)

M.G.'S BACKGAMMON FUDGE
A yummy Christmas goodie...make on a clear day!

Yield: 3 dozen
Preparation: 45 minutes

2/3 cup cocoa
3 cups sugar
1/8 teaspoon salt
1-1/2 cups milk
1/2 cup butter
1 teaspoon vanilla

Thoroughly combine dry ingredients in a heavy four-quart saucepan; stir in milk. Bring to bubbly boil on medium heat, stirring constantly. Boil without stirring to 234° (soft ball stage). Bulb of candy thermometer should not rest on bottom of sauce pan.
Remove from heat. Add butter and vanilla. DO NOT STIR. Cool at room temperature to 110°. Beat until fudge thickens and loses some of its gloss. Quickly spread in lightly buttered 8 or 9" square pan. Cool.
If recipe doubled, reduce cocoa to 1-1/4 cups instead of 1-1/3.

Mary Gladys Rogers Bitter (Mrs. K. F.)

Pickles & Jams

MY MOTHER'S BEST BREAD AND BUTTER PICKLES

Must do ahead

1 gallon (about 8 lbs.) medium
   cucumbers
8 small white onions
1 red pepper (sweet)
1 green pepper (sweet)
1-1/2 teaspoons tumeric
2 teaspoons celery seed
1 Tablespoon mustard seed
1/2 cup coarse salt
5 cups sugar
5 cups vinegar

Slice unpeeled cucumbers *thin*. Add sliced onions and peppers sliced in thin, narrow strips. Add salt and cover with cracked ice. Mix well and let stand 3 hours or longer. Drain. Combine remaining ingredients; pour over cucumber mixture. Bring to boil. Pack in sterilized jars and seal.

Adelene Barnett Watts (Mrs. Walter M., Jr.)

SWEET CUCUMBER PICKLES

Must do ahead
Yield: 7-9 pint jars

7 lbs. cucumbers—sliced
   crosswise
2 gallons of water
3 cups powdered lime
5 lbs. sugar
3 pints vinegar
1/2 box pickling spices—
   in cheesecloth bag

Soak sliced cucumbers in lime water 24 hours. Drain; soak in fresh water 4 hours, changing water every hour. Drain well. Mix sugar and vinegar and add spice bag. Put in cucumbers and let stand overnight (about 12 hours). Next morning boil for one hour. Seal in warm jars while pickles are still hot, covering pickles with juice.

Susan Murray Daniel (Mrs. John N., Jr.)

ICE BOX PICKLES

Must do ahead

4 cups sugar
4 cups vinegar
1/2 cup salt
1-1/4 teaspoon tumeric
1-1/4 teaspoon celery seed
1-1/4 teaspoon mustard seed
3 onions, sliced
3 cucumbers, sliced

Mix sugar, vinegar and spices cold. Pack in jars, pour syrup over pickles. Let pickles soak several days before serving.

Ann Huntington Westall (Mrs. Jack W.)

MOUNTAIN-STYLE PICKLES
With all outdoor picnic-type meals—simple but really quite good.

Can do ahead
Yield: 1 gallon pickles

1 glass gallon jar with lid
Enough sliced cucumbers to
　fill jar
2 large onions
4 cups vinegar
4 cups sugar
1 teaspoon salt
1-1/3 teaspoon mustard seed
1-1/3 teaspoon celery seed
1-1/3 teaspoon tumeric

Fill jar with sliced cucumbers and large onions—pack tightly. In separate bowl, mix vinegar and sugar, mustard, celery seed and tumeric. Pour over cucumbers and onions. Seal. Put in refrigerator and leave for 5 days. Pickles may be left in refrigerator for as long as a year—if they last that long!

Recipe given to me by a "mountain woman"—my special friend and advisor on ways of country living.

Mary Dallam Gennett (Mrs. Andrew)

SWEET GARLIC PICKLE
Good on cocktail buffet

Must do ahead
Yield: 1 gallon

1 gallon whole sour pickles
5 lbs. sugar
6 to 8 sections garlic (sliced)
4 sticks cinnamon (broken)
Box mustard seed
1/2 box whole black pepper

Pour off pickle juice—discard pickle ends and cut into one-half inch thick rounds. Put all ingredients back into jar. Mix by turning upside down. When sugar has dissolved pickle is ready to be chilled and served.

Ruth Wellman Jameson (Mrs. James L., Jr.)

PICKLED OKRA

Must do ahead

5 lbs. okra
1 quart white vinegar
2 quart water
1 cup salt

IN EACH JAR ADD:

1/2 teaspoon dill seed
2 garlic buds
1 red hot pepper
1 green hot pepper

Heat vinegar and salt to boil. Put dill seeds, garlic buds and hot peppers in each jar—pack okra in whole. Pour other ingredients over the okra and seal jars. Let set for 3 weeks. Chill several hours before serving.

Camille Stone Roberts (Mrs. Pearce, Jr.)

GREEN TOMATO PICKLES

Must do ahead
Yield: 6 pints

7 lbs. green tomatoes
3 sticks cinnamon
2 Tablespoons whole allspice
2 Tablespoons mixed pickling
    spices or cloves
4-1/2 lbs. sugar
1/2 gallon vinegar
8 Tablespoons lime (and
    enough water to cover
    tomatoes)

Slice tomatoes and soak in lime water for 24 hours. (Be sure tomatoes are covered with lime water—a porcelain roaster works well for this.) Rinse tomatoes. Mix vinegar, sugar and spices (tie in cheese-cloth bag) and bring to a boil. Add tomatoes and boil for 20 minutes. Pack in jars and pressure cook to 10 pounds and turn off.

Martha and Bruce Weaver

WATERMELON RIND PICKLES

Must do ahead
Yield: 12-14 pints

1 large or 2 small melons
18 cups sugar
9 cups vinegar
5 cups water
1 Tablespoon allspice
1 Tablespoon cloves
2 sticks cinnamon

Cut off the outside green peel and the red meat inside from 1 large or 2 small watermelons. Cut for pickles. Soak overnight in lime water (2 tablespoons lime to 1 gallon water). Next morning soak 5 minutes in alum water (1 tablespoon alum to 1 gallon water). Place in strong ginger water (1 can ginger root). Take out of ginger water and plunge seven times in cold water. Put in syrup made of sugar, vinegar, water, allspice, cloves and cinnamon. Boil slowly for 3 hours. Pack in jars and seal.

Helen King Turner (Mrs. Franklin H., Jr.)

CHUTNEY

Must do ahead

4 lbs. peeled, seeded peaches,
    pears or apples
1 cup crystallized ginger
1 Tablespoon salt
1 Tablespoon chili powder
1-1/2 lbs. sugar
1/2 cup chopped onions
1/2 lb. raisins
2 Tablespoons mustard seed
3 cups cider vinegar

Cut fruit and onions into slivers. Add all other ingredients. Put in heavy kettle over high heat until mixture begins to boil, reduce heat and simmer 2-3 hours or until thick. It should have a little syrup and not be cooked to mush. Put in jars and seal while hot.

Frances Hall

DILLY GREEN BEANS
A great cocktail food

Must do ahead

Whole green beans to fill
   a 1 pint jar
2 cloves garlic (per jar)
1 red and 1 green hot pepper
   (per jar)
2 heads dill or 1 teaspoon dill
   seed (per jar)
1 quart white vinegar
1 cup water
1/4 cup canning salt

Place 1 head dill in the bottom of the jar; pack with the beans, peppers and garlic. Top jar with 1 head dill. Boil the water, vinegar and salt together for 3-4 minutes. Pour over the beans, seal and process in water bath canner for 5-7 minutes. Let "ripen" for 2-3 weeks before eating. (This amount of pickling solution will fill 5-7 pint jars.)

Mary Jane Dillingham Westall (Mrs. Jack W., Jr.)

SWEET PEPPER RELISH

1 dozen green peppers
1 dozen red peppers
1 dozen onions
3 lbs. sugar
1 qt. vinegar
1 Tablespoon celery seed
1 Tablespoon salt

Wash peppers and remove seeds. Put peppers and onions through meat chopper. Scald and strain twice. Boil sugar and vinegar, put in other ingredients. Cook 15 minutes. Put in jars and seal.

Margaret Baumann

RED PEPPER RELISH

14 red sweet peppers
6 green peppers
7 large onions
1 jar banana peppers or 3 chili
   peppers
5 cloves garlic
5 cups vinegar
4 cups brown sugar
3 Tablespoons of salt
4 Tablespoons of ground clove

Grind peppers, onions and garlic. Pour boiling water over mixture and let stand 15 minutes. Put in colander and drain. Put mixture in large pot; add vinegar, sugar, salt and clove. After mixture comes to boil, cook 20 minutes. Fill hot jars and seal.

Eloise Saunders Frue (Mrs. William C. Jr.)

PATIO RELISH

Must do ahead
Serves: 8-12

1 green pepper, chopped
1 mild onion, chopped
1 cup celery—sliced
1 can each, drained:
  French cut green beans
  Leseur baby peas
  White shoe peg corn
  Bean sprouts
  Water chestnuts—sliced
  Mushrooms—sliced
  Pimento—sliced
3/4 cup oil
1/2 cup vinegar
1 Tablespoon salt
1-1/2 Tablespoons sugar
1 teaspoon pepper

Combine pepper, onion, celery, green beans, baby peas, corn, sprouts, water chestnuts, mushrooms and pimento and chill overnight in oil, vinegar, salt, sugar and pepper. Toss carefully before serving.

Susan Murray Daniel (Mrs. John N., Jr.)

RHUBARB MARMALADE
Different and delicious with homemade wheat biscuits.

Must do ahead
Yield: 3-1/2 pints

4 cups rhubarb
2-1/2 cups sugar
1 whole lemon

Wash and cut rhubarb—do not peel. Shave lemon rind thinly. Add to rhubarb with sugar and let stand overnight (use glass bowl; not aluminum.) Next day add juice of lemon to above ingredients and bring to boil. After it starts to boil, cook 10 minutes at rolling boil. Put in sterilized jars and seal.

Lynn Roda Smith (Mrs. Canie B.)

PEPPER JELLY

1-1/2 cups chopped green
  peppers
1/4 cup hot peppers
1-1/2 cups vinegar
6-1/2 cups sugar
1 6-oz. bottle Certo

Process peppers and vinegar in blender. Bring mixture to rapid boil. Add sugar and stir to dissolve. Cool 5 minutes; add Certo. Place in jars.

Helen King Turner (Mrs. Franklin H., Jr.)

Microwave Recipes

WASSAIL

Serves: 8-9
Preparation: 18 minutes

1 quart apple cider
1 teaspoon allspice
1/2 teaspoon ground cloves
1/4 teaspoon nutmeg
2 cinnamon sticks
1/2 cup orange juice
2 Tablespoons lemon juice
1/2 cup sugar
2 tart medium apples, thinly
    sliced

Place cider, allspice, cloves, nutmeg, cinnamon sticks, orange juice, lemon juice, sugar and apples in a 3 quart casserole. Microwave at HIGH 15 to 18 minutes, until hot. Strain and serve.

HOT CHOCOLATE

Serves: 6-8
Preparation: 9-11 minutes

2 (1 oz.) squares unsweetened
    chocolate
1/4 cup sugar
1/2 cup water
1/4 cup light molasses
1 quart milk
1/8 teaspoon salt
Whipping cream, whipped

Place chocolate in a 2 quart casserole. Microwave at MEDIUM 3 to 4 minutes. Stir in sugar to make paste. Add water, molasses, milk, and salt. Stir well at 2 minute intervals.
Microwave at HIGH 6 to 7 minutes or until hot, but not boiling. Stir well.
Pour into mugs and serve hot, topped with whipped cream.

BLUE MUSHROOMS

Yield: 24
Preparation: 10 minutes

24 fresh mushrooms, medium
1 Tablespoon butter
1/3 cup crumbled blue cheese
3 Tablespoons fine dry bread
    crumbs
1/4 cup snipped parsley

Remove stems from mushrooms; set caps aside. Chop stems. In 2-cup glass measure combine butter and stems. Micro-cook, on HIGH uncovered till tender, about two minutes; stir once. Stir in cheese and crumbs. Spoon about 1 teaspoon filling into each cap; sprinkle with parsley. Place 12 filled mushrooms in a glass pie plate; micro-cook, on MEDIUM covered, till hot, about 2 minutes, turning dish once. Cook remaining mushrooms.

RUMAKI

Yield: 40 hors d'oeuvres
Preparation: 30 minutes

1 lb. thin sliced bacon
1 can water chestnuts (8-oz.)
1/2 lb. chicken livers (about 20)
Ground cloves
Brown sugar

Partially cook the bacon, cut in half. Drain and cut each chestnut in half. Rinse and drain livers. Cut in half.

Sprinkle each bacon strip with ground cloves and brown sugar. Place one piece of liver and one piece of chestnut at the end of each bacon strip. Roll up, securing with toothpick. Arrange 10 in a circle on each of 4 paper towel lined paper plates. Cover with paper towel. Recipe may be refrigerated at this point.

Microwave each plate at HIGH 3 to 4 minutes, rotating dish 1/2 turn after 1-1/2 minutes. When microwaving from refrigerator temperature, increase time for each plate 1/2 to 1 minute.

GARLIC SHRIMP

Serves: 10
Preparation: 10 minutes

1-1/2 lbs. shrimp, peeled and
   deveined
4 whole garlic cloves
5 Tablespoons olive oil
1 Tablespoon lemon juice
1/2 teaspoon tarragon
Hot Lemon Butter

HOT LEMON BUTTER:

1 cup butter
Juice from 2 lemons
1/8 teaspoon salt

Place shrimp in a rectangular baking dish. Add garlic, olive oil, lemon juice, and tarragon. Microwave at HIGH 4 minutes.

Turn shrimp. Rotate the dish 1/4 turn. Microwave at HIGH 4 more minutes until shrimp are pink. Serve hot with Hot Lemon Butter.

Hot Lemon Butter: Combine all ingredients in a 2-cup glass measure. Cover with paper towel. Microwave at HIGH 2 to 4 minutes until butter is melted.

CRAB SOUP

Can do ahead
Yield: 2 quarts
Preparation: 20 minutes

1 (6 oz.) pkg. frozen crabmeat
2 cans celery soup, undiluted
2-1/2 cups milk
1 cup half and half
2 Tablespoons butter
2 hard-cooked eggs, chopped
1/2 teaspoon Worcestershire
    sauce
1/8 teaspoon garlic salt
1/4 teaspoon white pepper
1/4 cup dry sherry

Thaw, drain and flake crabmeat. Set aside. Combine next 10 ingredients in a 3 quart casserole. Cover and microwave at HIGH 4 minutes; stir well. Cover and microwave at MEDIUM 5 minutes. Stir in crabmeat; cover and microwave at MEDIUM 6 to 8 minutes.

BROCCOLI SOUP

Can do ahead
Yield: 1-1/2 quarts
Preparation: 20 minutes

1 (14-1/2 oz.) can chicken broth
2 pkg. frozen chopped broccoli,
    thawed
1/2 cup chopped onion
1/2 teaspoon Worcestershire
    sauce
1/4 teaspoon each, celery salt,
    pepper and salt
1/8 teaspoon garlic powder
2 cups half and half
2 Tablespoons cornstarch

Combine first 8 ingredients in a 3 quart casserole. Cover with plastic wrap; microwave on HIGH for 5 minutes or until broccoli is crisp-tender. Combine 1 cup half and half and cornstarch in bowl, blend well; stir in remaining half and half. Gradually stir cornstarch mixture into broccoli mixture. Cover and microwave at HIGH for 3 minutes; stir well. Cover and microwave at HIGH for 6 to 9 minutes or until bubbly, stirring at 2 minute intervals.

ORIENTAL CARROTS

Serves: 6
Preparation: 20 minutes

4 cups carrots, cut into 2" pieces
2 Tablespoons butter
1 11-ounce can mandarin
    orange sections, drained
1/2 teaspoon salt
1/8 teaspoon ground ginger

Place carrots and butter in a 1-1/2 quart casserole and cook covered for 10 to 12 minutes. Turn dish and stir halfway through cooking. Add oranges, salt and ginger. Cook 2 more minutes, covered.

CREAMED CELERY

Serves: 4
Preparation: 21 minutes

1/4 cup chopped onion
2 Tablespoons butter
3 cups sliced celery, 2 inch pieces
1/4 teaspoon basil leaves,
    crushed
1 cup White Sauce (recipe in
    this section)

Put the onion and butter in a covered casserole.
Microwave on HIGH for 3 minutes. Add the
celery and basil. Cook, stirring twice, about 10
minutes until tender. Set aside.
Make 1 cup White sauce. Stir it into the celery.
Reheat for 1 minute.

BARLEY, Instead

Serves: 6
Preparation: 35 minutes

1 cup barley
1/2 cup butter
1 medium onion, chopped
1 5-oz. can water chestnuts,
    chopped
1 pkg. dry onion soup mix
2 cups beef broth
1 8-ounce can mushrooms,
    sliced

In a 1-1/2 quart glass casserole, micro-cook
butter 30 seconds. Add chopped onion and barley
and cook 6 minutes, stir every 2 minutes. Add
remaining ingredients and cook 6 more minutes.
Stir. Cook covered on low setting for 20 minutes.
Add more water if liquid is absorbed before
barley is cooked.

ZUCCHINI MEDLEY

Serves: 4
Preparation: 15 minutes

1 medium zucchini, sliced
1 medium yellow squash, sliced
1 medium onion, sliced in rings
1/4 cup water
1 medium tomato, chopped
2 Tablespoons chopped fresh
    parsley
1/4 teaspoon each, oregano,
    salt, pepper
1/2 cup Parmesan cheese

Combine first 4 ingredients in a 2 quart casserole;
cover with plastic wrap. Micro-cook at HIGH
for 6 minutes; stir and give dish a half-turn after
3 minutes. Drain well.
Add remaining ingredients, except cheese; mix
well. Cover and micro-cook at HIGH for 2 to 3
minutes to heat. Sprinkle with cheese, tossing
gently.

TACO CASSEROLE

Serves: 6
Power Level: HIGH
Total Time: 25-1/2 to 29-1/2 minutes

1 lb. ground chuck
2 Tablespoons butter
1/2 cup onion, chopped
2 Tablespoons diced green
    chilies
1 (8 oz.) can tomato sauce
1 (14 oz.) taco seasoning mix
2 eggs
1 cup half and half
1 (6 oz.) pkg. taco chips
8 oz. Monterey Jack cheese,
    shredded
1 cup (8 oz.) sour cream
1/2 cup grated Cheddar cheese

Place beef in two-quart casserole. Microwave at HIGH 5 to 6 minutes, stirring after 3 minutes. Drain beef and remove from casserole. In 1 quart glass measure place butter, onions and chilies. Microwave at HIGH 2 to 2-1/2 minutes, stirring after 1 minute. Add tomato sauce, taco seasoning mix and 1/2 cup of water. Microwave at HIGH 1-1/2 to 2 minutes. Beat eggs, blend in half and half. Add this mixture slowly to tomato sauce, stirring constantly.

Place half of taco chips in same two quart casserole. Top with half of ground beef, half of cheese and half of sauce. Repeat layers. Microwave at HIGH 15 minutes, rotating 1/2 turn after 8 minutes.

Top with sour cream and cheese. Microwave at HIGH 2 to 4 minutes until cheese is melted.

Kathleen Fairburn Armstrong (Mrs. R. N.)

LEMON FISH FILLETS

Serves: 4
Preparation: 5 minutes

1/4 cup butter
2 teaspoons lemon juice
1 (16 oz.) pkg. frozen fish fillets,
    thawed
Salt and pepper to taste
3/4 cup seasoned dry bread
    crumbs
Paprika
Lemon slices

Micro-melt butter on HIGH for 30 seconds, stir in lemon juice. Sprinkle fillets with salt and pepper; brush both sides of each with butter mixture. Gently dredge fillets in bread crumbs, and sprinkle with paprika. Put fillets in a shallow baking dish with thick portion to outside. Cover with waxed paper. Micro-cook at HIGH for 3 to 5 minutes, giving dish one half-turn during cooking. Garnish with lemon and parsley.

HADDOCK ITALIANO

Serves: 4
Preparation: 10 minutes

1 (16 oz.) pkg. haddock fillets,
   thawed
2 Tablespoons olive oil
1 Tablespoon lemon juice
1 medium tomato, chopped
1-1/2 cups sliced mushrooms
1/4 cup chopped onion
1/4 cup chopped green pepper
2 Tablespoons chopped parsley
1 minced garlic clove
1/2 teaspoon dried oregano
1/4 teaspoon salt
Salt and pepper

Combine first 10 ingredients in a baking dish; stir well. Cover with plastic wrap; micro-cook at HIGH for 4 to 6 minutes, stirring once. Push vegetables to one side of dish.
Sprinkle fillets with salt and pepper; arrange in baking dish with the thickest portions to outside of dish. Spoon vegetables over fillets. Cover and micro-cook at HIGH for 2 to 4 minutes, giving dish one half-turn during cooking. Let stand 2 to 3 minutes.

CHICKEN DIVAN
A good way to use left over chicken.

Serves: 6-8
Preparation: 30 minutes

4 chicken breasts
1 cup water
1/2 teaspoon rosemary
1/4 teaspoon each salt and
   pepper
2 (10 oz. pkg.) chopped broccoli
2 (10-3/4 oz.) cans cream of
   chicken soup
1/4 cup white wine
1/2 cup shredded Swiss cheese
1/4 cup Parmesan cheese

Cut up chicken breasts into halves. Place in 1-1/2 qt. casserole; add water, rosemary, salt, pepper. Cover with clear wrap and cook on level 8 (MEDIUM HIGH) for 5-7 minutes. Drain and reserve 1/4 cup broth. Cook broccoli on HIGH 7-9 minutes. Combine soup, wine, cheese and broth, mixing well. Place chicken in 9x9 casserole. Pour in one-half of soup mixture and add broccoli. Pour remaining soup over broccoli and cook on level 6 (MEDIUM) for 9-11 minutes. Sprinkle with Parmesan cheese and cook on level 6 (MEDIUM) for two minutes.

Sandra Tucker Holt (Mrs. Stanley E.)

QUICK LASAGNA

Serves: 6-8
Preparation: 25 minutes

1 lb. ground beef
1/2 cup chopped onion
1 4-oz. can chopped
  mushrooms
1/4 cup chopped green pepper
1 clove garlic, minced
1 (30-oz.) jar spaghetti
  sauce
1/2 teaspoon dried oregano
1/4 teaspoon dried basil leaves
1/4 teaspoon salt
1/4 teaspoon pepper
4 oz. lasagna noodles, cooked
  and drained
  (6-7 whole noodles)
1-1/2 cups cottage cheese
1 8-oz. pkg. sliced mozzarella
  cheese

Crumble beef into a two quart casserole; add mushrooms, onion, green pepper and garlic. Cover with wax paper. Microwave on HIGH for 5 to 6 minutes, or until done, stirring twice. Drain off excess drippings.

Add spaghetti sauce and seasonings to meat mixture, stirring well. Cover and microwave on HIGH for 2-3 minutes, stirring once. Layer half each of the cooked noodles, cottage cheese, mozzarella cheese and meat mixture in a 9x9 baking dish; repeat layers. Cover and microwave at level 8 (MEDIUM HIGH) for 6 to 8 minutes or until well heated, giving dish one-half turn after 5 minutes. Let lasagna stand 10 minutes before serving. (Hint—Cook noodles while preparing meat mixture.)

Sandra Tucker Holt (Mrs. Stanley E.)

BEEF-SAUSAGE CASSEROLE

Serves: 6-8
Preparation: 20 minutes

1/2 lb. ground beef
1/2 lb. ground pork sausage
1/2 cup chopped onion
1/4 cup chopped green pepper
1 cup macaroni (cooked and
  drained)
1 (12 oz.) can whole kernel corn
2 (8 oz.) cans tomato sauce
1/2 teaspoon each ground
  oregano and salt
1/4 teaspoon pepper
1 cup (4 oz.) shredded American
  cheese

Crumble beef and sausage into a two quart casserole, add onion and green pepper. Cover with wax paper and cook on HIGH for 5-7 minutes, stirring twice. Drain drippings. Add macaroni, corn, tomato sauce and seasonings to meat. Mix well. Cover and cook on level 8 (MEDIUM HIGH) for 9-11 minutes or until well heated. Sprinkle with cheese, cover and microwave at level 6 (MEDIUM) or 2-3 minutes or until cheese melts. (Hint—cool macaroni first.)

Sandra Tucker Holt (Mrs. Stanley E.)

QUICK & EASY MEATLOAF

Can do ahead (refrigerate one day)
Can freeze (one month)
Serves: 3-4
Preparation: 5 minutes
Baking Time: 7 to 10 minutes. Let stand 5 minutes

1 lb. ground beef
2/3 cup (5 oz. can) evaporated milk
2 Tablespoons onion soup mix
1/4 teaspoon salt
2 Tablespoons brown sugar
1/2 teaspoon dry mustard
2 Tablespoons catsup

In 1 or 1-1/2 qt. (8x4) loaf dish, combine ground beef, milk, soup mix and salt; mix well. (Mixture will be very moist). Press evenly in pan. Combine brown sugar, mustard and spread over top of meat. Cook covered with wax paper 7 minutes (or 7-10 minutes. My microwave takes about 10 minutes) or until done. Let stand 5 minutes before removing to serving platter and slicing. If frozen, cook 8 minutes, rest 5, and cook 5 minutes more.

Nancy Johnson Weaver (Mrs. Pearce R.)

EASY BLACKBERRY PIE

Can make ahead
Serves: 6
Preparation: 25 minutes

2 frozen pie shells
1 quart blackberries or 4 cups
1 cup sugar
1/4 cup flour
4-6 Tablespoons sugar

Take crusts from freezer and thaw about five minutes. Remove crust from pie pan and place in two quart pyrex dish, gently pushing crust into corners and to the sides. In a mixing bowl, stir sugar and flour together. Add berries, coating well with sugar and flour mixture. Pour berry mixture into crust; dot with butter. Remove second pie crust from pan and place on top of pie, gently pressing to the sides. Slit top. Microwave on HIGH for 18 minutes, turning once.

Sandra Tucker Holt (Mrs. Stanley E.)

PECAN PRALINE CHEESECAKE

Can make ahead
Serves: 12-16
Preparation: 30 minutes

1-1/4 cups crushed graham
  crackers
1/4 cup granulated sugar
1/4 cup margarine
3 (8 oz.) pkgs. cream cheese
1 cup light brown sugar
1 (5-1/3 oz.) can evaporated
  milk
2 Tablespoons flour
1-1/2 teaspoon vanilla
3 large eggs
1 cup pecan pieces
1 cup light corn syrup
1/2 teaspoon cornstarch
2 Tablespoons brown sugar
1 teaspoon vanilla

In 9x9 or 2 quart rectangular dish, melt margarine for 30 seconds on HIGH. Combine graham crackers and granulated sugar with margarine and press on bottom and sides of dish. Microwave 3 minutes on level 7 (MEDIUM HIGH). Let cool.

Cheesecake: Place unwrapped cream cheese in large glass mixing bowl. Microwave 2 minutes on level 5 (MEDIUM) or until soft. With mixer beat cream cheese with 1 cup brown sugar, milk, flour and vanilla. Add eggs and beat until blended. Pour into baked crust. Microwave 12-15 minutes on level 7 (MEDIUM HIGH) until set, rotating once midway through baking. Cool at least 30 minutes before serving.

Topping: Sprinkle pecan pieces over top of cheesecake. In a 2 cup glass measure or pitcher pour corn syrup; add cornstarch, brown sugar and vanilla and microwave 3 minutes on HIGH. Drizzle sauce over cheesecake.

(Hint—Make sauce just before serving. Do not pour on earlier as it will make crust soggy. If only eating a portion at a time, drizzle sauce over individual slices. Depending on taste, additional sauce may be made.)

Sandra Tucker Holt (Mrs. Stanley E.)

S'MORES
An up to date Girl Scout treat!

2 graham cracker squares
1/2 plain chocolate bar
1 large marshmallow

Place 1 graham cracker on a paper napkin, top with chocolate and marshmallow. Microwave at HIGH 1/4 minute, or until marshmallow puffs. Place remaining cracker over top and eat like a sandwich.

SOUTHERN PRALINES

Can do ahead
Yield: 2 dozen
Preparation: 30-45 minutes
Cooking Time: 8 minutes

1-1/2 cup firmly packed brown
    sugar
2/3 cup half and half or coffee
    creamer, liquid
1/8 teaspoon salt
2 Tablespoons butter
1-1/4 cups pecan halves

Combine sugar, half and half or coffee creamer, and salt in deep three-quart casserole; mix well. Stir in butter, melted; microwave at HIGH for about 8 minutes or until mixture reaches soft ball stage (235 degrees), stirring once. Stir in pecans; cool about 1 minute. Beat by hand until mixture is creamy and begins to thicken (about 3 minutes). Drop by tablespoons onto waxed paper; let stand until firm.

Barbara Morgan Nesbitt (Mrs. Charles E.)

PEANUT BRITTLE

Can do ahead
Yield: About 1 pound
Preparation: 30 minutes
Cooking Time: 9 minutes

1 cup sugar
1/2 cup light corn syrup
1-1/2 cups salted peanuts
1 Tablespoon butter
1 teaspoon vanilla
1 teaspoon baking soda

Combine sugar and corn syrup in deep three quart casserole. Microwave at HIGH for 3 minutes. Add salted peanuts. Stir. Microwave at HIGH for 3-1/2 to 4 minutes or until light brown. Add butter and vanilla, mixing well. Microwave at HIGH for 30 seconds or until mixture reaches hard crack stage (300 degrees). Stir in soda; pour onto a buttered cookie sheet, spreading thinly. Let cool. Break into pieces.

Barbara Morgan Nesbitt (Mrs. Charles E.)

SWEET-TART LEMON SQUARES

Yield: 16 cookies or 9 desserts
Preparation: 10 minutes

1 can (15 oz.) sweetened
   condensed milk
1/2 cup lemon juice
1 teaspoon grated lemon rind
1-1/2 cups graham cracker
   crumbs
1/3 cup brown sugar (packed)
1/3 cup butter, melted

Mix together milk, lemon juice and rind until thick and smooth. Set aside. Mix together crumbs, sugar and butter. Place about 2/3 of the mixture in 8″ square dish and press firmly into bottom of dish. Add milk mixture and spread evenly. Sprinkle remaining crumbs over top and pat down gently. Microwave at HIGH 8 to 10 minutes, rotating dish 1/4 turn after 4 minutes. Cut into squares as cookies or in larger pieces as dessert.

QUICK CHOCOLATE SAUCE

Yield: 1-1/2 cups
Preparation: 2 minutes

1/2 cup light corn syrup
1 pkg. (6 oz.) semi-sweet
   chocolate pieces
1 Tablespon butter
1/4 cup dairy half and half
1/4 teaspoon vanilla or rum
   extract

Into glass measuring cup, measure syrup. Stir in chocolate pieces and butter. Microwave at HIGH 1-1/2 to 2-1/2 minutes. Stir until completely smooth. Blend in milk and vanilla. Serve warm.

FOOD SUBSTITUTIONS

1 teaspoon baking powder	1/4 teaspoon baking soda plus
	1/2 teaspoon cream of tartar
1 cup self-rising flour	1 cup all-purpose flour plus
	1-1/2 teaspoon baking powder and
	1/4 teaspoon salt
1 cup buttermilk	1 Tablespoon vinegar or lemon juice plus
	sweet milk to equal 1 cup
1 cup honey	1-1/4 cup sugar plus
	1/4 cup liquid
1-1/2 cups corn syrup	1 cup sugar plus
	1/2 cup water
1 square (1 oz.) chocolate	3 Tablespoons cocoa plus
	1 Tablespoon butter or oleo
1 cup dairy sour cream or milk	1 Tablespoon lemon juice plus
	evaporated milk to equal 1 cup
1 cup light cream	7/8 cup milk plus
	3 Tablespoons butter
1 cup heavy cream	3/4 cup milk plus
	1/3 cup butter
1 cup molasses	1 cup honey or
	1 cup dark corn syrup
1 Tablespoon minced fresh herbs	1 teaspoon dried herbs
1 teaspoon dry mustard	1 Tablespoon prepared mustard
1 lb. fresh mushrooms	6 oz. can or 3 oz. dried mushrooms
1-1/4 cup sweetened condensed milk	1 cup instant nonfat dry milk
	2/3 cup sugar
	1/3 cup boiling water
	3 Tablespoons melted butter
	Mix all in blender. Will keep in
	refrigerator several weeks.

METRIC

VOLUME

1 teaspoon	5 milliliters
1 Tablespoon	15 milliliters
1 fluid ounce	30 milliliters
8 fluid ounces	236 milliliters (approximately)
1 pint	473 milliliters (approximately)
1 quart	.946 liter

WEIGHT

1.1 ounces	30 grams
3.6 ounces	100 grams
9.0 ounces	250 grams
1.1 pounds	500 grams
2.2 pounds	1 kilogram

FOOD EQUIVALENTS

5 slices bread	1 cup fine dry crumbs
1/4 pound cheese	1 cup grated cheese
20 salted crackers	1 cup crumbs
30-36 graham crackers	3 cups crumbs
1 lb. coffee	5 cups
1 lb. flour	4 cups
1 medium lemon	2 to 3 Tablespoons juice
1 lemon rind	1 Tablespoon grated
1 marshmallow	10 miniature
1 gallon punch	20 servings
1 lb. raisins	2-1/2 cups
1 cup raw rice	3 to 3-1/2 cups cooked
1-1/4 cups raw spaghetti	2-1/2 cups cooked
1 lb. granulated sugar	2 cups
1 lb. powdered sugar	3-1/2 cups
1 lb. brown sugar	2-1/2 cups
1 cake yeast	1 level Tablespoon active dry

EQUIVALENTS

Dash	Less than 1/8 teaspoon
1 coffee spoon	1/4 teaspoon
60 drops	1 teaspoon
3 teaspoons	1 Tablespoon
4 Tablespoons	1/4 cup
1/2 cup	1 gill
1 gill	1/4 pint
2 cups	1 pint
4 cups	1 quart
8 quarts	1 peck
4 pecks	1 bushel
16 ounces	1 pound
32 ounces	1 quart
8 ounces liquid	1 cup
1 ounce liquid	2 Tablespoons

Index

311

313